Kierkegaard

OTHER TITLES IN THE ONEWORLD PHILOSOPHERS SERIES

Descartes, Harry M. Bracken, ISBN 1–85168–294–5
Nietzsche, Robert Wicks, ISBN 1–85168–291–0
Sartre, Neil Levy, ISBN 1–85168–290–2
Wittgenstein, Avrum Stroll, ISBN 1–85168–293–7

Kierkegaard

Michael Watts

ONEWORLD PHILOSOPHERS

ONEWORLD

OXFORD

KIERKEGAARD

Oneworld Publications
(Sales and Editorial)
185 Banbury Road
Oxford OX2 7AR
England
www.oneworld-publications.com

ISBN 1–85168–317–8

Cover design by the Bridgewater Book Company
Cover photograph © Corbis Stock Market
Typeset by Saxon Graphics Ltd, Derby, UK
Printed and bound in China by Sun Fung Offset Binding Co. Ltd.

Contents

Abbreviations

The following abbreviations are used in references to Kierkegaard's works:

CA *The Concept of Anxiety*, trans. Howard V. Hong and Edna H. Hong (Princeton University Press, 1980).

CA (E) *The Concept of Anxiety*, taken from *The Essential Kierkegaard*, edited by Howard V. Hong and Edna H. Hong. All the passages in this book are from *Kierkegaard's Writings* I–XXVI (Princeton University Press, 1978–2000).

CD *Christian Discourses*, ed. and trans. Howard V. Hong and Edna H. Hong (Princeton University Press, 1997).

CI *The Concept of Irony with Continual Reference to Socrates*, trans. H. V. and E. H. Hong (Princeton University Press, 1989).

CI (C.) *The Concept of Irony*, trans. Lee M. Capel (Indiana University Press, 1965).

CUP *Concluding Unscientific Postscript to the Philosophical Fragments*, vols 1 & 2, ed. and trans. Howard V. Hong and Edna H. Hong (Princeton University Press, 1989).

CUP (E) *Concluding Unscientific Postscript to the Philosophical Fragments*, taken from *The Essential Kierkegaard*, ed. Howard V. Hong and Edna H. Hong. All the passages in this book are from *Kierkegaard's Writings* I–XXVI (Princeton University Press, 1978–2000).

CUP (S.L.) Concluding Unscientific Postscript to the Philosophical Fragments, vols 1 & 2, trans. David F. Swenson and Walter Lowrie (Princeton University Press, 1960).

EO 1 Either/Or, vol. 1, trans. Howard V. Hong and Edna H. Hong (Princeton University Press, 1987).

EO 1 (E) Either/Or, vol. 1, taken from *The Essential Kierkegaard*, ed. Howard V. Hong and Edna H. Hong. All the passages in this book are from *Kierkegaard's Writings* I–XXVI (Princeton University Press, 1978–2000).

EO 1 (S) Either/Or, vol. 1, trans. David F. Swenson and Lillian Marvin Swenson (Princeton University Press, 1944).

EUD Eighteen Upbuilding Discourses, ed. and trans. Howard V. Hong and Edna H. Hong (Princeton University Press, 1990).

FT Fear and Trembling (with *Repetition*), trans. H. V. and E. H. Hong (Princeton University Press, 1983).

FT h Fear and Trembling, trans. Alastair Hannay (Penguin Classics, 1985).

JP Søren Kierkegaard's Journals and Papers, trans. Howard Hong and Edna H. Hong (Indiana University Press 1967–78). This is followed by volume and page or by entry number.

KAUC Kierkegaard's Attack upon 'Christendom' 1854–5, trans. Walter Lowrie (Princeton University Press, 1944).

Pap. *Søren Kierkegaard's Papirer*, ed. P. A. Heiberg, V. Kuhr, and E. Torsting, 16 vols in 25 tomes, 2nd edn, ed. N. Thulstrup, with an index by N. J. Cappelorn (Copenhagen: Gyldendal, 1968–78).

PC Practice in Christianity, trans. Howard V. Hong and Edna H. Hong (Princeton University Press, 1991).

PF Philosophical Fragments, trans. D. F. Swenson, rev. H. V. Hong (Princeton University Press, 1962).

PV The Point of View of my Work as an Author, trans. Walter Lowrie (Harper Torchbooks, 1962).

SKS Søren Kierkegaard's Skrifter, ed. Niels Jørgen Cappeløm, Joakim Garff, Johnny Kondrup, Alastair McKinnon and Finn Hanberg Mortensen (København: Søren Kierkegaard Forskningscenter/ Gads Forlag, 1997).

SUD The Sickness unto Death, trans. Howard V. Hong and Edna H. Hong (Princeton University Press, 1980).

SUD h The Sickness unto Death, trans. Alastair Hannay (Penguin Press, 1989).

SUD (E) The Sickness unto Death, taken from *The Essential Kierkegaard*, ed. Howard V. Hong and Edna H. Hong. All the passages in this book are from *Kierkegaard's Writings* I–XXVI (Princeton University Press, 1978–2000).

SUD (L) The Sickness unto Death, trans. Walter Lowrie (Princeton University Press, 1968).

SV Samlede Vaerker, ed. A. B. Drachmann, J. L. Heiberg, and H. O. Lange (Copenhagen, 1963–4).

TDO (E) Three Discourses on Imagined Occasions (29 April 1845), taken from *The Essential Kierkegaard*, ed. Howard V. Hong and Edna H. Hong. All the passages in this book are from *Kierkegaard's Writings* I–XXVI (Princeton University Press, 1978–2000).

Foreword

Not so long ago Kierkegaard tended to fuse in the popular mind with Hamlet as some shadowy competitor for the title 'melancholy Dane'. In David Lodge's *Therapy* it was only through looking up 'Angst' in a dictionary that the hero stumbled on the name. Today, however, outside the academy, and due not least to the kind of publicity a best-selling novel gives it, Kierkegaard's name is rapidly becoming a household word. In his home town, Copenhagen, where Kierkegaard as a lingering embarrassment to the establishment has long been kept under covers, the stooped figure, top-hatted and with cane under arm has even reappeared on the streets, in the form of a silhouette on bookshop windows as a boost to the tourist trade.

The Dane's writings have of course occupied scholars for close on a century. Now they are the subject, world wide, of a newly booming academic industry. Some measure of agreement might be expected, then, about what the works say, allowing reliable introductions for the beginning student to be readily available. That this is not the case is due to many factors, one of which is, as Michael Watts notes, that Kierkegaard is not 'an easy read'. There are other matters too, the pseudonymity for instance, but also the background against which the texts were read at or closer to his time, one that is in so many ways no longer ours.

That Watts has written an introduction which in spite of its self-imposed limits avoids the pitfalls, and thus allows the reader to do the same, is a fine achievement. It not only offers the beginner, both in Kierkegaard and in philosophy, a concise yet comprehensive survey of Kierkegaard's life and thought, crucially it does so in a way that allows the reader to see where the two interconnect. This is a tricky matter. Some interpretations of Kierkegaard, especially the early ones, tend to see the workings as a result of the life, while to be taken seriously as a thinker Kierkegaard himself would no doubt prefer the writings to carry with them a content that can be appraised or assimilated independently of the biography of their author. Before introducing the reader to the writings themselves via their main themes, Watts provides the biography that is needed to explain why these themes became important for Kierkegaard, and also a chapter giving tips on how to read the works themselves.

Kierkegaard has impressed people in so many different ways. Some see him as a (modern) Faust, others as a Mephistopheles, even a 'tragic Satan'. Another angle makes him a 'Don Juan of the intellect'. How sure can we ever be, in the face of such an elastic authorial personality, that we have a firm grip on his thought? For surely the idea behind an introduction must be to provide such a grip. Many scholars seem to assume they are in a position to provide it simply by virtue of a personal engagement in Kierkegaard's brand of thinking. Before explaining the thought to their readers, they frequently preface their discussions with a personal note recounting the impact of the master's works on their own spiritual growth.

My own view is that it is dangerous to assume that what we like in Kierkegaard is bound to be what Kierkegaard wanted us to find there, or alternatively, that what he wanted us to find there should be something we would immediately embrace. The therapeutic aspect may require just the opposite. It is a great merit of Michael Watts' introduction to Kierkegaard that its grip on the thought comes from the texts themselves and that the texts are well placed against the life, that is to say in a way that lets them emerge from that and to stand before us in relief, as matters to be approached in the way Kierkegaard suggests they should be, which, whatever else it mounts to, at least means that they are not to be dealt with as theories or theses to be expounded and defended in the time-honoured philosophical manner, but rather as topics and ways of seeing things about which to become freshly and self-critically aware.

Alastair Hannay, University of Oslo

Introduction

Born in 1813 in Denmark and today universally regarded as one of the most profound and influential thinkers of the nineteenth century, Søren Aabye Kierkegaard's 'philosophical star' is now clearly in the ascendant. An outstanding iconoclast and rebel of his time, his authorship evolved in conscious opposition to the cherished beliefs and conventions of the academic and religious institutions of his day. In his relatively short life of forty-two years, this deeply sensitive Danish religious philosopher wrote more than twenty-five books, all in the Danish language, and most of them under a variety of different pen-names.

During his lifetime he was virtually unknown outside of his homeland, and even after his death, when the first German translations began to appear in 1855 their impact was minimal. It was only very much later, when his ideas became associated with existentialist philosophy in the 1930s and 1940s, that his work finally began to achieve some international status and his books were then also translated into French and English. Today all of his works have been published in English as well as in various other major European languages, and, perhaps more surprisingly, even in Japan there is a long tradition of careful Kierkegaard scholarship.

His late arrival in the literary and philosophical world of Great Britain and the USA, as well as his relative obscurity during his lifetime, was influenced partly because he wrote exclusively in the Danish language, which only around two million Europeans spoke, and partly because he antagonised the Danish reading public through his cutting criticism of contemporary society. In addition, Denmark's policy of armed neutrality during the Napoleonic era did not assist in attracting interest in, or respect for, Danish accomplishments in the arts and sciences, and the fact that the predominant literary and philosophical ideals in Denmark were from Germany also did not help matters in this respect.

It also seems likely that Kierkegaard was relatively unconcerned about the influence of his writings abroad, for he was a fluent reader of the German language and a citizen of an international culture, and yet he never chose to develop sufficient fluency to write in German, French or English, which would have given his work worldwide exposure. Also, apart from one excursion to his family roots in Jutland, a day trip to Sweden and four visits to Berlin, Søren spent his entire life in and around Copenhagen – perhaps the journeys he made within the inner world of his own mind removed the need to broaden his horizons in the external world.

Although the histories of philosophy published ninety years ago scarcely mention Kierkegaard, today many regard his contributions as amounting to a philosophical revolution. Interest in his work is continually growing, as evidenced by the increasing number of studies of his writings appearing in current journals of philosophy and other philosophical publications. Indeed, the applicability of so much of his thought to modern life has caused many to regard him as a 'contemporary thinker' even though he died around one hundred and fifty years ago.

Kierkegaard the philosopher of everyday life

Kierkegaard's philosophy differs fundamentally from the great conceptual systems offered by philosophers such as Aristotle, Leibniz and Hegel who devote the greater part of their thought to abstract, logical and speculative thinking, dealing with subjects such as political theory and the foundations of science and logic. Although this type of philosophy has greatly influenced the history of Western culture, *the individual* only experiences its effects in a very indirect manner, filtered through the social institutions of religion, politics, science and other academic disciplines. Consequently, the ideas presented in this type of philosophy can rarely be adapted to the practical, ordinary everyday needs of the individual human being.

In direct contrast to this, Kierkegaard revolutionised our understanding of the *individual human condition*. His insights and advice go to the very core of the dilemmas that haunt the modern mind and spirit, and because he speaks directly and concretely to the individual person, in terms of how he or she actually lives, his words can have a deeply transformational effect upon the consciousness of receptive readers.

The multifaceted Kierkegaard

Kierkegaard has been described as 'the greatest Protestant Christian of the nineteenth century' and 'the profoundest interpreter of the psychology of the religious life ... since St Augustine'. Wittgenstein – the leading exponent of analytical philosophy of language – once described Kierkegaard as *the* most profound thinker of the nineteenth century. However, Kierkegaard's extraordinarily versatile writing and profound influence extends well beyond philosophy and theology, into the realms of literary criticism, devotional literature, fiction and psychology. Indeed, his exceptional psychological insight resulted in perhaps the first ever work of depth psychology, *The Concept of Anxiety*, in which he illuminates the clear distinction between what he calls 'Angst' – the feeling of *anxiety* or *dread* that exists independently of any apparent objective threat – and the experience of *fear* or *terror* which is caused by a genuine danger. He recognised that the mood of anxiety can potentially help us to find personal freedom, and he also saw the connection between anxiety and evil (sin) – a link that Sigmund Freud was to acknowledge nearly fifty years later. The highly literary, and often poetic, style of expression that he employs in much of his philosophical writing has even motivated some readers of his work to describe him as a 'kind of poet' (see Louis Mackey, *Kierkegaard: A Kind of Poet*, Philadelphia: University of Pennsylvania Press, 1971). His ideas are still constantly being explored and redeployed today by modern thinkers from a variety of academic backgrounds.

The goal of his authorship

Kierkegaard's 'authorship' as he calls it can, in a very general sense, be divided into two main categories: a collection of what he termed 'aesthetic' writings, which he wrote under a variety of pseudonyms, and a series of 'religious' works that for the most part were published under his own name. His aim in the first was to present various life-views on existence by providing the reader with a wide range of alternative ways of existing, in a manner that would enable the reader to see the false and empty values by which most people lead their lives. In his religious writings he wished to help his readers become aware of the true nature of Christianity.

Much of his writing does not address Christianity directly, but concerns itself instead with a detailed analysis of human existence. He considered this approach to be essential, because he regarded Christianity as being first and foremost a way of existing, and also felt that the erroneous beliefs that people had concerning the true nature of Christian faith were caused by a fundamental confusion or misunderstanding regarding the nature of existence, so to clear up the former misunderstanding he felt the latter must be carefully examined.

He was, however, without doubt fundamentally committed to one path in life – to deepen significantly people's awareness and to make them aware of the true essence of Christianity. He writes in his Journal: 'The category for my undertaking is: to make people aware of what is essentially Christian.' However, he regarded the Established Church as a serious hindrance to this objective: 'The Established Church is far more dangerous to Christianity than any heresy or schism.' 'Think of a hospital. The patients are dying like flies. Every method is tried to make things better. It's no use. Where does the sickness come from? It comes from the building; the whole building is full of poison. So it is in the religious sphere' (*KAUC*, pp. 139–41).

Kierkegaard is certainly not an easy read, for he combines extraordinary depth of insight with an ironical, ambiguous writing style that effectively camouflages his own philosophical position. This is because he does not want to be treated as an 'expert' or spiritual 'authority', offering a new philosophy or theology of life. Instead, he wishes to excite and provoke readers to question their own life and discover the 'truth' for themselves via their *own* very personal experience of reality.

Kierkegaard the existentialist

His astute observations on modern times and contemporary Christianity take place in the nineteenth century, but are equally applicable today. Roger Poole points out in the preface to his book *The Laughter is on My Side*, 'Kierkegaard emerges as a thinker whose wisdom is ahead of us, not behind. The nightmare of total bureaucratic control, and the impersonal and ruthless manipulation of vast international financial forces, is only the updated forms of those forces that Kierkegaard knew and named.'

Kierkegaard emphasised above all the need to become a 'true individual', passionately committed to a path that has been *personally* chosen. He observed that the majority of people merely exist as part of an anonymous 'public', simply conforming to the dominant way of living and thinking. In his *Concluding Unscientific Postscript*, he likens real existence to riding a wild stallion, and 'so-called existence' with falling asleep in a moving hay wagon.

Kierkegaard was convinced that in order to realise our true significance, we need to free ourselves completely from the influence of social, cultural and religious values and expectations. Instead, each person needs to develop a clear awareness of their life situation so that they can determine their own path by making conscious, responsible choices from among the alternatives that life offers them. He saw mankind's predicament as caused largely by a dissipation of energy via superficial interest in far too many things that renders existence a meaningless journey, devoid of real passion. It is evident from Kierkegaard's writings that he strongly believed that an essential precondition for developing a pure heart and a pure mind is that a person must focus the main energy of their will and their thinking on just one thing. In a journal entry in 1847 he writes that he must 'find a truth which is true *for me* – the idea for which I can live and die'. Kierkegaard saw this as a prerequisite to discovering genuine individuality and one's true self.

Individual, absolute and unconditional commitment to a fundamental path through life that one has freely and consciously chosen creates a genuine sense of meaning to existence, which then defines and becomes a focus for one's whole sense of reality – all other things standing out or receding into insignificance on the basis of this ultimate concern. For Kierkegaard, this meant personal commitment to the path of Christianity.

These views on personal, individual responsibility and freedom of choice as well as his awareness of the absurd, paradoxical nature of existence (though not the Christian paradox that he emphasised) are fundamental to existential philosophy, and it is widely acknowledged that Kierkegaard 'set the stage' and provided the conceptual tools for much of twentieth-century existentialist thinking, which employs numerous Kierkegaardian themes, though divorced from their original religious setting and used in an atheistic sense. Consequently, in the middle of the last century he became known as the 'father of existentialism'. This label, however, is anachronistic, since the movement of existentialism is a twentieth-century phenomenon and in spite of various close similarities, there are also vast, crucial differences between Kierkegaard's thought and existentialism. Indeed if one believes that existentialism denies the existence of human essence, then one could offer a reasonable argument *against* the assertion that Kierkegaard is an existentialist.

Nevertheless his ideas certainly did inspire many existentialist philosophers and writers – Martin Heidegger's key work, *Being And Time*, took much from Kierkegaard's writings, as did the philosophy of Jean-Paul Sartre (though neither Heidegger nor Sartre was prepared to acknowledge this great debt). Amongst the many other great thinkers whom Kierkegaard influenced were the twentieth-century theologians Tillich and Barth, the poet W. H. Auden and authors Albert Camus, Franz Kafka, August Strindberg and Henrik Ibsen.

Recently, he has also been seen as a precursor of postmodernism, which is a credible assertion since he rejects classical foundationalist epistemologies and uses elusive literary techniques such as pseudonyms. Postmodernists have heatedly examined ways in which Kierkegaard's thought breaks away from the type of Enlightenment thinking associated with modernity, in particular, through its confrontation with rationalistic epistemologies (see Merold Westphal, *Becoming a Self: A Reading of Kierkegaard's 'Concluding*

Unscientific Postscript', Indiana: Purdue University Press, 1996, and Roger Poole, *Kierkegaard: The Indirect Communication*, Charlottesville, Va: University of Virginia Press, 1993).

Kierkegaard the outcast

His significant achievements however were not always held in high regard. He passionately opposed the intellectualism and aestheticism of his era, and his provocative manner and extremely radical way of thinking were incompatible with nineteenth-century Danish religious and philosophical thought. As a result, eventually he became an outcast from his social and intellectual environment, but it is very evident that this situation was to a large extent intentionally manufactured. For instance, it is clear from entries in his private journals that he was fully aware of the hostile reactions towards him that would be generated by the publication of certain articles in well-known local newspapers. Throughout his lifetime, much of his philosophical, literary, psychological and theological authorship was ignored, criticised or even derided by most of his contemporaries in the Danish academic world.

In addition, as a result of his cutting attacks on the Established Danish Lutheran Church, which he regarded as worldly and corrupt, he was angrily dismissed by them as an eccentric, potentially dangerous, fanatic. His own brother, Peter Christian Kierkegaard, greatly criticised Søren's way of thinking – especially his negative attitude towards established religion and philosophy – and even in Søren's funeral oration Peter made comments which obviously implied that Søren was mentally unstable.

For more than two decades after his death, Kierkegaard's work remained in almost complete obscurity. Even much later, when psychoanalysis was at its zenith, it was quite fashionable to view his thought principally as a means of delving into a very interesting and special psychological make-up – his ideas were often treated primarily as the manifestations of a melancholic mind. The renowned Danish literary critic and biographer Georg Brandes wrote the first ever book about Kierkegaard's philosophy and life in 1877, claiming that he did so in order to free the Danes from his influence. Subsequent Danish philosophical appraisals of Kierkegaard were equally critical.

The growing acceptance of Kierkegaard's work

Ten years after he wrote his critique, however, Brandes changed his viewpoint. He wrote to Friedrich Nietzsche strongly recommending that he read Kierkegaard, and he became the first person in Denmark to give formal academic lectures on Kierkegaard's thought. He also recommended Kierkegaard to the Swedish author and playwright August Strindberg.

Around the same time the Norwegian dramatist Henrik Ibsen became interested in his work, and Kierkegaard's fame began to spread throughout Scandinavia. His writings became increasingly influential in Central Europe in the early part of the twentieth century when all of his texts were translated into the German language prior to World War One. In spite of this, in Denmark, as late as 1919, another respected Danish philosopher, Harald Hoffding, stated in his book *Søren Kierkegaard as a Philosopher* that Kierkegaard had very low philosophical acumen. Then, in the 1930s, primarily as a result of the association of his work with the modern existentialist movement, he began to capture the attention of the international philosophical community.

Kierkegaard had accurately predicted his posthumous fame – he foresaw that his work would become the subject of serious study and would achieve acclaim for its originality and depth of insight. He mockingly anticipated that after his death, the individuals who would praise him would be 'professors' – future members of the very same academic institutions that during his lifetime had strongly opposed his way of thinking.

Within the world of British philosophy, however, Kierkegaard's work remained virtually unknown until 1938, when the single-handed editorial efforts of Charles Williams at the Oxford University Press resulted in the publication (in England) of *The Journals of Kierkegaard 1834–1854*, translated by the Kierkegaard scholar Alexander Dru. This was the first time that a significant presentation of Kierkegaard's thought had appeared in the English language.

In this same year in America, the New York Office of the Oxford University Press released a second English publication, a biography entitled *Kierkegaard*, which was compiled and translated by the retired American pastor (and Kierkegaard scholar) Walter Lowrie. In the years between 1939 and 1944, the Press published fifteen more Walter Lowrie translations of Kierkegaard's work, and between the years 1936 and 1948 a publishing house in Minneapolis published around seven more translations, thanks to the dedicated work of another Kierkegaard enthusiast, David Swenson. The early translators, however, were theologians or philosophers of religion, so they tended to present a somewhat biased picture of Kierkegaard's thought that virtually disregarded the significance and subtleties of his irony, his use of pseudonyms and various other aspects of his indirect style of communication.

It is only since 1967 that there have been translations of Kierkegaard of a suitable standard for the learned world, in English. This has been thanks to the efforts of two dedicated Kierkegaard scholars and translators, Howard and Edna Hong, who have completed the translation of most of his writings.

The aim of this book

This book makes Kierkegaard's work accessible to the complete beginner. It also tries, wherever appropriate, to present a variety of alternative possible interpretations of his text, in an effort to avoid the error (often made by dogmatic theological scholars of Kierkegaard) of presenting a neatly packaged, unambiguous interpretation of his work that would clearly sabotage Kierkegaard's wish for readers to discover the truth for themselves. The material focuses primarily on the areas of his writing and thought that are especially relevant to the spiritual climate of the twenty-first century. The topics chosen comprise the very 'heart' of Kierkegaard, the core themes of his writings that best exemplify the essence of his thought and passion – his critique of systematic 'objective' philosophy, his insistence on the subjectivity of truth, his insightful psychological/spiritual analysis of despair, dread and faith and his description of the 'religious', 'aesthetic' and 'ethical' ways of living.

Throughout this book pseudonymously expressed viewpoints are frequently attributed to *Kierkegaard*, rather than to his *pseudonyms* as he would have wished, because this enhances the clarity and readability of the text. Whenever this occurs, however, the pseudonymously written material that has been used closely reflects Kierkegaard's personal opinions expressed in his private journals and signed works.

For the sake of maintaining an infinitely more comprehensible, harmonious and logical flow of ideas from one chapter to the next, the individual themes of each chapter do not represent a chronological sequence of the development of Kierkegaard's thought. For example Kierkegaard's work *Fear and Trembling*, the theme of chapter four, and *Concept of Anxiety*, discussed in chapter seven, were published in 1843 and 1844 respectively, so both of these works predate the theme of chapter three, *Objective and Subjective Truth and Faith*, which was largely derived from Kierkegaard's work *Concluding Unscientific Postscript to the Philosophical Fragments*, published in 1846. A concise and complete chronologically ordered list of Kierkegaard's writings is presented in chapter one.

The book begins with an easy-to-digest encapsulation of Kierkegaard's life – throughout his entire authorship there are subtle autobiographical references that will be missed completely by readers without this background knowledge.

The second chapter is especially important because it provides guidelines for readers who wish to read Kierkegaard's original text. It explains in detail various reasons for his use of indirect communication and examines his application of pseudonym, irony, humour and parable. Chapter four should also prove to be particularly useful for the more serious student of Kierkegaard, for it provides an in-depth analysis of his work *Fear and Trembling*, which is regarded by him, and numerous authors today, as being *the* most important contribution he made. No other introductory text focuses in detail upon this central work of his authorship which contains many major themes of his thought that are continued in the pseudonymous works and religious discourses which follow.

Chapter ten discusses Kierkegaard's views on death, and includes his personal reactions to the deaths in his family. Strangely, in spite of Kierkegaard's belief that a constant awareness of death was a prerequisite to true spiritual development, *none* of the introductory texts on Kierkegaard includes a chapter on this most important feature of existence, and even the more advanced literature on

Kierkegaard fails to emphasise the tremendous importance of this aspect of his work – perhaps we are dealing here with a serious problem of *denial* amongst Kierkegaardian scholars?

Finally, it is important to keep in mind at all times that in much of his authorship (though not in his signed works) Kierkegaard strives his utmost to avoid the use of *direct communication*, because he felt that this invariably provides only an *intellectual* understanding of truth. Instead he uses irony as well as many other modes of *indirect* communication to inspire readers towards their own subjective understanding of his ideas. Ultimately, therefore, he would vehemently disagree with *all* books offering *interpretations* of his work, because such authorship reverses and destroys this fundamentally important mode of communication – it changes his *indirect* communication back into *direct* communication!

Perhaps the most important aim of this book, therefore, is not *interpretation*, but *inspiration* – to awaken readers' interest in Kierkegaard's original works and to provide them with the necessary 'tools' and confidence to form their own *personal* understanding of truth as they journey inwards into the depths of Kierkegaard's original works. Embedded in his writings are metaphors and truths that will overwhelm and enlighten the receptive reader with their blinding clarity. However, extracting these truths requires hard work, for Kierkegaard's writings definitely cannot be understood merely with the intellect – one needs also to filter this understanding through the medium of personal life experience, so that the intellectual 'truth' of his words becomes *subjective* truth, for only then can there be a true comprehension of his insights that will lead to genuine inner transformation and personal growth. Perhaps Kierkegaard's most profound realisation was that truth is meaningless so long as it exists merely as objective understanding, unexpressed in a person's actions and manner of living.

Chapter One

A concise summary of Kierkegaard's life

Although Kierkegaard strives to his utmost to discourage his readers from using the facts of his life to interpret his work, perhaps more than with any other contributor to Western philosophy his writing and personal existence are inseparably intertwined. Kierkegaard was a subjective witness to the truth as he was living it, and he admitted on various occasions that personal themes are active in many areas of his authorship.

This connection between his life experiences and the evolution of his thinking was recorded in the extensive private journals which he kept from the age of twenty-one until his death. When examined closely alongside his works they unveil a mix of crystal clear pictures and vague, ambiguous impressions of the manner in which his authorship is enmeshed with the circumstances and events of his life.

Serious or advanced students of Kierkegaard's thought are advised therefore to study Alastair Hannay's recent book *Kierkegaard* (Cambridge University Press, 2001), as this 'intellectual biography' discusses the genesis of Kierkegaard's separate works, demonstrating clearly the way these individual works or topics, the development of his thought, closely intertwine with the events of his personal life.

Such a task is formidable and cannot be dealt with adequately in an introductory text such as this.

Consequently the aim of this chapter is merely to provide a short summary of his life, mentioning the key events, inner conflicts and relationships that shaped his personality and understanding of reality. Five relationships fundamentally conditioned his outlook – his relationship with his father, his broken engagement with Regine Olsen (the only love of his life), his strained relationship with his brother Peter, his conflict with *The Corsair* periodical and the general public and, finally, his battle with the Established Danish Lutheran Church. A general idea of the facts behind these relationships will help to bring to life the key themes of his thought, and it is hoped they will inspire the more enthusiastic reader to probe further into the biographical details of his existence with the help of specialist biographies such as the one mentioned above.

Søren's childhood

The story begins in central Copenhagen on 5 May 1813, when Søren Kierkegaard was born in the family home, 2 Nytorv, the youngest of seven children. This was the year the State bank had declared itself bankrupt. His father, Michael Pedersen Kierkegaard, a wealthy, influential merchant, was already an elderly man of fifty-six. His mother, Ane Sørensdatter Lund, at the time aged forty-five, was his father's second wife and a distant cousin who had formerly been a servant to Michael Pedersen. She had helped take care of his terminally ill first wife, Kirstine Royen, who died childless in 1796, after less than two years of marriage.

Kierkegaard's father had seduced Ane Lund, and when she became pregnant in 1797, shortly after his wife's death, he presented her with a harsh marriage contract which in the event of a divorce would have denied her custody of the child and left her with little money.

At the time of this second marriage he was forty years old, and he retired to support his future family on the more than sufficient income derived from his business, his properties and his investments.

Little is known about Søren's mother; this is not helped by the fact that in the thousands of pages of Kierkegaard's published and unpublished writings, which contain frequent references to his father, he never once even mentions her name. Eyewitness accounts at the time indicate that he loved her deeply and was profoundly distressed by her death – yet this intense sadness over her demise is not even hinted at in his journals.

Kierkegaard's mother, Ane Lund (1768–1834). From the Natural History Museum, Frederiksborg.

What is known about his mother is that she had been an illiterate servant woman born to a very poor, but respected, Jutland peasant family. She had left her home to serve in the family of her brother and sister-in-law in Copenhagen, prior to her employment with Michael Pedersen.

Søren's home education

Søren's childhood was extremely unusual. Since his father was already fifty-six when he was born, Søren knew him only as an old man. His father's stern manner, steady habits and serious, melancholic, religious temperament were a strongly dominating influence on the whole family. Already at a very early age, his father recognised and admired Søren's exceptional intellect and did his utmost to develop it. Consequently, Søren soon became the centre of his father's and the family's attention. Though only self-educated, Michael Pedersen was extremely knowledgeable, and by the age of seven Søren was already receiving a substantial education at home, which his father imparted in a rather odd, though highly creative, manner.

He allowed the boy to listen to the discussions that took place during dinner parties in his home. These were attended by guests who invariably belonged to Copenhagen's intellectual élite – the family regularly entertained the civic and religious leaders of the city, people such as Bishop Mynster, who discussed and argued the religious, social and political issues of a post-revolutionary era of increasing liberalism. Søren would listen attentively, captivated by the pros and cons of the logical arguments advanced by each guest and awaiting with eager anticipation for the final player in the game, his father, who, after ensuring that his opponents had their full say before he began his reply, would parry with a few well-aimed rapier thrusts all arguments that had been forwarded by the various visitors, clearly establishing the supremacy of his position. Afterwards, when all the company had departed, he would ask Søren to sit in turn in each of the empty chairs in order to present, one by one, the opinions and arguments of each of the dinner guests.

In addition, rather than just taking him on ordinary walks through the streets of Copenhagen, Søren's father would guide him on numerous sightseeing trips, but without ever leaving the house, for these journeys took place only in the imagination, in the family home. Later, Søren would be asked to describe, with meticulous attention to detail, the surrounding panorama of his 'virtual reality' experiences.

In an unpublished work by Kierkegaard from 1842–3, there is a passage describing such experiences through the eyes of one his future pseudonyms, Johannes, which several sources confirm is autobiographical. The admiration and gratitude that Søren felt towards his father is reflected in the following extract:

> His father was a very strict man, seemingly dry and prosaic, but beneath this homespun coat he concealed a glowing imagination which not even his advanced age could dim. When Johannes once in a while asked for permission to go out it was usually refused; but the father occasionally made amends, offering to take his hand and walk up and down the floor. This seemed at first a poor substitute; yet like the homespun coat it concealed something quite different. The offer was accepted and it was left entirely to Johannes to decide where they should walk. They went out of the city gate to a nearby country palace, or to the seashore, or about the streets – always just as Johannes wished, for everything was in his father's power. While they walked up and down the floor the father told him everything they saw; they greeted the passers-by, the carriages clattered past, drowning out the father's voice; the pastry woman's fruits were more tempting than ever. All that was familiar to Johannes his father described so exactly, so vividly, so directly down to the most trifling detail, and whatever was unfamiliar to him so fully and graphically, that after a half-hour's walk with his father he was overwhelmed and weary as if he had been out all day.' (See *Pap.*, IV B 1 (*Johannes Climacus eller de omnibus dubitandum est*), pp. 106–7).

Søren's religious instruction

The Christian instruction that Michael gave to his young child, however, would by today's standards be regarded as excessive and cruel. Being a devout member of the Lutheran Church, his religious convictions were founded upon austere Lutheran Protestant beliefs, which emphasised the sinfulness and innate depravity of mankind whilst preaching the necessity of strict self-discipline and rigid adherence to ethical obligations. In addition, Michael was also deeply influenced by the Congregation of Moravian Brothers (the

Herrnhuters) who were a strong influence within the peasant community. This section of Protestantism was anticlerical and preached an attitude of indifference to the lifestyle offered by bourgeois life. Instead it chose to accentuate to the extreme the central doctrine of Lutheranism, Christ's sacrifice. In their emotional sermons and religious meetings, they would discuss his brutal, sadistic crucifixion in violently explicit detail, with gruesomely vivid descriptions of all his wounds and the unbearable suffering he endured.

Ignoring the fact that he was dealing with a child's innocence and sensitivity, Michael demanded absolute obedience from Søren and applied, without any censorship, Moravian-style religious instruction. He would show the little child cards, illustrated with coloured pictures that displayed famous events and figures such as William Tell shooting an apple from his son's head, or Napoleon Bonaparte on his fine horse, and encourage Søren to ask questions about what he had been shown. Then, suddenly, Michael would produce a picture of Jesus' violent crucifixion, answering in shockingly graphic detail all the questions this elicited from his son.

The traumatic effect this must have had on the young boy's brain was worsened by the fact that his father constantly emanated a feeling of religious guilt and melancholic despair, even though he was supposed to believe in the all-powerful *love* and providence of God. In a retrospective journal entry Søren recorded 'the dark background which, from the very earliest time, was part of my life ... the dread with which my father filled my soul, his own frightful melancholy, and all the things in this connection which I do not even note down' (*The Journals of Søren Kierkegaard*, trans. A. Dru, Oxford University Press, 1962, p. 273). Justifiably, Søren later described such religious instruction as 'insane' and 'cruel', and blamed his father for ruining his life by raising him in this harsh Christian manner which deprived him of a normal, healthy childhood. In other reminiscences, however, he acknowledged that his father had significantly shaped his imagination, intellectual development, dedication and religious calling, and for this he was sincerely grateful.

Søren's formal education

Søren attended a distinguished private school in Copenhagen, the School of Civic Virtue. He was not top of the class, but usually achieved second or third place, with a minimum of homework.

His schooldays however were not a happy time for him. From the beginning, he tended to be picked on by classmates and school bullies, partly because he was so different from the other children. He was exceptionally independent minded and provocative, and in addition his physical appearance did not help matters – unlike his eight-years-older brother Peter, who was healthy and strong with an athletic appearance, Søren was pale and freckled, small for his years, and also extremely frail, which he attributed to his being the child of his parents' old age. Acutely self-conscious, he did not participate in games, and his teachers described him as being like 'a little old man'.

At school, he was very much a loner who never invited classmates home or visited them in theirs. An isolated, self-contained child, he stood out from the rest, even in terms of the very unusual clothes his father chose for him that earned him the name 'Choirboy'. He was also sometimes referred to as 'Søren Sock' in reference to his father's lucrative but undistinguished line of work in the textiles business.

Once, when his sister asked him what he most wanted to be he replied 'a fork' – so he could 'fork' anything on the dinner table, and 'stab' anyone who came after him. Thus 'The Fork' became his family nickname, which seems an appropriate one in view of his natural wit and sharp tongue, which he skilfully employed at school, both in self-defence and sometimes purposely to antagonise other schoolboys. He was also unpopular with certain teachers. One complained about Søren's tendency always to have an answer ready even before hearing the question, and many regarded him as impudent. Even as a young child, he displayed a natural predilection for dispute, which set him against the general current of opinion – this was to become his most immediately striking characteristic later in adult life.

Perhaps his arrogance was partly due to the fact that he was the youngest in the family and the spoilt favourite. Consequently he did not possess authority over anyone and therefore, unlike on his siblings, there was no real pressure on him to 'grow up'. Maybe this is why the metaphor of being allowed to 'grow up' was of central importance to him regarding the acknowledgement of his own work and also in reference to the 'little people' of Denmark – the ordinary common folk – whom he felt were rather like eternal schoolchildren, restrained and controlled by social superiors who taught them what to think and how to behave.

Kierkegaard's father, Michael Pedersen Kierkegaard (1756–1838). From Bymuseum, Copenhagen.

Søren's father

The roots of Søren's complex, melancholy nature extend far beyond his own childhood and birth, to circumstances and events in his father's early life.

Michael Pedersen Kierkegaard (1756–1838) was born a serf, one of nine children in a peasant farming family that was technically bound to the local priest, whose land they had once worked. This probably accounts for the family surname Kierkegaard, an earlier spelling of 'Kirkegaard', which in literal Danish means 'churchyard', though the usual translation is 'graveyard'.

He spent his early childhood living in poverty in his family home in the village of Sædding on the western coast of Jutland, an isolated and inhospitable part of Denmark. At the age of ten, he was already working as a shepherd boy. According to one of Michael Pedersen's sons, their father 'suffered from hunger and cold, or at other times was exposed to the burning rays of the sun, left to himself and the animals, lonely and forlorn'.

In spite of his strict religious upbringing, the young Michael Pedersen could not understand or accept that God could allow him to suffer so much hardship. One day, in a fit of childish despair, anger and frustration – whilst he was tending sheep on the bleak, windswept heaths near his home – he climbed atop a high rock and solemnly cursed God for allowing him to endure so much adversity and suffering. This behaviour would obviously have been considered an extreme sin in the Lutheran Pietism in which he had been raised.

Not long after this, his life rapidly began to improve – when he was twelve years old, one of his uncles who lived in Copenhagen offered him an apprenticeship in his cloth trade, and later, at the age of twenty-one, he was officially released by the priest from his serfdom.

He had up until this point worked for his uncle, demonstrating excellent initiative and industriousness as an errand boy and then as a shop assistant. Now he received his citizenship and set up his own business, rapidly achieving success first as a travelling salesman of Danish woollen clothing and then later as a leading wholesale importer of cloth and textiles.

At the age of twenty-nine he had already accumulated sufficient wealth to purchase a house. Nine years later, at the height of his business career, he married his first wife, Kirstine Royen, who was a business partner's sister. Two years later, in 1796, he inherited from Niels Andersen, his benefactor and uncle, a substantial business that he continued to expand.

Just prior to the stock exchange crash in 1813 he invested a significant part of his wealth in guaranteed gold-convertible bonds – he was now one of the richest and most respected citizens in Copenhagen, occasionally even entertaining royalty in his home.

In spite of his peasant roots, which would have been obvious to the respectable bourgeoisie of Copenhagen, he managed to bridge the gap between these two worlds through his notable financial achievements and also because he hedged his bets socially through his shrewd religious connections. On weekdays his family attended evening prayer with the rural religious community, but on Sundays they worshipped at the Church of Our Lady where he established a close personal relationship with its pastor, Jacob Peter Mynster, a key figure amongst the Danish intellectual and pious élite. Given the social structure of Denmark at the time, it was a remarkable achievement for a married couple of such humble origins to make their way into the upper middle class.

The family curse

In spite of his excellent life situation, Michael Pedersen's existence was overshadowed by a deep anxiety. He was obsessed with the idea that God had planned a fierce revenge on him and his family, on account of his sins, in particular for his cursing of God on the hillside in Jutland. This fear steadily intensified with the passage of years and there seems little doubt that the genesis of his obsession was a biblical phrase he must have known well, 'the sins of the father will be visited upon the sons'.

Then in 1819, his worst suspicions began to be confirmed when Søren's twelve-year-old brother, named Søren Michael, died from a brain haemorrhage after a school playground accident. At the time, Søren was only six years old. A couple of years later, in 1822, the family was dealt a second terrible blow when Søren's eldest sister,

Maren Kirstine, died unmarried at the age of twenty-five of Bright's disease (kidney inflammation). Then in September 1832, Michael Pedersen's daughter Nicoline Christine died in childbirth when she was only thirty-three. The following year, in September 1833, the grim reaper returned to collect Søren's brother Niels Andreas, who died in a hotel room in Paterson, New Jersey, USA, of galloping consumption, at the age of twenty-four. His death had an especially depressing effect on the atmosphere at home because on his deathbed he had asked to be remembered to his dear mother but had not mentioned his father – they had argued before he left because he refused to continue the family's trading tradition. Shortly after that, in the summer of 1834, Søren's mother died of typhoid – an event which deeply distressed Søren, especially since he did not manage to get home in time to say goodbye (when it happened he was on a two-week holiday at the coast in Gilleleje). About six months later, in December 1834, Søren lost his youngest and last remaining sister, Petrea Severine, who died at the same age (thirty-three) and in the same way (after childbirth) as her sister two years previously. Søren had been very close to Petrea and had frequently spent time with her and her three children.

Søren's rivalry with Peter

Aside from their father, only Søren and his eldest brother Peter Christian remained. Unfortunately, in spite of the great sadness they each must have felt, there was not sufficient closeness between the two siblings for them to be able to seek emotional support from one another.

Søren's relationship with his brother Peter had always been far from wholesome. There were irreconcilable differences in their temperaments, and virtually from the beginning there had been a conspicuous rivalry between them, perhaps because they both wanted to be the primary recipient of their father's respect and recognition. In addition, Søren felt he was not taken seriously by his brother and resented the elder brother's position of authority over him.

Moreover, Peter was a highly competent, hardworking high achiever with a forceful intellect, considered by his teachers to be an ideal student. Consequently, wherever Søren went – the School of Civic Virtue and Copenhagen University – an elder brother who had set extremely high standards preceded him. Furthermore, Peter physically surpassed his frail younger brother, with his hikes around northern Sweden and his large, strong, robust frame.

Peter was working on his doctoral thesis in Germany when seventeen-year-old Søren enrolled as a student at the University of Copenhagen in October 1830. In his first year Søren passed with distinction the majority of his preliminary courses, which included physics, mathematics (his best results were in these two subjects), history, Latin, Greek, Hebrew and philosophy. His lectures in theoretical and practical philosophy were by two professors, Frederick Christian Sibbern and Poul Moller, who became Kierkegaard's personal friends. Moller, Kierkegaard's first and only true mentor in the university, had a lasting influence on his way of thinking. A champion advocator of personal truth who was quick to spot any form of affectation, Moller clearly saw the limitations of Hegel's purely abstract, speculative philosophy, and in his later years openly criticised the System (a fact pointed out in a footnote by Kierkegaard's pseudonymous author of *Concluding Unscientific Postscript*). After Moller's death, in a dedication to him in *Concept of Anxiety*, Kierkegaard described him as 'the mighty trumpet of my awakening', and in unpublished declarations he also wrote of the 'confidant of my youth' and 'lost friend'.

In his second year he began reading for a degree in theology, but his progress was very slow, for he had no real heart for the subject. Søren, however, seems to have been able to count on his father's respect and support no matter what he did – even when he put off taking his theology exams, his father tolerated this without any complaint or display of disappointment, though according to Peter it caused him great suffering. It is likely that Peter would have resented Søren for the unconditional love, support and acceptance that he received from their father, and he was also angry that Søren appeared to attach no value to Peter's sense of family honour and adherence to duty.

There were numerous other differences between the personalities of the two brothers. Peter was cautious and economical and he behaved in a socially acceptable, emotionally controlled, predictable manner. Søren at times was extremely eccentric, passionate and impetuous, as well as extravagant and highly self-indulgent, lavishly spending money on luxuries. Indeed in his journals for March 1842, Peter records that he had written to his brother advising caution in financial matters and requesting Søren's written authorisation for certain transactions (which clearly he believed to be ill considered).

A further dissimilarity between the two brothers can be seen in their attitudes to marriage. Peter, who was married twice (his first wife died), was extremely calculating in his choice of partners – both

Kierkegaard's elder brother Peter Christian Kierkegaard (1805–88). From the Royal Library, Copenhagen.

women were of high status and extremely useful to him for the advancement of his religious career. Søren, on the other hand, to everyone's great shock and surprise, scandalously cancelled an engagement to a woman he loved, who was of high status and potentially a great asset to his future career and social standing, and he subsequently neither married nor dated anyone for the rest of his life – there were a variety of reasons for this turn of events which are explained in detail later in this chapter. With so many marked differences between the two brothers, it seems hardly surprising that their relationship with one another was incompatible and filled with conflict.

The great earthquake

In the summer of 1835, upon returning from the earlier mentioned vacation in Gilleleje, it seems that Søren's father, who was drunk at the time, hinted to Søren that he had done something very bad in his past. Though he does not reveal his father's actual words, Søren mentions the occasion in a journal entry: 'His father is a man of note, God-fearing and strict; only once, when he was drunk, did he drop a few words that made the son suspect the worst. The son has no other intimation of it, and never dares ask his father or anyone else' (*Pap.*, V A 108, from 1844; *Papers and Journals: A Selection*, p. 183).

Søren's realisation of the possibility or probability that his father – whom he had so much admired for his strict, pious God-fearing nature – might be guilty of serious sin is likely to have at least partially contributed to the alteration, around this time, of his entire intellectual and moral outlook, and it undoubtedly was a causal factor in the breakdown of the relationship with his father that occurred in this same year.

In an earlier journal entry, possibly written sometime in 1838, there is an important passage in which Søren speaks retrospectively about an unnamed traumatic revelation that he describes as an 'earthquake' which deeply influenced his whole outlook on existence:

It was then that the great earthquake occurred, the terrible upheaval which suddenly pressed on me a new infallible law for the interpretation of all phenomena. It was then I suspected my father's great age was not a divine blessing but rather a curse… . I felt the stillness of death spreading over me when I saw in my father an unhappy person who would survive us all… . A guilt must weigh upon the entire family, God's punishment must be upon it; it was meant to disappear, struck out by God's almighty hand, deleted like an unsuccessful attempt' (*Pap.*, II A 802–6, from 1838; the last four in *Papers and Journals: A Selection*, pp. 117–18).

There has been much speculation as to the nature of this 'earthquake'. Some have suggested that it refers to Søren's discovery of his father's childhood act of blasphemy towards God and his belief that, as a result of this, the entire family was cursed.

There is no doubt that Søren had knowledge of his father's cursing of God. This fact is clear from a journal entry in 1846: 'How dreadful, the thought of that man who as a small boy tending sheep on the Jutland heath, in much suffering, starving and exhausted, once stood up on a hill and cursed God! – and that man was unable to forget it when he was eighty-two years old' (*Pap.*, VII A 5 *Papers and Journals: A Selection*, p. 204).

The most well known speculator of this whole matter, the eminent Danish literary critic Georg Brandes, suggested that the 'earthquake' in question was caused by Søren's discovery that his father was guilty of marital infidelity.

Whatever speculation is correct, it is certain that as a result of Søren's traumatic discovery and revelation, he underwent a profound change in consciousness that altered the course of his life, and he now became convinced that he and Peter would not survive beyond their thirty-third year and that the family would be 'deleted' because no offspring would remain.

Søren and the Romantics

Søren could no longer see value in the bourgeois life of virtue for which he had been raised and which his elder brother Peter had chosen for himself, and his rejection of this way of living led him to a serious analysis of the only other alternative that seemed to be available at the time: a form of drop-out individualism that had been advocated by a group of young rebels known to later generations as 'Romantics'.

Kierkegaard had read the Romantics widely and enjoyed reciting Romantic poetry. His early journals, especially between 1835 and 1838, are filled with references to his reading and evaluation of these writings and it is clear that he strongly agreed with Romantic thought in its criticism of the whole Idealist development. Novalis, Hoffmann and the Schlegels especially influenced him because he saw in them a force that could counteract and save his times from Hegelianism. Their emphasis on the world of individual, subjective human experience – which cannot be understood through logical concepts – made room for values completely incompatible with Hegel's all-consuming systematic structure. Most of all, Kierkegaard appreciated and was influenced by the Romantic notion of Lebensanschauung, a life-view. The Romantics saw it as the unavoidable duty of every individual to create their own individual personal life-view rather than following the ready-made channels of existence offered by society. Like Kierkegaard, they too had firmly rejected the straitjacketed, predictable and superficial bourgeois way of living, striving instead to make their lives as interesting and creative as possible.

Their revolutionary, ironical outlook on existence and their style of living with its emphasis on non-conformity, freedom and the development of individuality leading to radical social and cultural change became a model of rebellion for the first half of the nineteenth century, and Kierkegaard was deeply influenced by them.

The period of dissipation

On 1 September 1837, Kierkegaard moved out of Nytorp with his extensive library to an apartment at 7 Lovstraede.

He was now economically independent, owing to a yearly allowance from his father, and theoretically was now responsible for his own debts, though just a few months later Kierkegaard was to receive from his father a lump sum of more than one thousand rixdalers (the equivalent today of around twelve thousand dollars) to pay his debts from the previous year to various retailers, including coffee shops, bookshops, clothes shops and tobacconists, to mention just a few. Having almost completely neglected his theological studies at the university, Kierkegaard had entered a period in his life of extravagant living, spending lavishly on food, alcohol, fashionable clothing and constant entertainment. He was a regular guest at the theatre and opera and a frequent customer at cafés and restaurants – often in the company of a chosen circle of student admirers. In addition, he was an active participant in the city nightlife through his attendance at numerous private parties. He described his own appearance during this period as 'a man in modern dress, glasses on his nose and a cigar in his mouth'.

It seems, however, that his outer appearance of gaiety was merely a thin veneer, for the entries in his journals throughout this period show that his extravagant lifestyle concealed feelings of emptiness and frustration arising from his inability to find any meaning or direction in life. In the spring of 1836, Kierkegaard underwent a deep crisis of despair in which he was overcome by unpleasant insights into his own existence. He realised he had been completely corrupted by cynicism – the sharp-witted, sarcastic cigar smoker who could be the life and soul of social settings was in fact standing on the edge of an inner abyss of meaninglessness. In a journal entry at this time, he wrote, 'I have just come back from a party where I was the life and the soul. Witticisms flowed from my lips. Everyone laughed and admired me – but I left, yes, that dash should be as long as the radii of the earth's orbit – and I wanted to shoot myself' (*Pap.*, I A 161, from 1836; *Papers and Journals: A Selection*, p. 50).

To resolve his predicament, he realised that he needed to discover a life-view or an idea that would inspire his wholehearted commitment, and he mentions as examples 'great men', who irrespective of the cost have passionately committed themselves to projects they considered supremely worthwhile. This dramatic contrast between his outer life and inner experience led Kierkegaard to compare himself to Janus, the two-faced god, saying, 'with the one face I laugh, with the other I weep' (*The Journals of Søren Kierkegaard*, trans. A. Dru, Oxford University Press, 1938).

The critique of Romanticism

Having closely analysed and experienced many aspects of the Romantic viewpoint, he reached the firm conclusion that this way of living was still a very inadequate approach to existence.

Later Kierkegaard presented a disguised critique of the Romantic outlook in his aesthetic works, and he formally discussed this way of thinking in his earliest writings, *From the Papers of One Still Living* and *On the Concept of Irony*.

Kierkegaard believed, unlike the Romantics, that repentance and renunciation are intrinsic to the religious view of existence and essential for the attainment of personal maturity – to ignore this fact is to deny the true nature of reality. Although the subjective human spirit of the Romantics, combined with their masterful use of irony, had successfully undermined the validity of Hegel's pompous system, Kierkegaard saw that their creation of a brand new way of being had given them an exaggerated sense of man's creative power and importance in the world, causing them to live in an illusory reality in which the distance between man and God is ignored, and instead God and the true spiritual self are unified and submerged out of view.

Kierkegaard then understood that in the Romantic state of consciousness one can exist in a deluded state of ecstasy and grandeur that is only a prelude to disillusionment, boredom and despair. Their ironical stance towards life leaves the experiencing subject out of touch with all reality, including their own reality, and he concluded that the world of literature and poetry have a validity only as long as they are rooted in a genuine awareness of God.

The death of Søren's father

The momentum of Søren's superficial extravagant lifestyle began to diminish following reconciliation with his father in 1838 through which he also regained his lost belief in God's fatherly love. Not long after this, there occurred in May 1938 the most powerful religious experience of Søren's lifetime – it was characterised by an over-whelmingly intense religious joy. It was this event that inspired and initiated his dedication to the problems of religious existence.

Then, very suddenly on 9 August 1838, at two a.m., Søren's father died at the age of eighty-two. This greatly shocked Søren, who had assumed for some time now that it was God's plan that his father should outlive all seven children (in the Bible, the number seven had mystical significance). Forced to reinterpret events, he now became convinced that his father's death must have been some sort of 'sacrifice', made on his behalf so that he could make something of his life.

Two days after his father's demise, Kierkegaard wrote in his journal: 'My father died on Wednesday night at 2am. I did so earnestly desire that he should live a few years more, and I regard his death as the last sacrifice his love made for me, because he has not died *from* me but died *for* me, so that something might still come of me' (*Pap.*, II A 241, 11 August 1838; *Papers and Journals: A Selection*, p. 98). This seemingly strange conclusion had probably been subliminally influenced by something his father had once said to him: 'In fact it would be good for you if I were dead; you might then still make something of yourself; that won't happen as long as I'm alive' (see Bruce H. Kirmmse, *Encounters with Kierkegaard*, trans. Bruce H. Kirmmse and Virginia R. Laursen, Princeton University Press, 1996, p. 229 (315)). It is clear from this statement that Michael Pedersen believed his presence exerted an inhibiting effect on Søren's development and the truth of his supposition is confirmed by Søren, who later claimed that he would never have graduated if his father had not died.

In this light, and to the surprise of all who knew him, Søren now decided to fulfil his father's wish by completing his theological studies and becoming a pastor. This decision – an act of respect towards his father's memory and also partly motivated by guilt – was made in spite of the fact that his inheritance had removed any practical motivation for graduating. His father's demise had left him with a substantial fortune, equivalent today to more than four hundred thousand US dollars, a fact which would later allow him to devote himself to writing without any thought of having to earn a living from it. Indeed, for the following ten years he would not only live very comfortably on his inheritance, but also use it to cover the self-publication costs of his first nineteen books.

Søren's graduation and engagement to Regine Olsen

Leaving his self-indulgent life of idleness far behind him, he now dedicated himself to serious study. Less than a month after his father's death he published his first book, a critical study of Hans

Andersen's limitations as a novelist, entitled *From the Papers of One Still Living*. Though some have claimed that this title reflected Søren's surprise that he had outlived his father, in fact this is not the case, for it was written long before that event. The book was a satirical review of Hans Christian Andersen and the aesthetic outlook on existence, and was the first of Kierkegaard's works that attempted to deal with principles that during Kierkegaard's youth had influenced his way of living.

In July 1840 he was finally awarded his degree in theology, and by September of the same year he announced his engagement to Regine Olsen, who was the daughter of Terkel Olsen, a high-ranking civil servant.

He had first met her on 8 May 1937 during one of his regular visits to a family by the name of Rordam who had a daughter, Bolette, whose company Kierkegaard enjoyed. The family had invited her as company for a young girl who was staying with them over the weekend. Even though she was only fifteen years old at the time, the intensity of emotion he felt from the very first meeting threw him completely off balance, as is confirmed by a journal entry later that same evening. He writes that he had never been more afraid of instantly losing his mind, and he thanked God for not letting this happen.

In spite of their ten-year age difference, Kierkegaard began to form a deep attachment to Regine, though he did not pursue her formally. However, later he wrote in his journals that whilst he was studying for his theology degree, Regine's existence had been 'twining itself' around his own and that even prior to his father's death he had set his sights firmly on her. In the years prior to his formal courtship he did his best to create a close rapport with her family and even befriended her boyfriend Fritz. He found out all he could about her personality and behaviour, which placed him in a perfect position to influence her aesthetic tastes.

Regine willingly agreed to read various books that Kierkegaard had carefully chosen for her, whilst he imparted his views on the way they should be interpreted – it seems that he saw her as his spiritual protégé. Although inwardly he may have experienced her erotically and with great passion, his outward behaviour was characterised by intellectual detachment.

From around 9 August 1840 through the rest of the month, Kierkegaard began a serious courtship of Regine (just over a month after his graduation in theology, on 3 July). He was now twenty-seven and she eighteen. Then, on 8 September, alone with Regine in her family home, he proposed to her and the same day informed her father, who gave him an appointment to return on 10 September – it

Regine Olsen at the time of her engagement to Kierkegaard. Bymuseum, Copenhagen.

was on this day that Regine accepted his proposal. The engagement party took place and an official announcement appeared in the paper. The following year, in November 1841, he commenced a training course at a pastoral seminary and simultaneously began working on his doctoral thesis. On 29 July 1841 he successfully defended it in Latin, as tradition demanded, and it was published in September 1841 under the title *On the Concept of Irony with Particular Reference to Socrates* (in spite of the reservations of some examiners who expressed distaste for his style of communication, which was extremely wordy and convoluted). He received the authorised diploma in October 1841.

He now seemed destined for a conventional, bourgeois existence as a respected, responsible married man in a solid professional career. However, appearances would once again prove to be deceptive.

The broken engagement

Following the engagement, Kierkegaard had seemed genuinely happy with his decision, visiting Regine daily and taking frequent walks and coach rides with her, but his friend and tutor Sibbern, who often chaperoned them, noted a growing disharmony in the relationship.

It seems that from the start Kierkegaard had harboured ambivalent feelings towards the whole idea of marriage – in a retrospective journal entry, he describes an experience he had whilst returning from his father's childhood home a couple of weeks prior to his engagement. It seems to be a clear forewarning of coming events:

> On the road to Aarhus I saw the most amusing sight: two cows roped together came cantering past us, the one gadabout and with a jovial swing to its tail, the other, as it appeared, more prosaic and quite in despair at having to take part in the same movements – Isn't that the arrangement in most marriages?

The day after his engagement, he already regretted making the proposal, realising it had been a serious mistake. However, he concealed this truth behind a façade of behaviour that created the opposite impression.

He still seemed to be headed for a career as pastor or perhaps even a professorship, and even when enrolled in the Royal Pastoral Seminary he continued this charade. As the months passed, however, he became utterly convinced that emotionally, physically, psychologically and spiritually he was totally unsuited to living a married life or a normal existence.

Various journal entries pieced together like a jigsaw puzzle suggest the following reasons for his decision to break up with Regine. Earlier, he had overlooked any potential problems that might arise from the marked contrast in their temperaments – her happy, simple spontaneity, compared with his introspective, inaccessible, melancholy nature. But the prospect of marriage now caused him to view her spontaneous behaviour as a symptom of an unreflective, unspiritual character that could never be altered. He now realised he was 'an eternity too old' for her, since she could never travel with him along his path of critical reflection and resolute commitment.

Later, however, he would claim that he was totally captivated with her and would have found it impossible to live without her if he hadn't been so sure of the fact that his 'melancholy and sadness' – which he saw as a blessing in disguise and an intrinsic and essential part of his nature – were serious obstacles barring the success of the relationship. In addition, owing to certain secrets he felt unable to reveal, he felt the marriage would be based on a lie.

> Had I not been a penitent, not had my *vita ante acta* (life before actions) not been melancholic, marriage to her would have made me happier beyond my dreams. But even I, being the person I unfortunately am, had to say that without her I could be happier in my unhappiness than with her (**Pap.**, X 5 A 149, from 1849; *Papers and Journals: A Selection*, p. 414).

He also wrote in his journals of a 'thorn in his flesh' given to him by God to prevent him from leading a 'normal' life, so that he could fulfil the purpose God had set forth for him. Even on his deathbed he mentions to his friend Emil Boesen 'I have a thorn in the flesh, like St Paul; so I couldn't enter into ordinary relations'.

What is certain is that Søren believed he was faced with insurmountable obstacles barring him from marriage. Finally, although he did not yet know what direction his life was to take, he was convinced that his destiny lay in a 'higher' purpose; he knew that he wanted to devote himself to writing and to God, which would require him to sacrifice everything else for the sake of this path.

Consequently, on 11 August 1841, less than one year after his engagement, he returned his ring to Regine, in a letter, asking her to forget him and forgive him as someone who was incapable of making a girl happy. The letter was later reproduced in *Stages on Life's Way*. On receiving the letter she went immediately to his apartment, and not finding him there, sat down and wrote a desperate letter begging him 'with tears and prayers', for the sake of Jesus Christ, and in memory of his dead father, not to desert her. She added that he could 'do anything with her, absolutely anything' and she would 'still thank him all her life for the greatest of blessings' (**Pap.**, X 2 A 3, 7 September 1849; *Papers and Journals: A Selection*, p. 421). This spirited resistance aroused in him a deep respect and admiration for her as someone who was not the innocent child he had taken her to be, but an adult who was demanding her rights.

In the two months prior to the final break, he entered what he called a period of 'deceit', a strategy of careless indifference towards her and her suffering, partly to induce Regine to end the relationship herself by making her feel she would be better off without him, and partly because breaking off an engagement in the social circles of the time would have placed the woman in an unfavourable position, so Kierkegaard resolved to take all the blame on himself by publicly behaving in an irresponsible, despicable manner that would damage his reputation.

He aroused the indignation of public opinion, the intense disapproval of friends and the anger of Regine's family, except for her sister who still believed in his goodness. In his journals, Søren describes his cruel behaviour to her as 'fearfully painful' for him, stating that she would have 'won' the fight to keep him if he hadn't believed there was 'divine opposition' to the marriage.

He suggested to Regine that she break the relationship publicly so that he would share her humiliation, but she replied that she would endure anything rather than release him. Finally, on 11 October, Kierkegaard told Regine that the break was final, and after an emotionally intense conversation he went straight to the theatre.

That same evening and the following morning he returned at the request of her father, who related Regine's utter despair and, fearing for her life, begged him not to leave, but Kierkegaard would not change his mind.

Kierkegaard writes,

> I made her see reason. She asked me: Will you never marry? I answered: Yes, in ten years time, when I have had my fling, I will need a lusty girl to rejuvenate me. It was a necessary cruelty. Then she said to me: Forgive me for what I have done to you. I answered: I'm the one, after all, who should be asking that. She said; Promise to think of me. I did. She said: Kiss me. I did – but without passion – merciful God.

His broken engagement precipitated the beginning of his authorship, and his first books are partly an attempt to explain, in an indirect and symbolic manner, his reasons and justifications for not marrying her. He wrote in his journals that Regine saw his decision to leave her as merely a symptom of his severe depression, his 'madness, a melancholy bordering on craziness'. She had not realised it was based on a spiritual incompatibility – a tragic conflict of interests and motivation on the spiritual level which he termed a 'religious collision'. He remained obsessed with the event throughout his life, relentlessly dissecting his actions and reactions with ruthless honesty in numerous journal entries and in disguised references to it that appeared throughout his authorship. Even when he lay dying in hospital he mentioned to his friend Boesen, with great affection and sadness, the terrible suffering that he had caused Regine. The act of his broken engagement which began as an agonising choice was eventually to become his work *The Agony of Choice* – the dilemma that he saw as facing all of humanity. His personal question, 'What am I to do?', evolved into the universally applicable question 'How are we to live?'.

In later years he came to believe that his failure to marry was due to the fact that he lacked sufficient faith that all things are possible for God – he saw his 'melancholy' as a symptom of doubting that Christ had truly broken the power of inherited guilt through his sacrifice. Yet he also acknowledged that it was the commitment he initially made to Regine that had allowed him to realise his special calling from God.

His deep bond with Regine is reflected in a letter to his brother that accompanied his will, which explains that Regine was to inherit everything because he wished to express the fact that he had always considered his engagement to her as binding as marriage. (Regine declined the inheritance but later claimed that it was her husband who had refused it on her behalf.)

Søren's substantial authorship

After leaving Regine Søren began an isolated, bachelor existence, totally immersing himself in his work. He realised that in order to clear the path for his own thoughts on the nature of reality and purpose of human existence he would need to undermine thoroughly the validity of Hegel's system, which he viewed as a highly articulate codification and defence of bourgeois ideals and a prime influence on the intellectual élite in Germany and Copenhagen at the time.

Consequently, less than a month after breaking his engagement, Kierkegaard travelled to Berlin to attend lectures given by the German Romantic-Idealist philosopher Schelling, who had been closely associated with Hegel in his youth but who was now well known for his uncompromising opposition to the latter's ideas.

During his stay, Søren also worked furiously on a manuscript, which may have been his main reason for travelling to Berlin – shortly before he left Copenhagen there is a journal entry in which he begs God that he might succeed in writing and finishing this manuscript. He later claimed that this work, which was well over seven hundred pages, took him only eleven months to write. This extensive book, published in two volumes, was entitled *Either/Or: A Fragment of Life* and it was the first of a series of books with literary, psychological and philosophical themes which he wrote in extraordinarily rapid succession over the next few years.

Though Kierkegaard maintained a façade of indifference to Regine's fate, whilst in Berlin he secretly kept track of what was happening to her through correspondence with his friend Emil Boesen. It seems that the suffering he had caused Regine and himself by breaking up with her had become a self-flagellistic 'food' for his soul that fired him with creative inspiration. The whole drama had provided an experiential basis for favouring a religious life-view, and marriage had now become something he could 'think' rather than 'endure'. Indeed he would later admit that his being able to become a writer was due to a combination of his financial independence, his melancholy and his experience with Regine. He even suggested that Regine had helped him to develop a relationship with God and to find his true self.

In a revealing letter to Boesen that he wrote from Berlin, he speaks of his broken engagement and its effects on him:

> In the course of these recent events my soul has received a needed baptism, but that baptism was certainly not by sprinkling, for I have descended into the waters, all has gone black before my eyes, but I rise to the surface again. Nothing, after all, so develops a human being as adhering to a plan in defiance of the whole world. Even if it were something evil, it would still serve to a high degree to develop a person. So just write, and if I may say so, a little more clearly whenever you receive any intelligence (about Regine). I don't shy away from the thought of her, but whenever I think of the poor girl – and yet she's too good to give – to call a poor girl – and yet she is a poor girl – and yet my strength of mind has been guilty of breaking the proudest girl – as you see I am in a treadmill and all I need is to tread for an hour a day like this, and then let my hypochondria be a surly coachman who shouts Giddyap all the time and hits the most sensitive places with his whip, and that's exercise enough for the day, then I need all possible strength of mind to say, Stop, I will now think of other things. And yet my soul is sound, sounder than ever before. (*Breve og Aktsykker*, I, p. 74 (93); letter no. 50).

Kierkegaard returned to Copenhagen with the *Either/Or* manuscript towards the end of 1842, and it was later published in February 1843 under a pseudonym – or, more correctly, a series of pseudonyms. In this work Kierkegaard suggests that there are two fundamental ways that we can live our life, the aesthetic and the ethical. Everyone has the opportunity to make a conscious choice as to which way of life he or she adopts. One must accept full responsibility for this choice that will characterise all aspects of one's entire existence. (Note here the seeds of modern-day existentialism which emphasised the necessity of individual freedom of choice and the acceptance of full responsibility for one's existence.)

Also contained in the same manuscript is a work entitled *Diary of a Seducer*. In this pseudonymous fictional story, Kierkegaard describes the seduction of a young innocent girl by a man who studies her every gesture. The reader of the story soon realises that the girl has no way of escaping the eventual seduction owing to the thoroughness of her seducer's planning. It seems reasonable to speculate from the content of this work that Søren wanted Regine to believe that he was no better than the 'Seducer' he wrote about. Those who were aware of the meticulousness of the strategy Kierkegaard employed to win Regine's heart felt that Kierkegaard had indeed trapped her.

In spite of this and the enormous suffering she endured as a result of the broken engagement, when Kierkegaard discovered a few months after his return from Berlin that Regine had become engaged to Johan Fritz Schlegel (the man she had known before she met Kierkegaard), he reacted with bitterness, which is evident from his criticism of her 'faithlessness' in a section of text that had been intended for his work *Repetition*. In a later work in which he examined the topic of love, there are clear indications that Kierkegaard had thought that he and Regine would pursue their God-relationships in parallel and that he would be assisting with her future spiritual development – that the success of this endeavour would compensate and even justify their broken engagement. Her new engagement now rendered all this impossible. Later, however, he would give her relationship his blessing, though there were tinges of irony in the words he used.

After the publication of *Either/Or*, Kierkegaard continued to write obsessively and at an incredibly fast pace, publishing one book after another under various different pseudonyms. Following the publication of *Either/Or* in February 1843, three more books were published in the same year, on the same day, October 16: Johannes de Silentio published *Fear and Trembling*, Constantine Constantius published *Repetition*, and Kierkegaard published, under his own name, *Three Edifying Discourses*. He continued throughout most of his writing career to publish fifteen more of these *Edifying Discourses* (dedicating all of them to the memory of his father) alongside the pseudonymous books. Using simple, direct language, these specifically religious discourses were intended to make his readers aware of what the Christian ideal really was. They shared a common theme – man's religious obligation as an individual standing alone before a God who does not respect establishments, majorities or compromise. The next year, in 1844, Johannes Climacus published *Philosophical Fragments* and four days later, on 17 June, two more books arrived: *The Concept of Dread* by Vigilius Haufniensis and *Prefaces* by Nicolas Notabene. In April 1845, *Stages on Life's Way* by Hilarius Bookbinder was published.

All his works were published privately, and he used a go-between to make payments and collect whatever was due from sales in order to preserve the secrecy of his pseudonymous authorship. To support this deception, he assumed a façade of frivolity by carefully and masterfully manipulating the impression he made on the general public – the tree-lined ramparts circumnavigating the town, which he used for his daily strolls, the narrow cobblestone streets and squares with their cafés and restaurants and Copenhagen's theatre all became part of the scenery and setting for an 'existential theatre' that he produced and directed in a manner that succeeded in capturing and focusing the wandering, diffused attention of the Copenhagen public upon his published works.

In spite of his frenzied pace of writing, and remarkable volume of publication, during the daytime he was out on the streets maintaining his long daily strolls in order to create the completely false impression that he was solely a man of leisure with abundant free time. On his walks round the town he delighted in communicating in an unhurried manner with people from all walks of life, calling it his 'people bath'. In the evenings he used to visit the theatre between acts to give the impression that he was not working at night. He even had articles published in a newspaper called *The Fatherland* so that it would not occur to people that he was engaged in serious authorship. Not only did Kierkegaard express the process of dialectic through the formation of his two very different branches of writing, he also created a further dialectic by means of the marked contrast between the content of his written works and the 'content' of his way of living.

Despite his sociable behaviour he always remained an enigmatic character and closely guarded his privacy – no one was ever allowed entry to his private dwelling because his butler, Anders, was instructed to turn away all visitors. This contrast between his social presence and social 'absence' (his friendly public manner versus his elusive private personality and rejection of all visitors) is yet another example of Kierkegaard's dialectic manner of communication.

In February 1846, he published what he considered might be his final work, the gigantic manuscript *Concluding Unscientific Postscript to the Philosophical Fragments*. This was much longer than the book for which it claimed to be a Postscript, and it was neither scientific nor conclusive. In it, he discusses the central features of the subjective nature of experience, his philosophy of subjectivity, and he also brings to an acceptable close the various discussions and arguments that the pseudonyms had been having among themselves. Finally, at the end of this book, Kierkegaard confesses authorship of all the pseudonymous works.

The enormous productivity over the past half-decade, during which he had worked 'like a clerk in his office, perhaps without a single day's break', had left Kierkegaard mentally exhausted. He now considered abandoning his career as an author in order to live in the countryside as pastor. On 7 February 1846, five weeks after the manuscript of *Concluding Unscientific Postscript to the Philosophical Fragments* was delivered to the printer, Kierkegaard wrote,

> My idea is now to qualify for the priesthood. For several months I have prayed to God to help me further, for it has long been clear to me that I ought not to continue as an author, which is something I want to be totally or not at all. That's also why I haven't begun anything new while doing the proofreading, except for the little review of *Two Ages*, which is, once more, concluding (*Pap.*, VII A 4, 7 February 1846; *Papers and Journals: A Selection*, p. 204).

Søren's private journals

Incredibly, in spite of his massive workload throughout his authorship, he still continued adding extensive new entries to the private journals that he had first begun in April 1834. These personal notes provide a vivid picture of the intellectual and religious setting of his time that was influenced by the combination of Romantic aestheticism, the Danish Lutheran Church and Hegelian thinking. In addition, one can see in his journals the birth and evolutionary development of many key images and notions that would feature, much later, in his published works. One key image is that of the Archimedean point, and it recurs frequently in the journals.

Kierkegaard, like Descartes, was influenced by the story of Archimedes' search for a 'leverage point'. Descartes found his Archimedean point, around which he could construct his thought, in what he considered to be the indubitable truth that the certainty of one's existence is confirmed whilst one is thinking.

Kierkegaard believed that his Archimedean point existed, not in this world of space and time or in any sphere of theoretical existence, but in the development of a stable life-view. Much later, in 1840, during a trip to his father's native province of Jutland, Kierkegaard arrived at the conclusion that man's true home, his true Archimedean point, can only be found in the realisation of God's fatherly love for us, providing us with a stable life-view which frees us from both pride and despair. Kierkegaard later came to define this life-view as being rooted in a compassionate commitment to God through the example of the way of life epitomised by Jesus Christ.

His Journals form a crucial and fundamental part of his authorship, shedding valuable light on the hidden recesses of his unusual, complex disposition and original manner of thinking. Kierkegaard's observations, recollections, work sheets and plans for the future, as well as his extremely honest, intimate personal confessions and prayers which are recorded in these journals, were only intended for publication after his death, in another time and place, destined for readers yet unborn. Though Kierkegaard lacked sufficient openness and trust to confide in his contemporaries, he provided for later generations, especially in his earlier journals, a most valuable source of insight into the inner workings of his mind. In acknowledging and describing his neurotic, and often negative, thoughts and moods, he was a forerunner of a revolution in which people would come to regard the analysis of complex feelings and attitudes as a pathway towards improved mental health. Aside from the cathartic benefits of self-expression and the potential rewards of posterity that his journals could yield, Kierkegaard also valued them as a means of recording fugitive ideas and elusive overtones, of capturing a thought in the warm freshness of mood 'with the umbilical cord still attached'.

The early journals also discuss his fascination with criminality, especially in the form of 'the master thief', who for Kierkegaard symbolises the complete outsider to society who sees the flaws in the system and challenges it, with a willingness to accept the consequential punishment this may well entail. Kierkegaard once admitted to a friend 'an enormous desire to carry out an actual theft, and then live with his bad conscience in fear of discovery' (Kirmmse, *Encounters*, pp. 207–8 (285–6)). In a symbolic sense, his wish largely came true – later, he would 'steal' Regine's heart, anxiously hiding from her, behind a façade of indifference, the true motives for his actions, and he lived the rest of his life with a bad conscience over the tremendous suffering and stress he had caused.

At the age of twenty-two, living away from home, his journals also reveal a period during which he became interested in Faust, the legendary German necromancer who sold his soul to the devil in exchange for money and power. Kierkegaard writes that Faust's relationship with evil was made in order to 'feel all the sluice gates of sin open within his own breast, the whole kingdom of boundless possibilities' (**Pap.**, II A 605, from 1837; *Papers and Journals: A Selection*, p. 108). Kierkegaard was primarily interested in Faust as a representation of the intellectual who doubts religion and has the courage to reveal the truth of the world's secrets. There seems an obvious similarity between Faust's monogamous attraction to the simple and unreflective Gretchen, which then proved to be an obstacle in the way of his search for knowledge, and Kierkegaard's attraction to Regine's refreshing innocent spontaneity that he later decided was incompatible with his search for truth.

He was also fascinated by the way of life symbolised by the character of Don Juan, as depicted by the hero of Mozart's *Don Giovanni*. He attended every performance of the opera following his first visit on 10 November 1835. Fours years later he wrote of the opera in his journals: 'In some ways I can say of *Don Giovanni* what Elvira says to the hero: "You murderer of my happiness" – for to tell the truth, it is this piece which has affected me so diabolically that I can never forget it; it was this piece which drove me like Elvira out of the quiet of the cloister' (*Pap.*, II A 491, from 1839; *Papers and Journals: A Selection*, p. 104). This passage seems to suggest that Kierkegaard's period of dissipated living, though perhaps related to the revelation of his father's 'sin', was also given fuel by the indulgent lifestyle portrayed in the opera, and this ultimately led him to commit an act that he deeply regretted.

Søren's dark secret

There are passages in Kierkegaard's journals that suggest that he might have had relations with a prostitute. Perhaps this was the 'secret' that he could not reveal to Regine – one of his reasons for not marrying her. The picture gradually emerges from various journal entries.

In a note in 1843 in which he discusses the pros and cons of taking up a position as pastor as against continuing as an author he says:

> There's an ethical requirement. By taking up a definite position in the State as a teacher of religion I am committed to being something I am not. A guilt I bear opens me at every moment to attack from that quarter. Once I am a cleric the confusion will be a sorry one because I kept quiet about something that happened before I entered that estate. As an author the situation is different (*Pap.*, VII A 221).

In another note from 1843 we read under the title 'Layout':

> Someone in his early youth has in an overwrought moment succumbed to the temptation to visit a public woman. The whole thing is forgotten. Now he wants to get married. Angst is awakened. The possibility that he is a father, that somewhere in the world there is a living creature who owes him his life, tortures him day and night (*Pap.*, IV A 65).

This suggests that he is referring to a prostitute since in the case of a love affair or seduction the man would know if he had conceived a child. From the title, and the manner in which Kierkegaard writes this piece, it appears that either he is thinking of this outline as a plot for a short story, or he wishes the *reader* to believe that this is the case. Alternatively, he may have intended that readers should look beneath surface appearances and read it as a plain piece of autobiography.

As mentioned previously, a journal entry dated February 1846 shows that Kierkegaard had pondered giving up his authorship to become a country pastor. However, it seems that prior to this entry, Kierkegaard had already started a chain reaction that would sabotage this possibility and alter the course of his life.

The *Corsair* saga

The following dramatic episode, which culminated in the relentless public persecution of Kierkegaard, proved to be a crucially important turning-point. From the facts of the case, it appears as if Kierkegaard had intentionally designed what happened to him – but why would he do this? The answers to this question are obviously speculative; there are some clues that hint at potential reasons for his behaviour.

One possibility is that he used the intense suffering to inspire the renewed cycle of writing that he later expressed within the privacy of his journals. This seems confirmed by journal entries expressing gratitude for what transpired, stating that the experience had 'put new strength into my instrument, forced me to publish even more'. The question here, however, is did Kierkegaard *consciously* provoke his own persecution because he foresaw a positive outcome, or is this merely retrospective acknowledgement of beneficial side-effects?

One might also speculate on the existence of a martyr complex in his personality – an unconscious wish to be attacked by society that began with his childhood antagonism of classmates. In an essay in 1848 he wrote that although he was 'a genius who might be martyred for the truth, I am not capable of being a martyr for Christianity, for I cannot call myself a Christian to that degree' (*Pap.*, IX A 302, from 1848).

Alternatively, was there the desire, consciously or unconsciously, to attract public attention to himself because his writings had been largely ignored – better negative attention than no attention at all?

Finally, he would have been aware that any suffering he endured would capture Regine's attention and sympathy – perhaps this was sufficient reason for him to provoke his own suffering?

Readers can form their own conclusions after examining the following description of the events involved.

Prior to the completion of *Postscript*, Kierkegaard appears to have contemplated the idea of provoking an attack on himself, supposedly in order to rescue his work from associations with a popular periodical called *The Corsair*. This widely read, weekly satirical tabloid was renowned for its scathing attacks on the haute bourgeoisie of Copenhagen. It publicly ridiculed, using sharp satire, the embarrassing private weakness of local prominent figures within every section of the society – no intellectual ideal or political institution eluded its sharp, cynical, levelling criticism.

Kierkegaard had been a notable exception to *The Corsair*'s policy of criticism. *The Corsair*'s talented editor, Meir Aaron Goldschmidt, had received Kierkegaard's blessing when the paper had first appeared in 1840, and he personally liked and admired Kierkegaard, warmly praising his book *Either/Or*, first in 1843, and then again in a review in 1845, in which he wrote that the name of its editor/author, Victor Eremita, would survive when all other Danish writers were forgotten.

Following the publication of *Either/Or*, Goldschmidt even hosted a banquet in Kierkegaard's honour, which Kierkegaard did not attend because he wished to distance himself from this magazine, since he felt that positive acknowledgement by a scandal periodical, which supposedly served liberal political causes by satirising the establishment, could serve only to misrepresent his authorship.

Though at first Kierkegaard only *imaginatively* insulted *The Corsair* through derisive comments about it in his private journals, his attacks were soon to materialise on the physical plane. At the end of December 1845 a collection of literary essays published in *Gaea, Aesthetic Yearbook*, a literary annual, included a review of the year's literature that contained an appraisal of Kierkegaard's *Stages on Life's Way*. The article incisively criticised Kierkegaard's book and contained a covert condemnation of his treatment of Regine Olsen. The author of the article and editor of the magazine, Peter Ludwig Moller (reputedly the model for the immoral character 'Johannes the Seducer' in the 'Diary'), was a writer, poet and literary critic with academic ambitions whom Kierkegaard had known during his student years (not his university mentor Poul Moller).

The day the article appeared Moller sent Kierkegaard an invitation to respond, addressed to 'Victor Eremita'. Under the pseudonym Frater Taciturnus, which Moller had attacked in his article, Kierkegaard immediately published a response that appeared on 27 December 1845 in a newspaper called *Faedrelandet* (The Fatherland). At the end of this article, in which he contemptuously spoke of Victor Eremita's humiliation at being made immortal in *The Corsair*, he wrote in Latin 'Where there is spirit, there is the church; where there is P. L. Moller, there is *The Corsair*' – thus exposing Moller as being a secret contributor to this gossip paper.

Moller wrote a non-aggressive reply the same day in the same newspaper, and a week later there was a reply to Kierkegaard in *The Corsair* that had a playful yet respectful tone. Kierkegaard used this response as an excuse to attack the periodical viciously in the *Faedrelandet*, on 10 January 1846. Under the pseudonym Frater Taciturnus, he wrote,

> One can engage *The Corsair* to throw abuse at people just as one can engage an organ grinder to make music.... *The Corsair*'s faded brilliance ought to be ignored from a literary standpoint, along with its hidden helpers, the professional traders in vulgar witticisms, as are prostitutes in ordinary life. Anyone insulted by being praised in this paper, if it should happen to come to his notice ... can retort: 'Please throw abuse at me, for it is really too much to be made immortal by *The Corsair*. I can do no more for others than to request that abuse be thrown at me too.

In retaliation for being humiliated in this manner, Goldschmidt responded to Kierkegaard's challenge with a relentless and devastating personal assault that continued for over a year. Using the services of a caricaturist called Klaestrup, Kierkegaard was pilloried in every issue, verbally, with circumstantial reports of his habits and manner of speech, and graphically, by grotesque and comical caricatures of his mode of dressing, crab-like manner of walking, thin legs and curved spine. His physical appearance and eccentricities now became a standing joke, and he was openly mocked in the streets by young children, laughed at by shopkeepers and called nicknames such as 'old man either-or', and 'the great philosopher with uneven pant legs'.

In his journal he speaks of acquaintances whose company he formerly enjoyed being embarrassed or irritated by his presence because they feared being included in *The Corsair*'s victimisation campaign, and none of his influential friends tried to help him. As a consequence, Kierkegaard now abstained from the daily walks and street conversations that he had enjoyed so much.

However, he writes in his journals that the whole matter had gone according to plan, that he was pleased with the result because now there was no longer a risk that his authorship would lead people to classify him as an authority. In addition, he saw a value in being despised by his fellow citizens, because he felt that rejection by 'the crowd' served to strengthen his individuality and made him realise the necessity for a true individual to stand alone if necessary against 'the crowd', and this inspired him to become a better Christian and confirmed his belief that Christianity and 'the public' are incompatible. 'The individual' would later become a key category in his thought.

Though publicly he displayed an air of indifference, the enormity of his suffering is evident from a line in his journal: 'God in heaven! If there were no interior in man where all this can be forgotten in communion with you, who could endure it?' (*Pap.* VII 1 A 97 and 98, 9 March 1846; *Papers and Journals: A Selection*, pp. 213–17).

Kierkegaard, however, was not the only loser in this drama. His exposure of Moller effectively sabotaged Moller's strong chances of gaining a professorship at the University of Copenhagen, and he left Denmark, dying a few years later in poverty and obscurity abroad. Goldschmidt closed down his paper, because he claimed that his victory over Kierkegaard and the consequential damage to someone he so much admired had left a very bad taste in his mouth. Kierkegaard, however, chose to believe that *The Corsair*'s closure signified that he had won the battle against the paper.

Søren's new direction in life

Kierkegaard abandoned his previous idea of retirement to a country parsonage partly because he feared now that it might be misinterpreted as 'running away' due to *The Corsair* bringing his writing career to a halt. More importantly, the great suffering he had endured utterly convinced him that he had been chosen by God for a special purpose – to speak out in the name of the truth of Christianity.

His experiences with *The Corsair* inspired him to study the phenomenon of 'the public', and the press. In 1847 in a review of a novel by Fru Gyllembourg called *Two Ages*, he included the insights that resulted from his bitter experiences. He noted that the press, which was the impersonal tool of the public, was responsible to no one and was only interested in profit, and he understood through personal experience how the influence of the press, combined with the public spreading of anonymous rumours, was capable of corrupting every level of society. 'Journalists are animal-keepers who provide something for the public to talk about. In ancient days people were cast to the wild animals. Now the public devours the people – those tastefully prepared by the journalists' (*JP*, III, p. 321).

Throughout the campaign against him, even those who knew the incredible unfairness of the attack – highly educated literary people as well as representatives of the Church and State – submitted to the majority opinion and maintained a cowardly silence.

Kierkegaard believed that this behaviour of the Copenhagen public had its roots in contempt for the independent-minded individual, induced by Hegelian philosophy and its theological counterpart. This motivated Kierkegaard to publish in February 1846, at the height of all this controversy, his unremitting attack upon Hegelianism, *Concluding Unscientific Postscript to the Philosophical Fragments* (which had already been completed prior to the article he had written against Moller).

Søren's later works

Kierkegaard saw clearly that the lifestyle of contemporary society was polluted by self-deception, complacency and hypocrisy and that this manifested itself most clearly in the religious sphere. Consequently a primary aim of his writing now was to shock people into self-awareness so they could understand the shallowness of their so-called Christian manner of living.

He became convinced that the unavoidable consequence of assuming individual responsibility as a witness of the truth, living a genuine Christian existence, is that one must endure persecution by the majority. He observed that this Christian demand had been ignored, diluted or only poetically contemplated by the representatives of Christianity and that it was his calling to enter into battle with the Established Church over this negligence.

Consequently, following his war with *The Corsair*, the outline of his criticism of more specific issues of contemporary Christianity began to emerge in his *Edifying Discourses in Various Spirits* (1847), *Works of Love* (1847), *Christian Discourses* (1848), and *Lilies of the Field and Birds of the Air* (1849).

In 1848, he experienced his second major religious experience, in which he became passionately convinced that it was God's destiny for him that he should speak out openly about the truth of Christianity. After making his final investigation of religious psychology in *The Sickness Unto Death* and the theoretical difficulties of religious authority in *Two Minor Ethico-Religious Treatises*, which both appeared in 1849, he began his condemnation of the Church of Denmark, a divine mission to which he was passionately devoted until he died. He carried out an important part of this task in his three hard-hitting books that appeared between 1850 and 1852. *Practice in Christianity*, *For Self-Examination*, and *Judge for Yourselves!* clearly presented Kierkegaard's conception of true Christianity, which in its most fundamental form is perfectly exemplified by the life of Jesus Christ.

His full-frontal attack on established religion

Kierkegaard's major battle with the Established Church was triggered by a remembrance speech given for Bishop Mynster, the Danish Primate, following Mynster's death, on 30 January 1854.

In this speech the Bishop was described as 'one of the holy chain of witnesses to truth which stretches through the ages from the days of the Apostles'. Kierkegaard responded by making it clear that he regarded Mynster's 'Christianity' as self-serving hypocrisy, and Mynster himself as a self-interested, materialistic servant of the State, someone who perfectly represented the status quo of public mediocrity, the State Church and all other aspects of Establishment. 'The truth was, that he was very worldly wise, but weak, pleasure-mad, and great only as an orator...' (*SV*, 1. XIV. 10).

Formerly, Kierkegaard had believed that Mynster's viewpoint was not so far from his own. He had sincerely hoped that Mynster might support his notions on Christianity and the nature of 'the single individual' and true faith, thus helping these ideas gain widespread acceptance through Mynster's official stamp of authority as Primate of the Danish Church.

He realised with certainty that this was not to be the case when he met Mynster about a month after the September 1850 publication of *Practice in Christianity* (which had been written in 1848). Although Kierkegaard did not mention his name in the book, Mynster told him that it was clear he was the main target and that Kierkegaard wanted him out of the way. Though Kierkegaard denied this, Mynster's conclusion was perfectly rational – since the book scathingly attacked the Danish Church and Mynster was its most important representative.

Prior to this meeting, Kierkegaard had hoped that Mynster might help him to get a pastorate or perhaps a position at a pastoral seminary that would allow him to escape his current activity of working intensely and at an expense he could no longer afford. The tone of their conversation and the fact that Mynster offered him no help now convinced Kierkegaard that Mynster was out to get him. Kierkegaard also realised that Mynster could not accept the truth that as 'the single individual' one stands alone face to face with God and if no one else could demonstrate this truth, upon which 'the cause of Christianity stands or falls', not even the primate of the Danish Church, then perhaps he would have to be the one to do so.

Kierkegaard's decision to attack the Church through Mynster was made easier by the fact that he harboured a grudge towards the Bishop. A late journal entry on 29 June 1855 (one of Kierkegaard's last entries) suggests that he had resented the Bishop for around seventeen years, following a meeting with him that took place on 9 August 1838, when he informed Mynster of his father's death. Søren relates that Mynster shocked and dismayed him by seeming at first unable to remember the old man even though he had been a key figure in the father's life and had eaten frequently in the family home. Kierkegaard never forgave this extraordinary act of snobbery, condescension and disrespect.

He was also distressed by a recent public remark Mynster had made, in which he equated Kierkegaard and Goldschmidt (the now former editor of the scandal paper *The Corsair*) in terms of their talent. Kierkegaard had very politely informed Mynster that the comparison was *weak* since Goldschmidt had 'talent' whereas Kierkegaard was 'gifted'. Journal entries reveal, however, that Kierkegaard was outraged by the comment, which he regarded as an attempt to damage his reputation.

More importantly, he now saw the Bishop as a manifestation and symbol of everything that was wrong with contemporary Christianity. On his deathbed he confided to his friend Boesen, 'You have no idea what a poisonous plant Mynster has been, no idea; it's monstrous how widely it has spread its corruption.'

Kierkegaard now commenced his subversive, single-handed campaign against the Church Establishment's hypocrisy in twenty-one articles published over a period of around a year in the public press, and in nine issues of a satirical periodical called *The Instant*, which Kierkegaard had founded, financed and published himself. In these articles he criticised and satirised not just the academic halls and churches but also attacked all parsons who were earning a living out of Christianity, and he also included in his criticism their families and their sacramental ministrations.

Søren's final stand

On 2 October 1855, shortly after the completion of the tenth issue of *The Instant*, he was struck down in the street with paralysis of his legs. He was taken by carriage first to his home, where he then asked to be transported to Frederik's Hospital. Two weeks prior to this he had fainted at a party and again the following day whilst getting dressed at home. It is perhaps not by chance that Kierkegaard's collapse perfectly coincided with the moment that he had exhausted the last of his father's money – he mentioned to his friend Emil Boesen, 'But there's also the fact that I'm financially ruined and now have nothing, just enough for the burial.'

His niece, Henriette Lund, who visited the hospital with her father soon after Kierkegaard's arrival, reports that she saw radiating from his face, 'mixed with the pain and sorrow', a 'blissful feeling of triumph'. Never had she witnessed 'the spirit break through the earthly sheath in such a way and convey to it a lustre as though it were itself the body transfigured in the dawn of the resurrection'.

On 19 October 1855, his brother Peter came to visit him at the hospital, having travelled a considerable distance from his parish in west-central Zealand. Søren refused to see Peter, who was now a 'royal official' of the State Church, and Peter returned home the next day. That same day Søren was visited by his friend Emil Boesen, who asked him if he wished to receive the Eucharist. 'Yes', replied Søren, 'but from a layman, not a pastor.' When Boesen responded that this would be difficult, Søren stated, 'Then I will die without it.' He defended this decision by explaining that 'pastors are civil servants of the Crown – they have nothing to do with Christianity' (from Kierkegaard's hospital conversations with Emil Boesen, in *Af Søren Kierkegaards efterladte Papirer*, 1954–5, pp. 596–7).

These two events, the rebuttal of his brother and his rejection of the Eucharist, created scandals with repercussions that continued long after Søren's death – an outcome that he had clearly intended.

His lifelong friend Emil Boesen kept a record of Kierkegaard's last month on earth. To the very end, Kierkegaard would not take back a word he had written and he continued adamantly to refuse communion from a priest. His condition steadily declined, and on 11 November 1855, six weeks after his arrival in hospital, he died peacefully. The tentative diagnosis was 'paralysis – (tubercul?)', which was probably tuberculosis of the spine marrow. No post-mortem was carried out.

Although Søren had stopped attending church and had called upon all people of integrity to 'cease participating in public worship' (*SV*, 1. XIV. 85), his funeral service was, against what he would have wished, held on a Sunday, in between two scheduled religious services, in the Church of Our Lady, the nation's principal place of worship.

At the funeral was one of Søren's nephews, Henrik Lund, who had been amongst several physicians attending Kierkegaard in the hospital. Henrik openly mocked the clergy represented by Peter Kierkegaard and the Archdeacon, protesting against the Christian burial as being against Søren's principles. In addition, angry theology students from the university expressed their fury at the way in which the Established Church had taken over in death the man who had so bitterly opposed them until his last breath.

His brother Peter, who gave the eulogy, added a final insult to Søren by comparing him to a brave but foolhardy Norwegian peasant who in the year 1135, in a highly drunken condition and without the support of his friends, helped to defend local townsmen from pagans by fighting eight attackers, killing six and putting the other two to flight. In this speech he was hinting that his brother had needed *help* rather than criticism, that he had not been of sound mind when he was attacking the Established Church.

Peter felt deep guilt concerning his behaviour towards Søren, and this haunted him until his death. He had inherited Kierkegaard's estate, which Regine had declined, but later he donated to charity the money that had accumulated from the royalties inherited from the sales of new editions of Søren's books, of which two were published by Peter. He decided finally that he no longer deserved to be a Bishop and that perhaps he never had done, and resigned in 1875. In 1879 he returned all his royal decorations to the government and in 1883 he sent a letter to the Probate Court which was returned opened to the family by a friend, but is now lost. According to Peter's own journal records, it began with the text of I John 3:15, 'Anyone who hates his brother is a murderer, and you know that no murderer has eternal life abiding in him.' Finally, in 1884, he renounced his legal right to take care of his own affairs, thus assuming the legal status of a child, and died a ward of the State on 24 February 1888, aged eighty-two, in the 'darkness of insanity' (a quote from his biographer).

Chapter Two

How to read Kierkegaard – irony, parable and other indirect communication

The elusiveness of Kierkegaard's writing style

Aside from being dubbed the founder of existentialism, Kierkegaard has been labelled a 'mystic', a 'religious ascetic' and even a 'brilliant poet'. To a far greater degree than with any other recent thinker, interpretations of his work are influenced by and adapted to the reader's own subjective viewpoints. There are even German translations of his work (by Emanuel Hirsch) which attempt to relate his ideas to an existence theology adapted to National Socialism. Other theologians have asserted that Kierkegaard provides a radical 'Christian apologetic', and yet atheistic and agnostic thinkers with widely diverging political views have also welcomed him.

Kierkegaard's writings clearly possess a chameleon-like quality that enables readers from a wide range of different intellectual and ideological backgrounds to interpret his thought in a manner that chimes with, and supports, their own particular view of existence. A typical example of this phenomenon is reflected in the diaries of Franz Kafka in which the author writes of Kierkegaard, 'As I suspected, his case, despite essential differences, is very similar to mine…'.

This characteristic of Kierkegaard's work is the outcome of his often indirect, sometimes confusing manner of writing. Although some of his books are written under his

57

own name, Kierkegaard assigns the authorship of much of his material to a variety of different pseudonyms and creates further pseudonyms to represent the editors or compilers of these pseudonymous writings.

Sometimes he published on the same day whole series of works, some under his own name, and others under pseudonyms, and in his monumental book *Either/Or*, completely contrasting viewpoints are presented *simultaneously*, through the mouths of different pseudonyms. Added to all this is his regular use of irony and paradox, and his wide diversity of themes and writing styles. Often this makes his thought rather unclear and ambiguous, leaving most readers feeling somewhat disoriented, which was exactly his intention, for reasons that will be described a little later.

The art of reading Kierkegaard

Kierkegaard's authorship can be loosely grouped into his pseudonymous 'aesthetic' works and his 'religious' writings, which were usually published under his own name. The 'aesthetic' series commences with *Either/Or*, and is followed by *Fear and Trembling*, *Repetition*, *Stages on Life's Way* and other works. The 'religious' writings begin with several *Edifying Discourses* and continue with *Christian Discourses*, *Works of Love*, *Judge for Yourself*, *Practice in Christianity* and other religious works. Both his subject matter and writing style, therefore, vary considerably, and he presents a very wide range of different and conflicting religious, ethical and philosophical viewpoints on life without ever openly declaring his own position in any of his works.

Because of this great diversity and complexity of his writings, Kierkegaard realised that readers would naturally tend to search for some unifying theme to his work. Consequently, he explains in *The Point of View for My Work as An Author* that the *aesthetic* versus *religious* distinction in his authorship is not an indication that he was *firstly* an aesthetic author who later *evolved* or *changed* into a religious author. Rather, he asserts: 'The content, then, of this little book is: what I in truth am as an author, that I am and was a religious author, that my whole authorship pertains to Christianity, to the issue: "becoming a Christian"…' (*PV*, p. 43).

To corroborate this claim, Kierkegaard points out that the two categories of his literature are *simultaneous* rather than *successive* – the *Edifying Discourses* being written at the beginning of his authorship, thus accompanying the aesthetic writings. His strongest argument, however, is that to presume that he was initially, or was always, an aesthetic author means that the religious writings cannot be explained. Whereas if he had been a religious author throughout his entire writing career, then his aesthetic writings can be understood as a means of 'getting on the same wavelength' as his audience, for Kierkegaard observed that the vast majority of the people in Christendom spend most of their existence living an aesthetic lifestyle. Therefore, exploring and writing about this mode of existence enabled him to capture the interest of his readers, thus making them more receptive to the core theme of his authorship: 'becoming a Christian'.

Kierkegaard stated, quite rightly, that the ultimate test of the validity of this explanation of his aesthetic work depended upon the reader's judgement as to whether or not this manner of reading his texts allows one to make better sense of them.

Some critics have suggested, however, that Kierkegaard's claim concerning the religious nature of all his texts is retrospective, simply the way in which he wished readers to view his work and thus not representative of his motives at the time of writing but rather a conclusion he reached at the end of his entire authorship. Kierkegaard does indeed admit that when he started writing he did not have a clear or precise understanding of what he was doing, but explains that this unity of his authorship must therefore be attributed to the role of divine 'Governance' in his life. Even if one does not accept this 'divine guidance' explanation, the fact that the fundamental purpose and unity of Kierkegaard's work only became apparent to him during the later stages of his writings does not necessarily imply that his claim is suspect – in the literary world there are many examples of writers who, rather than planning the whole enterprise in advance, tend to work things out and ascertain what they want to say *during* the actual process of writing.

This indirectness of his writing, however – in particular his use of pseudonyms and subtle irony – has caused a great deal of controversy regarding the question of how one should study his work. This has given rise to two main schools of Kierkegaardian scholarship.

There are those who follow the counsel of Walter Lowrie (the early authority and English translator of Kierkegaard), who advises that the entire authorship should be regarded as an expression of Søren Kierkegaard's personal philosophical and religious views. This school tends to approach Kierkegaard's work armed with the question 'what does it all mean?' It views his writings as containing specific philosophical doctrines that can be unambiguously defined by the academic philosopher. If Kierkegaard were alive today, he would undoubtedly criticise Walter Lowrie's approach, since although he eventually exposed the fact (what everyone by then knew) that he was the author of all the pseudonymous works, he also stated, 'In the pseudonymous works there is not a single word which is mine. I have no opinion about these works except as a third person, no knowledge of their meaning except as a reader, not the remotest private relation to them' (CUP (S.L.), p. 551). And in his journals he expressed his explicit wish that anyone quoting from his books should cite the name of the respective pseudonymous author. It would seem evident, therefore, that he does not want any of his pseudonymous texts to be read as *Kierkegaard*. Instead he wishes them to be simply an expendable vehicle that allows his readers to reach their *own* understanding. In spite of this, Lowrie blatantly refuses autonomy to the pseudonyms.

In contrast to Lowrie's approach, the poststructuralists treat the entire authorship, even his private journals and signed works, as though it were *all* the product of pseudonyms. According to this school of thought, Kierkegaard's writings invariably refrain from offering any conclusive meaning – they do not intend to clarify any issues or assert objective truths, nor do they present any definite doctrine. Instead Kierkegaard's work seems to be asking each individual reader the question 'what do *you* think?' A well-known book published in 1971 even suggests in its title (*Kierkegaard: A Kind of Poet*) that Kierkegaard should be approached using primarily the tools with which one reads a poet – literary criticism.

It would seem reasonable to assume that the 'Lowrie approach' is undoubtedly very misguided since it blatantly contravenes Kierkegaard's wishes. The poststructuralists respect Kierkegaard's request to acknowledge pseudonymous material, but perhaps are too extreme in suggesting an 'anything-you-want-to-make-of-it' approach by claiming that one cannot attribute *any* viewpoints to Kierkegaard.

'Middle ground' approach to reading Kierkegaard

The following more 'middle ground' approach might perhaps appeal to most readers.

1.   Material that expresses views on established religion and the essence of Christianity, in texts that Kierkegaard personally signs, can be regarded as a reflection of his own views (except when he is using irony).

2.   Respect Kierkegaard's wishes, by treating all opinions expressed in his pseudonymous writing as belonging to the corresponding pseudonym and *not* to Kierkegaard, unless point (3) is applicable.

3.   Whenever a viewpoint expressed by a pseudonymous author is the same, or nearly the same, as one that is expressed in Kierkegaard's personally signed writings, one may assume that this viewpoint is almost certainly Kierkegaard's. In this book, the author frequently applies point 3, and thus often attributes pseudonymous material to *Kierkegaard* rather than to his *pseudonyms*, as Kierkegaard would have wished, because this serves to make the material less confusing and far more readable. The author has however closely followed the requirement of point 3 by only using this approach with pseudonymously written material which *very* closely reflects Kierkegaard's personal opinions (as revealed in his signed works).

4.   In keeping with the spirit of Kierkegaard's intentions, do not use any viewpoints attributable to him for the purpose of compiling any form of conclusive 'doctrine' or 'philosophy of Kierkegaard'. Kierkegaard definitely does not want anyone to adopt his, or any other, philosophy or understanding of life – the fundamental aim of his writing is to motivate his readers to form their *own* conclusions about life and choose their *own* way of existence.

It might appear that this *complete* existential 'freedom of choice' that Kierkegaard seems to promote is not *genuinely* meant, given his feelings about Christianity. However, one might reasonably argue that there is no contradiction here because it seems clear from Kierkegaard's writings that he realised that the 'true' Christian existence can only be achieved if it is *freely chosen* by the individual, and it also seems evident from the ideas he expresses that this is only likely to happen when a person has first seen through the emptiness of all other ways of living. Without the freedom to choose and experience alternative modes of existence, such insight is unlikely to occur.

Therefore it seems reasonable to conclude that to motivate his readers to form their own conclusions about life and to choose their *own* way of living is *still* the fundamental goal of Kierkegaard's work, in spite of his deep-rooted conviction that ultimately Christianity is the *only valid choice* for human existence. One could reasonably assume, therefore, that it may simply be Kierkegaard's hope that his writings will eventually catalyse a realisation in his readers that will inspire them to *choose willingly* the true Christian path.

The fundamental reasons for using indirect communication

Kierkegaard's pseudonymous work *Concluding Unscientific Postscript* contains the most comprehensive discussion of his theory of indirect communication. In spite of the pseudonymity of the text, we can nevertheless assume that this theory does represent Kierkegaard's own views because he had previously developed an outline of this same theory – for a projected lecture course – in his personal *Journals and Papers*. Additionally, there is a very close relation between Kierkegaard and the pseudonymous author Johannes Climacus – which is pointed out by Kierkegaard himself on pp. 31–2 in *The Point of View of my Work as an Author*.

Kierkegaard perceptively observed that although *direct* communication can be very effective in communicating facts or information, it *cannot* adequately catalyse the realisation of *subjective truth*, which is the only type of truth that potentially can evolve a person's consciousness – for this purpose an indirect tactic is need. Kierkegaard states, 'All communication of knowledge is direct communication. All communication of capability is indirect communication' (*JP*, I, p. 282). In the case of the aesthetic works, his method, he says, is to deceive:

> It means that one doesn't begin *directly* with what one wants to communicate, but … going along with the other's delusion. Thus one begins by saying, not 'I'm a Christian, you are not,' but 'you are a Christian, I am not.' Not by saying 'It is Christianity I preach, and the life you lead is purely aesthetic,' but by saying 'Let's talk about the aesthetic.' The deception is that one does this precisely in order to come to the religious. But according to the assumption, the other is also under the delusion that the aesthetic is the Christian, since he thinks he is a Christian and yet lives the life of immediacy (*The Point of View of my Work as an Author: A Direct Communication – Report to History*, *SV*, 18, p. 105).

So Kierkegaard observed that people frequently *choose not* to know themselves and thus he saw that a fundamental task in his work was to find a way to overcome the psychological defences of his readers – to gain the co-operation of their *will* so that they would be willing to transform their existence.

It is evident from the following analogy that Kierkegaard realises the tremendous difficulty of successfully achieving this aim.

> To stop a man on the street and stand still while talking to him, is not so difficult as to say something to a passer-by in passing, without standing still and without delaying the other, without attempting to persuade him to go the same way, but giving him instead an impulse to go precisely his own way. Such is the relation between one existing individual and another, when the communication concerns the truth as existential inwardness (*CUP (S.L.)*, p. 247).

He recognised that his battle was not against objective *theories*, which could be proved wrong, but with various *styles of living*, which were both subjective truths and also illusions. Thus a radical attack was called for – an attack at the roots of the various prevailing illusory styles of living. This attack had to be indirect because humans find it remarkably easy to dismiss any direct forms of attack that others launch on their way of thinking and behaving. 'No, an illusion can never be destroyed directly, and only by indirect means can it be radically removed…. That is, one must approach from behind the person who is under an illusion' (*PV*, p. 24).

To take an extreme example, if you presented a paranoid schizophrenic with clear proof or evidence that his beliefs were false and that therefore his paranoia was completely irrational, he would be able to neutralise all your arguments instantly, simply by classifying you as part of 'the plot' against him. In other words, you would be absorbed into his illusion. In a similar manner, someone who criticises the views of a devout communist might easily be discredited due to their 'bourgeois morality'; an opponent of Christianity would be discounted by Christians on account of their 'sin'; the detractor of psychoanalysis would be labelled by their therapist as suffering from 'resistance'. In each case the attack would not be taken seriously because every approach to dealing with existence has its own techniques for explaining away critics as 'part of the problem'. All direct assaults on a person's lifestyle are therefore doomed to failure.

Kierkegaard describes how people react to the direct critic: 'First and foremost, they do not bother about him at all ... the next step, they ... settle themselves securely in their illusion: they make him a fanatic' (*PV*, p. 24). It is really no great surprise that people do respond in this manner, because any serious challenge to a person's lifestyle is at the same time a direct threat to their self-image and self-esteem – the very core of their experience of self.

Kierkegaard undermines the effectiveness of such defences by avoiding them. He avoids them by challenging them undetected, through 'approaching from behind'. If one does this effectively, the person's defences can be bypassed or sufficiently weakened, before they notice they are 'under attack', and in this way, one can subtly undermine the confidence they have in their approach to existence.

So Kierkegaard's approach is to enter imaginatively into the various points of view and emotional positions that might be held by his readers, and from this 'insider position' he demonstrates how these views differ from alternative outlooks on life. Through identification with the characters he describes who have similar values and lifestyles, readers are subtly guided into a detached, clear awareness of their own life situation and attitude to existence, and this provides them – often for the first time ever in their life – with the opportunity to become aware of and challenge their unconscious, fixed, routine manner of living and thinking. This leads to deep insight into their own motives for adopting a particular way of existence and the limitations that are inherent in it. Now they are in a position to choose between remaining where they are, and opting for a fundamental change. This indirect approach allows his readers to preserve their personal integrity and individual freedom of choice, because any subsequent decisions they might make are now based upon their *own* insights rather than upon recommendations coming from some outside authority.

So Kierkegaard's indirect style of writing effectively helps his readers to appropriate and assimilate his material in a manner that makes his thought *their own*, so that it becomes a subjective experience of reality which then potentially can inspire a genuine transformation of their existence.

He insisted that his writings were not attempting to communicate or defend a set of specific propositions but were more like poetry – though not the same because his literary form had a religious purpose. Like his beloved model Socrates, Kierkegaard wished to make people think for themselves, use independent judgement and act with deliberate choice. This approach was based upon his realisation that existential truth – truth that potentially can transform a person's outlook and manner of living – couldn't be communicated directly in an effective manner. For existential truth presents insights that all people must adapt to their own unique experiences and outlook, and Kierkegaard felt that this could be best achieved via 'indirect communication'.

Why did Kierkegaard use pseudonyms?

The most fundamental mode of his indirect communication was his use of pseudonyms. The primary task of the pseudonyms was certainly not to conceal his identity, for Kierkegaard knew very well that some of his more learned readers would instantly have recognised Kierkegaard as the author behind these texts.

However, his use of pseudonyms did serve several other important purposes. To begin with, it prevented his readers from treating his work as 'authoritative knowledge', which helped to stop his thought from being mutated into yet another 'system' for human existence. His use of pseudonyms also allowed him to reveal more of what he thought and felt than would have been wise or proper if the works were signed. It is also possible that Søren may have believed that others would not consider him an 'authority' worth listening to, but by using pseudonyms he was able to distance himself from his own works, thus overcoming this problem and freeing himself to say whatever he wished without being concerned whether or not he had the 'authority' to do so.

Kierkegaard also wished to present his ideas about life from various different points of view, and none of these viewpoints was to be taken as correct or authoritative. This obliges his readers to make up their own minds regarding the variety of conflicting ideas that are being expressed. Therefore, in a sense, his pseudonymous characters sometimes function rather like fictional characters in a novel, with their own opinions, behaviour and outlook on life. Kierkegaard's hope is that readers will recognise in themselves aspects of the lifestyle and manner of thinking represented by these fictional characters and that this will inspire inward reflection.

His great masterpiece *Either/Or* includes a section entitled *Diary of a Seducer* that presents perhaps his most elaborate applications of pseudonyms. In the preface to this work, 'A' states that he is the editor of this 'diary', which he stole from a friend called Johannes. Victor Eremita, however, suggests that in fact 'Johannes the Seducer' is probably just a name that 'A' has invented and that A's editorial claim is simply 'an old novelist's trick'. Then the whole issue of the manuscript's authorship is complicated further when, in the preface to the entire work, Victor Eremita suggests that his own editorial claims may also be a similar disguise. Kierkegaard creates all this confusion because he had set himself a very difficult task; he wished to conceal his identity as author behind a pseudonym, but simultaneously he wanted to make it obvious to the reader that this *was* a pseudonym (or series of pseudonyms). In addition, he did not want overtly to expose himself as the author of the autobiographical text of *Diary of a Seducer*, for it was composed as a coded message to his jilted fiancée Regine, expressing his thoughts and feelings about his relationship with her. However, from the content of the diary it seems obvious that he nevertheless wanted Regine to know that he wrote it for her.

Adopting an ironic perspective on life

Another favourite mode of indirect communication employed by Kierkegaard was an ancient literary technique dating back to the fifth century BC that today is known as Socratic irony. Socrates' primary form of communication was irony. The most well-known examples of this were his assertion of his own ignorance. When told that the oracle at Delphi had named him as the wisest man in Athens, Socrates pretended to be shocked. How could this be true if he knew nothing? But after some consideration he admitted that he was wiser than others because, though he knew nothing, he *knew* that he knew nothing, whereas other people also knew nothing, but thought they knew something. This claim of 'ignorance' by Socrates served the purpose of undermining the condescending pretence to knowledge by his opponents.

Kierkegaard carried out his most in-depth analysis of the subject in his university thesis, *The Concept of Irony with Continual Reference to Socrates*, and he made good use of irony in some parts of his authorship which has given rise to some controversy over what *was* or was *not* written with irony. What is certain, however, is that a knowledge of his views on irony and other aspects of his indirect communication is essential to a correct reading of his texts.

Kierkegaard and his contemporaries were more interested in irony as an expression of a person's overall attitude towards existence than as a mere verbal strategy. So he devoted his thesis on irony primarily towards the question of what it means to *live* entirely from within an ironical perspective in terms of one's attitudes and behaviour within the world. The ironic perspective on life is characterised by a complete inner detachment of oneself from the surrounding world. It is an assertion of oneself as a radically independent entity. Although the 'ironist' participates in life, he does not take his involvement seriously. The normal motives behind various activities are not *his* motives, for he sees that in comparison with the 'big picture' – infinity – all human endeavours are insignificant and ultimately meaningless. Therefore he no longer defines himself in terms of his social roles or career, for he has risen above society and is basically indifferent to what others think of him. And yet in spite of his feelings of alienation from society, and his complete *inner* disengagement from the world, he makes no attempt to protest against existence or withdraw from the world; instead he acts as though he were a sincere participant.

Kierkegaard describes an essential flaw in adopting this ironic perspective as a permanent way of life:

> For the ironic subject, the given actuality has lost its validity entirely; it has become for him an imperfect form that is a hindrance everywhere. But on the other hand, he does not possess the new. He knows only that the present does not match the idea.... He is continually pointing to something impending, but what it is he does not know (*CA*, p. 261).

This ironic stance towards existence, if taken as an end in itself, provides only *negative* liberation in the sense that it detaches one from *inappropriate* forms of existence without providing a *constructive alternative* – in other words, though it is a mode of consciousness that potentially *may* catalyse the transition to a more evolved way of living, if the ironic stance becomes a person's permanent way of life, so that the detachment is for its own sake and not used for the purpose of finding a positive alternative, it can only lead to despair, for in this negative use of irony 'the whole of existence has become alien to the ironic subject and the ironic subject in turn alien to existence' (*SKS*, 1, p. 259). Irony levels all values to indifference, and good and evil and other contrasts appear at bottom to be the same. It thus leaves the person in a type of 'limbo' state, on the edge of existence, a non-participant in life.

It should also be noted that a *perfectly* pure ironical outlook does not in fact exist, because the ironist cannot include his own *ironical self* as one of the objects of his irony. In his self-disengagement from existence, he does not disengage himself from his *own self-disengaging*. Even if he wished to do this it would not be possible because it would result in an infinite regression of ironic disengagement from ironic disengagement ad infinitum.

Mastered irony

However, Kierkegaard regarded the ironical attitude as an important stage in the evolution of a person's self-understanding and emotional maturity – he describes this use of irony in his thesis as being 'the awakening of subjectivity', and later in *Concluding Unscientific Postscript* the ironical attitude is identified potentially as a transitional stage between the aesthetic and the ethical spheres.

He regarded 'mastered irony' as an invaluable tool for evaluating one's life, because he saw that an ironic stance towards oneself was absolutely essential to developing the detachment necessary for objectively and accurately evaluating the totality of the way one lives. One must, however, in spite of this detachment, at the same time remain committed to one's own values. To be detached is objective, whereas to be committed requires one to be subjective. So in mastered irony a person must be simultaneously a subject – the centre of commitment – and object – that which is analysed by the self. These are opposing tendencies that can never live together harmoniously, and consequently the attempt to maintain a balance between these contradictory forces, which one is obliged to do, always produces anxiety.

> When irony has first been mastered it undertakes a movement directly opposed to that wherein it proclaimed its life as unmastered. Irony now limits, renders finite, defines, and thereby yields truth, actuality, and content; it chastens and punishes and thereby imparts stability, character, and consistency.... He who does not understand irony ... lacks *eo ipso* what might be called the absolute beginning of personal life (*CI*, p. 339).

So mastered irony potentially provides us with deep insight into our strongest beliefs and commitments, and the courage to assess these objectively, through the lens of detachment, without personal bias. Without this skilled detachment a person is unable accurately to evaluate himself or herself and this can lead to fanaticism or dogmatism. Mastered irony allows one to be firmly committed to one's life whilst still being able to see other points of view objectively. 'Most men are subjective toward themselves and objective toward all others, ... but the task is precisely to be objective toward oneself and subjective toward all others' (*JP*, vol. 4, 4572).

Most importantly, Kierkegaard considered that the detachment provided by an ironic stance towards existence is an essential stage in the process of spiritual development, the preliminary requirement that must be cultivated and allowed to run its course, for the purpose of extracting oneself from the grip of the ordinary unreflective way of life that is characterised by mere desire-satisfaction. The feelings of alienation towards this lifestyle that are provided by an ironic perspective help to deepen a person's resolve to make a transition to the next level of existence, the ethical realm. Ironic detachment also protects the self-awareness that is already present by preventing the person from becoming re-involved with the superficialities of the finite world of form – the inner self, through its consciousness of finitude as a limit, interprets itself as poised before possibilities that transcend that limit. Interestingly, it was whilst he was writing his doctoral dissertation on the subject that he himself 'first gained a clear understanding of what he himself wanted to do and what he was capable of' (Kirmmse, *Encounters with Kierkegaard*, p. 29).

The use of verbal irony

Kierkegaard considered verbal irony to be, even at its highest level of expression, merely a manifestation of an ironic life, though usually it is not even that. 'Irony is an existence qualification, and thus nothing is more ludicrous than regarding it as a style of speaking or an author's counting himself lucky to express himself ironically once in a while' (*CUP*, pp. 503–4).

He saw no value whatsoever in clichéd verbal irony that quite obviously conveys only one meaning, which is the opposite of the literal meaning, such as when someone says 'lovely weather isn't it?' when in reality it is pouring with rain. He regards this as a deficient or weak use of irony that 'cancels itself; it is like a riddle to which one at the same time has the solution' (*CI*, p. 248).

A more subtle example of verbal irony might be the following remark in a letter of recommendation for a stockbroker candidate, which says, 'This man is a quick learner and good at his job – you won't have to continually remind him about the dangers of stress caused by overwork.' In this example the reader has to make a little bit more effort to decipher what might be implied because the sentence is open to more than one possible interpretation, but there is still an intended meaning behind the statement.

Kierkegaard points out a still higher stage of irony, when what is said can be interpreted in a variety of ways but there is no intention, on the part of the author, that the reader or listener should interpret anything at all – if the person *does* choose to interpret what is said as meaning something, that is entirely their own responsibility.

In direct, non-ironic modes of speech in which the assertion belongs to us, our views can be challenged, but when we say something that can be interpreted in various possible ways, and we have no interest in communicating anything in particular, we make no commitment to what we have said and are thus free from responsibility. Consequently, we cannot be judged or criticised for what is interpreted by the reader. This is verbal irony in its most extreme and purest form – the mode of communication that Kierkegaard attributes to Socrates and which Kierkegaard used in various parts of his authorship.

The humorous approach

Throughout his authorship, an important part of Kierkegaard's indirect approach was to 'disarm' his readers with his keen ironical wit, so as to make them more receptive to his more provocative statements.

> It is with existence as it was with my doctor. I complained of feeling ill. He replied: 'You are probably drinking too much coffee and not taking enough exercise.' Three weeks later I again consult him and say I am really not feeling well, but this time it cannot be the coffee for I do not touch it, nor the lack of exercise for I walk all day. He replies: 'Well then, the reason must be that you do not drink coffee and take *too* much exercise.' There we have it; the lack of well-being was and remained the same, but when I drink coffee it comes from the fact that I drink it, and when I do not drink coffee it comes from the fact that I do not drink it. And so with us human beings in general. Our whole earthly existence is a kind of illness (*CUP*, pp. 402–3).

The type of humour that is of *primary* importance to Kierkegaard, however, and which he considers in itself as distinct from irony in his discussions of the subject, is not humour as a mode of literary 'style' or verbal communication, but humour when it has become an expression of an individual's overall attitude towards existence –

71

their general *stance towards life*. In other words, in the same way that Kierkegaard is far more concerned with the *ironist* – irony as a complete outlook on life – rather than with *irony* as a *technique*, similarly with regard to humour he is chiefly interested in the *humorous outlook* on existence.

So a major similarity between humour and irony is that *both* have the potential to form a person's total perspective on the world and both have a levelling effect upon everything in the world. Humour is similar to irony in that it depends on 'not coming to terms with the world' (*Pap.*, I A, p. 154, April 1836; *Papers and Journals: A Selection*, p. 50). Both states of consciousness see the emptiness of worldly values and practices that are traditionally regarded as meaningful in various ways. But according to Kierkegaard, whereas irony's only suggestion is that one should 'admire nothing' (complete disengagement from the world), the scope of humour is greater since it includes the ironist as well. In 1836 Kierkegaard wrote that irony and humour 'may well unite in one individual'. Later, in a journal entry from 1837, he relates irony to humour when he speaks about the dialectical potential (inner tension which can give birth to something positive) of Romantic irony, by likening the Romantic view of existence to 'a see-saw whose ends designate irony and humour' – a continual oscillation between the humorous and ironical perspectives on existence that finds a certain 'rest and equilibrium' in the fluctuation between the two. In the same entry he writes that an individual can only 'survive' the despair of irony when he enters a state of complete detachment from everything, including himself, and from this raised vantage point sees the full extent of his own insignificance. Kierkegaard states that irony 'kills itself' only when 'with humour it has scorned everything including itself' (*Pap.*, 11 A, p. 627; *Papers and Journals: A Selection*, pp. 109–10).

Kierkegaard saw other fundamental similarities between the two states. Just as the ironic stance can serve as a type of borderline zone (between the *aesthetic* and the *ethical* spheres of existence), which potentially can facilitate a 'shift' from the aesthetic to the *ethical* mode of existence, similarly Kierkegaard asserts that humour also can potentially serve as a borderline or transitional stage between the *ethical* and the *religious* existence. 'Irony is the boundary between the aesthetic and the ethical; humour the boundary between the ethical and the religious' (*SV*, 3 10, p. 179). In both cases, the boundaries are related to existential tensions that first become apparent to subjective reflection and steadily increase in intensity the longer one remains at this stage.

In the borderline zone of irony, the individual has become aware of the contradiction between the way he feels and exists in his innermost being and his failure to express this in his outer behaviour. At this intermediate stage there is detachment and disidentification from the *given self*, but not yet complete identification with an *ethical self*. Instead, the would-be ethicist now identifies with his activity of detachment, his *ironical self* – irony becomes his 'incognito'. By ironising the relative nature of the finite world of form he conceals and protects the purity of his deepest ideals and escapes the delusion that he is satisfying his innermost needs. To other ironists, however, this ironical stance may be viewed as a manifestation of inwardness that is being concealed and defended.

Humour is used in a similar way; the person with religious aspirations who has not yet reached a pure state of religiousness uses humour to conceal his spiritual preoccupations from others and protect whatever religiousness he has already developed – as well as his inner unfulfilled religious ideals – from being disturbed by any behaviour he exhibits that appears to contradict these values. Such behaviour would include not only 'aesthetic' behaviour characterised by 'immediacy' and governed by purely external contingencies of reality, but also all behaviour motivated by the desire to become an ideal *ethical self*.

So, like irony, the humorous outlook attempts to conceal and protect inwardness and restrains its open expression. In addition, both humour and irony can potentially signal the presence of inwardness to others who share this same characteristic. Kierkegaard's pseudonym Johannes Climacus, in *Concluding Unscientific Postscript*, asserts that if you are looking out for a religious person, then you should be on the look-out for humour. Yet he also points out that in the case of a truly religious person, the presence of humour does *not* mean that this person is a humorist – the humour is merely an incognito – an act or façade, 'strictly speaking the religious person is infinitely higher than the humorist', and is essentially *serious* because the moment a person truly turns inward and away from the world, their 'hidden' inwardness, which excludes all consideration of earthly goals, provides no foothold for humour. However, Kierkegaard also points out through his pseudonym that 'religiousness with humour as the incognito is the unity of absolute religious passion (inwardly deepened dialectically) and spiritual maturity, which calls religiousness back from all outwardness into inwardness and therein it is again indeed the absolute religious passion' (*CUP (E)*, VII, p. 440). In addition, the pseudonym asserts that if a supposedly religious person were to be offended if others were to laugh at his religious values, then this indicates he lacks inwardness and thus needs to be consoled by the illusion that others share the same beliefs.

In contrast to this, the person who is *essentially* humorous – the *existing humorist* – is *not* a façade. Climacus says that an 'existing' humorist 'presents the closest approximation to the religious person' (*SV*, 3 10, p. 133). For the *existing humorist* exists in the transitional stage between the ethical and the religious, for he has reached the point where committing oneself to the infinite (God) makes sense, and he sees the contradiction between the conception of God and the values of our finite existence, but he postpones dedicating himself to God in religious passion – his humour conceals his inwardness and protects him from taking this final step into the state of genuine spiritual commitment which he knows is essential to him, he 'parries with his jest' (*SV*, 3 10, p. 134) – at this stage, the humorist realises that he himself is now comical. Unlike the systematising or theoretical philosopher, who believes that whatever cannot be spoken is of secondary importance, the humorist is deeply aware of his (and other people's) limitations concerning the ability to express the true nature of existence which is immeasurable and inexpressible, and for him it is those facets of existence that *cannot* be verbally expressed which are the deepest expression of fundamental truth. Climacus also describes this type of humorist as someone who has the ability to recognise the comedy 'present in all stages of life' (*SV*, 3 10, p. 189).

In contrast to the *existing* humorist, a person who is simply a *humorist* without any religiousness lacks that *inner mode of existing* which contrasts with the humorous exterior – so there is nothing in their *own* attitude to existence that they find comical. This person is very much aware of, and responds to, the demands and challenges of existence by helping *others* to understand and deal with *their* existential suffering, whilst simultaneously ignoring their *own* suffering, much like a psychoanalyst who administers therapy to his anxious clients whilst ignoring his own neuroses.

Kierkegaard's use of parody

Kierkegaard also used parody in his writings, usually as a means of indirectly attacking Hegel's system. The titles of some of Kierkegaard's works are parodies of various Hegelian viewpoints. For instance, Hegel believed that his philosophical 'System' had solved almost all philosophical problems, but admitted that there may be a few loose ends that needed tying together. He claimed however that this could be achieved simply via a brief postscript to his System that would eventually be compiled by his followers. Reacting to this pompous assumption, Kierkegaard wrote *Philosophical Fragments* which consisted of *fragmentary* rather than *systematic* philosophy, and then he followed this work with a postscript to *Philosophical Fragments* entitled *Concluding Unscientific Postscript* that was *four times* longer than the book.

Kierkegaard – 'master of parable'

Aside from Socrates, Kierkegaard was also influenced by another ancient historical figure who used indirect communication. In the Synoptic Gospels (Matthew, Mark and Luke) Jesus rarely, if ever, 'tells it like it is'; instead he preaches through different indirect modes of speech, one of these being the 'parable'. No writer in the world of Western philosophy has made more use of this medium of communication than has Søren Kierkegaard. He loved parables as a source of entertainment and, more importantly, as an inspiration for intense self-examination leading to increased self-awareness and intensified spirituality.

In a literary sense, a parable must be memorable, express metaphorical imagination, aesthetic balance and economy of words, and it should also be able to stand alone, to transmit a message even when detached from its original or historical context – it should withstand the test of time through its relevance to passing generations.

Kierkegaard frequently uses parables to underscore and make more transparent the essential message of a longer essay. His parables perfectly fit the requirements of indirect communication, because they are precisely 'dialectical knots' presented by 'nobody' (pseudonymous authors) and readers must untie the dialectical knot entirely through their *own* efforts, rather than reading another's interpretation, in order to reap the full transformational benefits of the communication hidden within. The parables require readers to think for themselves and form their *own* conclusions rather than those of an outside 'authority'.

Kierkegaard saw this literary form as a valuable weapon for attacking the philosophical assumptions of his day, in particular the passionless Hegelian logic that he regarded as undermining our human potential for spiritual self-development.

> A thinker erects an immense building, a system, a system which embraces the whole of existence and world history etc. – and if we contemplate his personal life, we discover to our astonishment this terrible and ludicrous fact, that he himself personally does not live in this immense high-vaulted palace, but in a barn alongside of it, or in a dog kennel, or at the most in the porter's lodge. If one were to take the liberty of calling his attention to this by a single word, he would be offended. For he has no fear of being under a delusion, if only he can get the system completed ... by means of the delusion (*SUD*, pp. 176–7; *SV*, XV, 100).

He also used parable to inspire his readers towards true self-hood:

> unfortunately this is the sorry and ludicrous condition of the majority of men, that in their own house they prefer to live in the cellar. This soulish-bodily synthesis in every man is planned with a view to being spirit, such is the building; but the man prefers to dwell in the cellar, that is, in the determinants of sensuousness (*SUD*, p. 176; *SV*, XV, 100).

Sometimes he used parable simply for his own literary satisfaction and for its entertainment value:

There was a man whose chatter certain circumstances made it necessary for me to listen to. At every opportunity he was ready with a little philosophical lecture, a very tiresome harangue. Almost in despair, I suddenly discovered that he perspired copiously when talking. I saw the pearls of sweat gather on his brow, unite to form a stream, glide down his nose, and hang at the extreme point of his nose in a drop-shaped body. From the moment of making this discovery, all was changed. I even took pleasure in inciting him to begin his philosophical instruction, merely to observe the perspiration on his brow and at the end of his nose (*EO 1 (S)*, p. 295).

Objective and subjective truth and faith

Since the fundamental objective of all philosophy is to discover the truth of reality, perhaps the single most important area of Kierkegaard's work is his investigation and discussion of objective and subjective truth and the role they play in determining our understanding of existence. His book *Concluding Unscientific Postscript to the Philosophical Fragments* (1846), written under the pseudonym of 'Johannes Climacus', provides the clearest explanation of his insights in this area.

Objective truth

The first category, objective truth, traditionally (since the time of Plato) attempts to understand the truth of existence via specific *criteria* or *theories* that are used for assessing true or false propositions. For instance, the standard definition of truth used today is the 'correspondence theory', which requires statements to be verified or 'proven' by the 'facts' – judgements, statements or propositions are correct or true only if they factually 'match' the object or situation they are referring to. A proposition is either true or it is not. There are no degrees or graduations of truth or untruth. In all such systems, truth is something that occurs only within the perimeter of specific 'rules' or 'conditions' that are used for its assessment.

Objective truth provides only *factual* or *theoretical* information about things in the world. This manner of interpreting reality creates an artificial but fundamental rift between an *apparently* isolated 'subject' who is the 'knower' (and merely the detached observer of events), and an *apparently* independently existing realm of 'objects' that are 'known' – the objective thinker's task is to deal with what is *in* the mind *only* in relation to what is *outside it*.

Objective truth completely ignores the *essence* of living things. For instance, an objective observation or 'truth' about a 'dog' will be based entirely upon objectively intelligible general information such as its breed, size, weight or colour, physical composition and history, descriptions of its behaviour and potentials and its similarities or differences to other entities. In the meantime, however, the dog's actual *existence*, its *existing* 'isness' or 'essence', the living, primordial 'source' of all its attributes, is completely ignored. In the realm of objective truth the dog now 'exists' only as a *thought* or *idea* – it no longer has any physical or *concrete* existence. In other words the dog, in a sense, has disappeared, and what is left is an *abstraction* of the dog, not the *reality* of the dog. For objective truth is based wholly upon *representations of existence*. Therefore 'objective' truths or thoughts about reality are merely conceptual *approximations* or *possibilities* of concrete existence and this, quite definitely, is *not* existence itself. Even the *word* 'existence' is not that to which it refers, as the truth of existence is experienced in a *wordless* dimension of consciousness.

Another significant flaw in the objective approach to under-standing reality is that ultimately we can never be rationally *certain* of anything, since what we 'know' is either based on *facts* derived from *historical* information, or on logically derived data received through our senses. But since existence is an ongoing, constantly changing process, the laws of change affect both historical infor-mation and sensory perceptions. So we can never be certain about the truth of any *objective* knowledge, even that which we acquired through personal experience, for there is no way of proving to ourselves that the information is *still* correct.

What chiefly concerns Kierkegaard (which he expresses through his pseudonym Johannes Climacus), however, is that the objective approach to matters of personal truth cannot shed any light upon that which is *most* essential to our lives, for the objective approach cancels out or ignores the essential significance of the individual existence of the 'knower' or subject from which questions of personal truth arise and for whom such truth matters. Kierkegaard asserts:

> All essential knowing pertains to existence, or only the knowing whose relation to existence is essential is essential knowing ... all essential knowing is therefore essentially related to existence and to existing. Therefore, only ethical and ethical-religious knowing is essential knowing. But all ethical and all ethical-religious knowing is essentially a relating to the existing of the knower (*CUP (E)*, VII, p. 166).

These essential truths of our existence – described by Kierkegaard as being our ethical and/or religious values – are rooted in the *essence* of who we are, our 'existence' or 'existing'. Our actual *existence* and our human values do not have *objectively* measurable properties or characteristics. Also, my existence is 'hidden' from other people's view, for it exists *inside* me, not *outside* of me. This is why no one else can ever know the truth of *my existence* – only I (and, in Kierkegaard's view, God) can *know* the truth of my existence. 'If a person does not become what he understands, then he does not understand it either' (*JP*, IV, p. 347).

Kierkegaard's subjective truth

This is why Kierkegaard calls this type of truth *subjective truth* or *inwardness*, 'subjectivity, inwardness, is truth ... the inwardness of the existing person is the truth' (*CUP (E)*, VII, p. 171).

Kierkegaard clearly accepts the relevance and necessity of *objective truth* for the study of subjects such as history, maths or science, and he would not deny that it plays an important role in certain matters of daily survival – for instance, on an African safari trip, it might be useful to inform very young children of the objective truth that it is dangerous to stroke the 'giant pussycats'. But this way of viewing truth, according to Kierkegaard, is also *existentially indifferent* in the sense that it does not shed any light on man's *inner* relationship to existence – unlike *subjective* truth it cannot deal with human values such as the nature of freedom and moral or spiritual insight.

Kierkegaard therefore strongly criticises all systematic, rational philosophies for their futile attempts to know life via theories and through the assimilation of objective knowledge about reality. At best, this can only yield 'truths' that provide a severely narrowed perspective on life that has little to do with one's actual *experience* of reality. Detached or observational modes of thought can never comprehend human *experience*. 'True sentences' are merely true sentences, but the primary ground of truth is in actual existence which resides in the living process of existence itself, as it is unfolding – existence and living humans are *not* 'completed entities' available for categorisation, so rather than being the relationship between a subject-knower and the object-known, human truth is something that is continually *occurring*. For just as a tree cannot truly be appreciated or understood when it has been uprooted and removed from its place of growth, so Kierkegaard asserts that a human being cannot find truth *separate from* the subjective experience of his own individual existing, which is the fundamental essence of who he is, defined by the values that determine his way of life.

The nature of subjective truth

Kierkegaard regards subjective truth as the highest truth available to mankind, and he makes it clear that by 'subjective truth' he does not mean that a belief is true simply because one believes it to be true. Instead, he is referring to the subjective experience of being, or living, *within* truth – of immersing oneself in the subjective, inward activity of *experientially* exploring and discovering truth of one's own self in the *process of existing*, which is the *process of becoming*, a direct personal involvement in the living moment-by-moment process of unfolding reality. This is why subjective truth is sometimes called *existential* truth because it is essentially related to one's *actual* existence; 'the inward deepening in and through existing, is truth' (*CUP (E)*, VII, p. 172).

Whereas objective truth is concerned with the *facts* of our being, subjective truth is about our *way of being*. For who we *are, our way of being* and the *significance* our existence has for us can only be understood within the context of the unfolding process of our life in terms of our values that determine the choices and decisions we make. And it is impossible to experience this *objectively* because the 'existing individual', who is the *source* of the subjective truth, cannot separate from himself and observe his existing from an outside vantage point. According to Kierkegaard, only God has access to objective truths about my existence.

So it is impossible for me to *analyse* my existence in any deeply meaningful way. Unlike objective truths that are 'finished' or final conclusions, the *truth* of my 'existence' is a *living, subjective experience* that is always in the process of becoming, so it defies all conceptual accounts. Any attempts to make my existence the *object* of my thinking would result only in a *conceptualisation* of my experience. 'The subjective thinker is continually in the process of becoming. The objective thinker has already arrived' (*CUP*, p. 73).

So my existence is a *happening*, a continually evolving, never-ending process that cannot be contained in a conceptual framework, and when it *is* eventually 'completed' by my death, then it is no longer 'existence'. Therefore from the viewpoint of the rational mind the human process of existence is an elusive phenomenon, a complete paradox.

> When subjectivity, inwardness, is truth, then truth, objectively defined, is a paradox; and that truth is objectively a paradox shows precisely that subjectivity is truth.... The paradox is the objective uncertainty that is the expression for the passion of inwardness that is truth. The eternal, essential truth, that is, the truth that is related essentially to the existing person by pertaining essentially what it means to exist is a paradox (*CUP (E)*, VII, p. 171).

When Kierkegaard speaks of the *inwardness* of subjectivity, he is in no way referring to introspective reflection on our own mental and emotional states, for this would merely be the mode of detached contemplation. Instead he is referring to *active involvement*, manifested by passionate self-commitment to one's innermost moral or spiritual commitments.

Although Kierkegaard gives absolute precedence to subjective truth for dealing with matters of moral and spiritual or religious truth – the truth about *how* humans should live their lives – he is not denying the existence of 'objectively' true moral and spiritual truths. He points out however that these truths can only be truly *known* and are only of *use* once they have become *inwardly appropriated* through subjective experience. An objective moral truth is merely an *approximation* and a *possibility* of a reality that has no *concrete* existence. Its *being* only comes into existence when expressed through the passionate commitment of inwardness, when it becomes part of a person's subjective experience of ethical or moral reality. In other words, *understanding* only takes place during the actual process of *experiencing*, not through an *intellectual knowing*. This experiencing of inwardness arises out of the state of deep silence. 'Only someone who knows how to remain essentially silent can really talk – and truly act. Silence is the essence of inwardness, of the inner life' (*The Present Age*, p. 49, trans. Alexander Dru and Walter Lowrie; London: Oxford University Press, 1991).

'The one who is truly resolved is silent. It is not as if being resolute were one thing and being silent another. No. To be resolute means to be silent; for silence alone is the measure of power to act' (*The Present Age*, pp. 82–5).

Kierkegaard points out the fairly obvious fact that a person can have objectively 'true' moral beliefs and still live falsely (e.g., religious hypocrites) or have objectively 'false' moral beliefs and yet still *manifest* truth (for instance, someone with 'wacky' spiritual beliefs whose actions display what Kierkegaard might label as 'Christian goodness') (*CUP*, p. 201). In the following well-known passage he contrasts this feature of subjective truth with his definition of objective truth:

> When the question about truth is asked objectively, truth is reflected upon objectively as an object to which the knower relates himself. What is reflected upon is not the relation but that what he relates himself to is the truth, the true. If only that to which he relates himself is the truth, the true, then the subject is in the truth. When the question about truth is asked subjectively, the individual's relation is reflected upon subjectively. If only the how of this relation is in truth, the individual is in truth, even if he in this way were to relate himself to untruth (*CUP*, p. 199).

To illustrate this point, Kierkegaard uses the example of two men at prayer. One is praying to 'the true conception of God' (which for Kierkegaard is the Christian conception) but this man is praying in 'a false spirit'. The other man is praying to his pagan, primitive idol, but with 'an entire passion for the infinite' (*CUP*, p. 201). In Kierkegaard's opinion, it is only the latter who is experiencing subjective truth, because he is praying 'in truth' with passionate inward commitment – his beliefs have been appropriated and have transformed his state of consciousness. The highest form of subjective knowing is passion. 'At its highest, inwardness in an existing subject is passion' (*CUP (E)*, VII, p. 166); 'the passion of the infinite is the highest truth' (*CUP (E)*, VII, p. 169).

Kierkegaard is by no means trying to imply that ultimately the validity of what you 'objectively' believe is unimportant, but of far greater importance is the question 'is your *heart* in the right place?' – does your faith, whatever it might be, manifest 'passion of inwardness for the infinite'?

Kierkegaard emphasises that it is *only* via *subjective* understanding that one can potentially achieve a true relationship with reality. Our morals and values are an intrinsic part of our sense of our individual identity. All our choices or decisions are based on such values that are entirely rooted in a subjective reality. Even when we think our decisions or actions are based on the *facts* of a situation, this is not true, for how someone responds to the particular facts facing them depends upon their values. If you truly believe something, such as God is love, or that causing others suffering is wrong, then these beliefs will be manifested in your behaviour. Therefore, if you change your beliefs, your behaviour will change and you will also become a different person. So in this sense you *are* your values, since your individual identity is a physical, emotional and psychic manifestation of the values you hold.

Kierkegaard asserts that there are no *objective* criteria by which one can judge moral values. For instance, the assertion that infidelity is immoral cannot actually be objectively 'proven', for there exist no objective standards of truth to do this. In the same way, someone who asserts 'Jesus loves you' cannot possibly back up this claim with any sort of objective criteria of truth. This means we can never be *objectively* certain that we have chosen 'the right values'.

This is why Kierkegaard describes the subjective experience of moral truth as an 'objective uncertainty'.

You *are* your subjective experience

The crucial significance of subjectively experienced truth in our existence becomes even more apparent when we realise that it can even influence what we perceive as being 'objective truth' – the so-called 'objective facts' of a situation. The 'facts' we perceive in life, and most certainly the way we respond to facts that we are presented with, is determined, sometimes entirely, by our values, for to have certain values is to be 'tuned into' life in a certain way, and this influences the nature of our understanding at any given moment. For instance, if a devout Catholic and a completely irreligious hedonist were taken to a religious retreat and then a whorehouse the 'facts' they see in each of these environments would probably differ significantly.

In other words, the values we hold 'create' the world in which we live. An entertaining illustration of this truth can be seen in the famous ambiguous drawing known as 'Wittgenstein's duck/rabbit', where the person's thoughts or attitude towards the picture determine whether they see it as a duck or a rabbit. This demonstrates that I cannot look at the world 'objectively' because the world is not, and cannot possibly be, 'outside' me, since I am – and always have been since birth – *in* the world existing as a *part of it*. I am inextricably enmeshed or rooted in the world, linked to all other entities in a *worldwide* web of significance. We can see in this argument the seeds of modern-day relativism, which rejects the whole idea of objective truth. There are also similarities to twentieth-century phenomenology, which considers consciousness as 'intentional' or purposive – the way we see the world determines what we intend to do to it. Similarly, as Wittgenstein pointed out, 'The world of a happy man is a different one from the world of an unhappy one'. Kierkegaard's hope was that his readers would realise, through his authorship, the subjective truth that they are the 'authors' of their life story and as such that they should assume responsibility for this fact, and decide whether or not they should stay with or change the values they have chosen that are determining their existence.

The transmission of subjective truth

According to Kierkegaard, subjective truth must be communicated *indirectly* because if spoken directly it will be only 'intellectually' or *objectively* grasped. 'Socrates was a teacher of the ethical, but he was aware that there is no direct relation between the teacher and the learner, because inwardness is truth, and inwardness in the two is precisely the path away from each other' (*CUP (E)*, VII, p. 208).

For example, although *intellectually* I might know that I possess freedom of choice regarding the way I live, it is only when I *subjectively* experience the truth of this fact, when I *feel it in my bones*, that I am likely to make any radical alterations to routine patterns of living that I dislike but have taken for granted. Being objectively informed about, or objectively recognising, my predicament is unlikely to catalyse a subjective realisation leading to inner and outer transformation of my existence. For Kierkegaard, a profound existential truth, like a seed, carries latent energy and just as a seed needs watering in order to release its latent energy, the latent energy of a profound, potentially life-transforming truth is only released when it is *subjectively experienced*.

Kierkegaard's emphasis on the pointlessness of 'intellectually grasped' truth makes good intuitive sense, for it explains why throughout history so few seekers have gained enlightenment from the 'great truths' provided by various enlightened men such as Jesus or the Buddha. For when the insights of these enlightened masters are spoken by them, or repeated and recorded by others, they are invariably experienced by those listening only as *objective*, or *intellectually* acknowledged, truths that do not carry the energy of the *subjective* experience from which these insights arise.

Also, because later generations of 'teachers' customarily use the mode of 'direct transmission' in the attempt to communicate these insights, seekers are rarely motivated to discover for themselves the *subjective* understanding of reality that is necessary for reaching an authentic understanding of these truths. For language cannot *directly* communicate the *subjective truth* of enlightened masters – their words are just *conceptual representations* of their subjective insights – signposts that merely *point towards* a reality that each individual must discover, or *subjectively* understand for themselves through their *own direct experience*.

We can see the truth of this on a more banal level. Most people, through alcohol, drugs, the splendour of nature or perhaps through an insight that arises from a book or movie, occasionally have experienced profound enlightening realisations. If, however, these are written down and read the following day, invariably they no longer impact on the consciousness. When the insight arose it was *subjectively* experienced whereas later it is only experienced intellectually or *objectively*. This is because enlightenment is a moment-by-moment experience. Subjective truths are the living fruits of awareness that exist only in the burning fire of subjective experience – when the fire goes out the truth becomes a lifeless, impotent, empty 'word husk'.

In contrast to this, objective knowledge – for example, the statistical results of an investigation – can be transmitted easily and effectively, in a direct manner. Subjective truth, however, requires an indirect transmission that creates in the reader's mind what Kierkegaard calls 'double reflection'. Double reflection refers to the dual process of first understanding a truth intellectually and then relating it to one's own life situation in a manner that gives rise to the subjective understanding of the truth through *direct personal experience*. So the communicator of ethical and religious truths must present not only the *content* of the truth but transmit it in a manner that triggers in the reader an inward, subjective understanding of it.

The Christian religion, for example, needs not only indirect communication but also *direct* communication, because, as Kierkegaard states, there is a necessity for preliminary knowledge: 'That there is an element of knowledge is particularly true for Christianity; knowledge about Christianity must certainly be communicated in advance. But it is only a preliminary' (*JP*, I, p. 289). Kierkegaard asserted that, ultimately, 'It is subjectivity that Christianity is concerned with, and it is only in subjectivity that its truth exists, if it exists at all; objectively, Christianity has absolutely no existence' (*CUP (S.L.)*, p. 116).

Faith – the highest subjective truth

Kierkegaard believed that, ultimately, the highest level of subjective truth available to a human being is faith – a state of consciousness of the infinite in which one is no longer confined to the perception of reality imposed by intellectual reasoning. This faith is a state of passionate surrender to what is rationally uncertain and paradoxical. Inwardness, which is subjectivity, is truth and the definition of this truth is 'An objective uncertainty, held fast through appropriation with the most passionate inwardness, is the truth, the highest truth there is for an existing person' (*CUP (E)*, VII, p. 170).

> The definition of truth stated above is a paraphrasing of faith. Without risk, no faith. Faith is the contradiction between the infinite passion of inwardness and the objective uncertainty. If I am able to apprehend God objectively, I do not have faith; but because I cannot do this, I must have faith. If I want to keep myself in faith, I must continually see to it that I hold fast the objective uncertainty, see to it that in the objective uncertainty I am 'out on 70,000 fathoms of water' and still have faith (*CUP (E)*, VII, p. 171).

Kierkegaard considered knowledge and faith to be polar opposites: knowledge is objectively certain, but cannot tune in to the living process of reality, nor can it embrace the infinite. In contrast to this, faith is highly uncertain, but allows us direct access to the infinite reality of our own being.

It is only through a 'leap to faith', for instance, that we can commit ourselves totally to a God whose existence is logically and rationally uncertain, 'the objective uncertainty maintained in the most passionate spirit of dedication is truth, the highest truth for one existing'. What is demanded here is a dedicated, passionate and resolute engagement of the whole being.

When Kierkegaard speaks of the fact that faith requires a 'leap' on the part of the individual, he is not talking about any type of 'blind leap' or 'a leap into the dark' which some forms of existentialism talk about. Rather, the 'leap' expresses Kierkegaard's acknowledgement of the fact that faith is discontinuous with what came before – it is not a development of any sort of potential skill or characteristic that is already present in the individual but a transition to a completely different dimension of consciousness. It is the coming into being of something brand new.

Kierkegaard had complete faith that the highest form of selfhood – man's highest form of self-realisation as spirit – is a religious existence defined by passionate self-commitment to the personal Absolute through the sustaining standpoint of faith; for him this meant Christian faith. It is only through the medium of faith that one can accept the paradoxical nature of Christianity and live in the presence of eternal, absolute truth.

According to Kierkegaard, the Christian concept of the incarnation also represents the 'Absolute Paradox' because it requires us to adopt the rationally impossible belief that the eternal entered the temporal sphere of existence, taking on the limitations of finite existence. 'What, then, is the absurd? The absurd is that the eternal truth has come into existence in time, that God has come into existence, has been born, has grown up etc, has come into existence exactly as an individual human being, indistinguishable from any other human being' (*CUP (E)*, VII, p. 176). Much of Kierkegaard's authorship explores this paradox of living in the face of absurdity. He writes, 'The paradox is not a concession but a category, an ontological definition which expresses the relation between an existing cognitive spirit and eternal truth'.

Whilst one's consciousness of existence remains trapped within the confines of the rational mind, this Paradox must be rejected for its complete absurdity. If, however, the reasoning faculty of the mind acknowledges its own limitations for dealing with this matter, the possibility opens for making the 'leap to faith', but Kierkegaard insists that making this leap requires 'divine assistance' – a prior transformation of the individual's nature through God's Grace.

> Truly, no more than God allows a species of fish to come into existence in a particular lake unless the plant that is its nourishment is also growing there, no more will God allow the truly concerned person to be ignorant of what he is to believe. That is, the need brings its nourishment along with it, what is sought is in the seeking that seeks it; faith is in the concern over not having faith; love is in the self-concern over not loving.... The need brings the nourishment along with it, not by itself ... but by virtue of a divine commandment that joins the two, the need and the nourishment (*CD*, pp. 244–5).

Because of the divine assistance required for the leap to faith, it too becomes a miraculous paradox. 'But in that case is Faith not as paradoxical as the Paradox? Precisely so; how else could it have the Paradox for its object, and be happy in its relation to the Paradox?

Faith itself is a miracle, and all that holds true of the Paradox also holds true of Faith' (*PF*, p. 81).

Religious faith versus faith in 'the Absolute Paradox'

Kierkegaard distinguishes true Christian faith – faith in this Absolute Paradox – from other forms of faith, including faith that is just in the existence of God.

> Socratic ignorance is an expression of the objective uncertainty; the inwardness of the existing person is truth.... The Socratic inwardness in existing is an analogue to faith, except that the inwardness of faith, corresponding not to the repulsion exerted by ignorance but to the repulsion exerted by the absurd, is infinitely deeper (*CUP (E)*, VII, p. 172).

He suggests that believing in the existence of God and the promise of eternal happiness requires faith in the face of 'objective uncertainty', but only in the sense that it is obviously impossible to present any rational evidence for this belief. The paradox of this belief is simply that the rational mind can neither comprehend God, nor prove his existence. Although this belief requires faith, this faith only requires an intensity of inwardness sufficient to deal with a paradox characterised by an *absence of reason*. But he points out that Christian faith requires much more than this and thus the faith is more intense – 'the more risk, the more faith' (*CUP (E)*, VII, p. 171). For Christian faith also demands that the individual 'risk his thought' by believing not merely in the *absence* of any rational basis, but *against* all rational understanding, for 'that which in accordance with its nature is eternal comes into existence in time, is born, grows up, and dies – this is a breach with all thinking' (*CUP (S.L.)*, p. 513). Logically speaking, historical or *temporal* properties cannot apply to an *infinite* God. To believe that an eternal God can exist in time, in the form of a man (Jesus), is therefore logically completely absurd.

Because this faith requires an intensity of inwardness sufficient to sustain belief that is *against all reason* – and from a rational standpoint, *utterly absurd* – the inwardness (subjectivity) in Christian belief is therefore 'intensified to the utmost degree' and thus it constitutes 'the highest passion in the sphere of human subjectivity' (*CUP (S.L.)*, p. 118). Such faith is 'precisely the contradiction between the infinite passion of the individual's inwardness and the objective uncertainty' and that faith is being 'out upon the deep, over seventy thousand fathoms of water' (*CUP (S.L.)*, p. 309).

Interestingly, Kierkegaard claims that the Paradox carries the same relevance for us today as it did for contemporaries of Jesus. He asserts that although the incarnation of God in the human form of Jesus took place thousands of year ago, that is *not* a historical event, because of its *eternal* nature. This is because although *history* occupies the realm of time, *the eternal* lies *outside* of time.

Witnesses of the actual event of his birth and the circumstances of his life were not in a better position than we are today to comprehend rationally what was happening, because an eternal event can only be known through *faith*, and faith posed the same challenge for those living at the time as it does for those of us alive today. 'In relation to Christ, there is only one time, the present. Eighteen hundred years makes absolutely no difference; they neither change Christ nor reveal who he was, for who he is revealed only to faith' (*PC*, pp. 62–3).

Consequently, although time must have distorted and falsified many facts surrounding the incarnation, the 'historical accuracy' of events at the time is completely irrelevant to the decision as to whether or not one should believe in the Christian concept of the incarnation. Those living at the time deeply believed in an eternal *non-human* God, and when they met Jesus they saw only a human being, so they too could only believe in 'Jesus, God incarnate' through pure faith. So the immense paradox of the incarnation and resurrection transcends the rational mind and all human senses, and therefore even *immediate* perception is ultimately of no value in supporting belief – faith was then, and is now, the only support.

So the capacity to believe, through faith, in Jesus Christ is equally available to those living today as it was to actual witnesses of his existence, and for those alive today who believe in the paradox that Christ was God incarnated in human form, this belief is *as real* as it was for those sharing the same belief during his earthly presence. 'There is no disciple at second hand. The first and the last are essentially on the same plane' (*PF*, p. 131).

Mankind – 'hybrid' of the infinite and the finite

Kierkegaard asserts that 'Existence is a synthesis of the infinite and the finite, and the existing individual is both finite and infinite' (*CUP (S.L.)*, p. 350). But what might he be implying here when he says that the self is a synthesis of the finite and the infinite? How could one justify this claim in a manner that would be acceptable to the modern mind?

To begin with, there is no limit to the way you can *imagine* the world to be. Thus human imagination, in this sense, belongs to the realm of *infinity* as it allows us to break with the natural realm. But a person can also discern reality – how the world actually *is* – this aspect of ourselves belongs to *finite* existence and limits the degree to which the natural realm can be transcended. Humans are both realistic and yet infinitely creative, down-to-earth and yet infinitely imaginative, and we are required to develop and balance these opposing characteristics of our nature.

In addition, although God or the universe is infinite, whereas man belongs to the finite world of form, in another sense, because man was *created* by the universe or God, he is therefore also a 'child of infinity', and just as children inherit their parents' genetics, it seems fair to conclude that mankind may have inherited the 'genetics of infinity' and thus is partly infinite. Indeed, perhaps it is only *because* of the infinite component of his being that man possesses the capacity – through the 'faith-mind' – to achieve a sense of oneness or unity with the infinite universe or God. However, because of the *finite* component of his make-up, he cannot make a 'once and for all' permanent transition to this state of being in which his consciousness is attuned to God or the universe – in other words our finite nature makes it impossible for us to remain in this highest form of spiritual or religious existence without *constant striving*. So this way of existing via a total self-commitment to God, or the universe, requires continuous effort – a constantly repeated self-commitment through faith that never ends throughout one's entire life. 'Existence is the child that is born of the infinite and the finite, the eternal and the temporal, and is therefore a constant striving' (*CUP (S.L.)*, p. 85).

Johannes claims that through the passion of faith it is possible to achieve a 'happy relationship' between human reason and paradox; but the rational mind has an imperialistic quality to it that resists any recognition or acknowledgement of its own limits. This causes it to reject instantly anything that makes no sense. For instance, if we are presented with the rationally absurd proposition 'cows can fly' we will confidently, without taking offence, reject this idea. When presented with the idea of 'faith', however, though we may reject the notion as ridiculous, there is simultaneously a subliminal awareness of the actual *reality* of faith because its *effects* are sometimes visible even if the *substance* or *basis* for faith lies beyond our rational senses. It is for this very reason that the rational mind finds the paradox of faith so offensive – faith threatens its position of 'absolute' power, because at the same time that it rejects faith outright, there exists in the mind a shred of doubt. If this doubt is justified, then the rational mind can no longer lay claim to its supremacy, for something incomprehensible and far more powerful transcends it.

Kierkegaard compares the reaction of finding faith offensive with the feelings that arise when a person's negative attitude blocks their potential to love. They react by feeling embittered and angry at love because they are deprived of the genuine happiness and fulfilment that it can provide. In a similar way the person who finds faith offensive experiences suffering because their attitude of refusing to acknowledge the limitations of their rational mind has cut them off from the healing and fulfilment that comes with genuine faith.

What is also interesting is that in spite of the fact that offence is the natural response of reason towards the paradox of faith, offence – like faith – is not rational. Both faith and offence are passions, and the roots of passion do not lie in reason. Although the offended individual in this case may claim that their complete rejection of faith is based on its irrationality, Kierkegaard's pseudonymous author, Johannes, points out that the accusations of 'irrationality' made by the offended mind are just 'acoustic illusion', an echo of what reason has learned from the paradox about its own limitations. Furthermore, the reaction of offence is itself a confirmation of the claim of the paradox to be something that reason is incapable of understanding – in other words, proof that the paradox is indeed a paradox.

To understand the 'communication barrier' between a person's faith and their rational thinking, it might help matters if we think of the mind as operating, in some senses, like a radio and the various different functions of the mind as being like different radio frequencies. The mind's capacity for rational, analytical thinking can be thought of as being like a radio frequency that receives distortion-free, easily decipherable broadcasts coming from stations transmitting logical, objectively verifiable information about *finite forms in existence* – stations broadcasting information outside of this category are either inaccessible via this radio frequency or else the sound quality of the transmission is too distorted to allow accurate comprehension.

Similarly, the radio frequency of our intuitive faculty can also receive transmissions only from channels broadcasting information about the factual, finite world of form – this time, consisting of sense perceptions of the world that are *subliminally analysed and processed* to provide us with our intuitive feelings and insights.

In contrast to this, our human capacity for faith is like a radio frequency that can 'tune into', and receive clearly intelligible broadcasts from, stations dealing with matters of infinity that are *prior to* and *beyond* the world of form – God, the cosmos, truth, and so on. Since the infinite includes the totality of everything, this means that the faith-mind also embraces, and can function within, the finite world of form.

So the information-processing systems of the rational mind and the intuitive mind can comprehend *only* data existing in the *finite* world of form, whereas our 'faith-mind', which is the highest level of brain functioning, is the only 'wavelength' of the brain that permits us to attune ourselves to, and realise both the infinite, formless realm *and* the finite realm of existence.

Perhaps when a person is fired by the passion of inwardness and total commitment to discover the truth of their own being, they gradually enter a state of deep connection or oneness with the process of their existing, and just as a guitar string will 'sympatheti-cally resonate' with a string of the same pitch that is vibrating nearby, it is possible that the 'existing force' of their being, as a mani-festation of divine creation, may sympathetically resonate with the awesome power of the infinite creative force, attuning them to the faith-mind that opens the door to the realm of infinite possibility.

Kierkegaard wants us to realise that, ultimately, we can *rationally* understand neither the world we live in nor our true nature or purpose in life. As a consequence we dissipate our energy and squander our lives in a variety of meaningless ways. Because there is no *rational truth* that can guide us towards an understanding of the meaning of human existence, the only *possibility* of salvation we have is via the miracle of divine enlightenment. But we cannot even know if there *is* a God in the universe who can provide us with such enlightenment.

Since it is impossible for us to work out what we need to do to become enlightened, we have two choices: to remain forever in a life of complete ignorance and uncertainty about what we ought to believe or how we should live, or alternatively we can choose to take 'the leap into absurdity', in other words, a 'leap to faith' in which we adopt the utterly irrational belief in an eternal, unchanging God who can take form *in time* and who can enlighten us if we passionately and whole-heartedly commit ourselves to him. Kierkegaard considers faith to be the most important of all human potentials, because he believes that an individual can only reach complete selfhood through faith.

To be one's true self, Kierkegaard asserted the necessity of becoming what he termed a 'single individual'. The single individual is central to all areas of his thought. At its highest level of evolution the single individual stands alone before God and is answerable first and foremost to God. According to Kierkegaard, it is only when a human realises that he stands naked before God that he becomes a fully fledged human being. To be a 'single individual' requires passionate self-commitment to a single purpose in life. Kierkegaard explains, 'Purity of heart is to will one thing.' 'Every call from God is always addressed to one person, the single individual. Precisely in this lies the difficulty and the examination, that the one who is called must stand alone, walk alone, alone with God' (*JP*, I, p. 100).

As a 'single individual', my *true self*, I create and choose my own values and way of life irrespective of whether or not it harmonises with the society in which I live. Total commitment to the funda-mental path that I have freely chosen in life is the key feature of this state of consciousness. This lends a sense of cohesiveness and integrity to my existence, for now my actions are a genuine expression of what I *really* want to be doing with my existence. As Kierkegaard states, an essential feature of true selfhood is:

> To be clear in my mind *what I am to do*, not what I am to know, except in so far as a certain understanding must precede every action. The thing is to understand myself, to see what God really wishes *me* to do; the thing is to find a truth which is true *for me*, to find *the idea for which I can live and die* (*The Journals of Kierkegaard 1834–1854*, pp. 15–20).

Chapter Four

The key themes of *Fear and Trembling*

With incredible accuracy, Kierkegaard prophesied the great rewards of posterity that would result from his classic work *Fear and Trembling*. 'Once I am dead, *Fear and Trembling* alone will be enough for an imperishable name as an author. Then it will be read, translated into foreign languages as well.'

Given the diversity of interpretations that have been read into the content of this highly controversial work, he could have added 'philosophical languages' to his prediction about 'foreign languages'. *Fear and Trembling* also serves as an excellent introduction to Kierkegaard's entire authorship since it contains the major themes of his religious and ethical thought that are continued in the pseudonymous works and religious discourses that follow it.

Contemporary interest in *Fear and Trembling* is not at all surprising. The tremendous importance of respecting a person's individuality within a society, one of the key messages of this work, has been repeatedly confirmed in the world, in a shocking manner, through the manifestation of its antithesis – the periodic appearance of dictatorial regimes. The portrayal of total religious obedience has potentially sinister implications in view of the intermittent emergence of dangerous religious cults and, more currently, the present world crisis stemming from the 'faith' of some so-called 'Islamic fundamentalists' who claim that their terrorist attacks are 'God's will'.

A controversial choice

Fear and Trembling, which is Kierkegaard's most complete account of the essential nature of genuine religious existence, uses the Old Testament story of Abraham and Isaac as a vehicle to illuminate the weaknesses of contemporary Christianity and Hegelian ethics, in the light of true Christian faith.

To modern man's consciousness this story could easily be viewed as a parable reflecting how power can intimidate or destroy the weak. A song by Bob Dylan beautifully reflects this: 'God said to Abraham, go kill me a son. Abe said, Man, you must be puttin' me on. God said, you can do what you want, Abe, but next time you see me comin', you'd better run. Well, Abe said, where you want this killin' done? God said, do it on Highway 61' (*Highway 61*). However, as a means of conveying to a 'Christian' audience the essential qualities of Christian faith, Kierkegaard's selection could not have been better.

It is important also for readers to be aware of the wider religious significance of his choice, which seems especially relevant today, as evidenced by the fact that fairly recently, the story of Abraham and Isaac was chosen for the front cover and central feature of *Time Magazine* (30 September 2002). In this article Kierkegaard was mentioned and a passage quoted from *Fear and Trembling* – yet another confirmation of his earlier prophecy of fame.

The article points out the fact that the central biblical figure Abraham represents the first man in the Bible to devote himself in complete faith, and through free choice, to One God – an act that represented a radically new understanding that formed the foundation of Western civilisation. Most importantly, he is also an 'interfaith superstar', beloved by Jews, Christians and Muslims. Aside from God, Abraham is the only biblical figure who enjoys the unanimous acclaim of all three religions. It is for this reason that since the late 1800s, and especially following the 11 September attack on New York, interfaith activists have sought to locate in the patriarch a true symbol of accord to heal the chasm between Islam and the West.

Unfortunately, however, Abraham appears to be a flawed vessel for reconciliation – if he is the father of three faiths, then he is like a father who has left a bitterly disputed will. Since these religions began, all of them have interpreted the biblical story to their own advantage, throwing out what they want to ignore, adding what they want to believe, tailor-fitting it to their own unique religious viewpoint.

The Jews regard the story of Abraham and Isaac primarily as demonstrating God's great mercy, and claim (anachronistically) that Abraham spoke Hebrew and adhered to the Law of Moses. In addition, the Torah states that Abraham's Covenant with God gave the Jewish people exclusive rights to the Holy Land.

In contrast, the Koran asserts that Abraham was not a Jew but Islam's first true believer – so pure is his submission to God that Muhammad later stated that his own message is merely a restoration of Abrahamic faith. Muslims claim that if Allah ever had made a pact with the Jews as a race, it had been broken because they didn't keep their faith. In addition, they assert that it was Ishmael, not Isaac, whom Abraham offered for sacrifice.

Christians honour Abraham as a paragon of perfect Christian obedience and faith, and he is of central importance in the Roman Catholic Mass. Early Christians claimed that Abraham found grace outside the Jewish law, since his Covenant with God long predated the Jewish law delivered by Moses, and also they point out that God had declared Abraham to be 'righteous' years before his circumcision. This was offered as proof that to be a believer, and be redeemed by God, one did not need to belong to the Jewish race or follow Jewish law – the way of Christ was enough.

Later, the second-century Church claimed that Judaism's Abrahamic Covenant was rendered null and void by Christianity, though in the early 1960s the second Vatican Council re-acknowledged the Covenant made between God and the Jews as irrevocable, thus rehabilitating the notion of Abraham as father of the Jews.

So the controversy and scandal that Kierkegaard created by suggesting (and demonstrating) that contemporary Christianity and Hegelian ethics had misunderstood and ignored genuine Christian faith was achieved, ironically, and somewhat appropriately, with the assistance of a fascinating biblical character whose own history constitutes a kind of scandalous controversy.

An encapsulation of the biblical story

Abraham was a hereditary tribal leader of the Hebrews, whose faith was put to the test by God in a most severe manner. At the age of seventy-five, God commanded him to take his people on a journey to a land God would show him, and God made a Covenant with Abraham, promising him that his sixty-six-year-old barren wife, Sarah, would produce a son who would father a great nation. Later God repeated his promise to Abraham, who still had faith in God's word even though he was now ninety-nine. Following this, Sarah conceived and gave birth to Isaac, who became Abraham's only beloved son (years earlier he had banished to the desert his first-born son Ishmael, whom he had conceived at his wife's request – because she doubted God's prediction – with her Egyptian slave, Hagar). Then came the horrifying night described in Genesis 22: 1–2, when Abraham awoke to the voice of God commanding him to sacrifice his son atop a mountain in the land of Moriah. Without hesitation, and telling no one, Abraham took Isaac on a three-day journey and climbed an appointed mountain to sacrifice Isaac. Just as he was about to make the fatal thrust with the sacrificial knife the angel of the Lord stopped him, and informing Abraham that he had passed the test, allowed him to sacrifice in Isaac's place a ram that he caught nearby. So Abraham got his son back and lived in blessedness with his people for the rest of his life. Since then he has been cele-brated as a worthy father of nations and the true 'father of faith'.

This story is not meant to be read as a test of Abraham's faith in the *existence* of God, since this is taken for granted from the way the story is told. Instead, it is a test to see if Abraham truly believes that, even if he carries out God's command to sacrifice Isaac, Isaac will be returned to him again *in this world*.

The multidimensional structure of *Fear and Trembling*

In many senses, this book is like a 'magic mirror', reflecting multidi-mensional levels of meaning that are gradually disclosed as the reader's gaze penetrates more deeply. Convinced that profound existential truth does not reveal its innermost significance when directly communicated, Kierkegaard conceals beneath the obvious messages contained in this text carefully hidden, interrelated layers of meaning that become steadily more subtle the further one probes.

This work is illuminating in another important way. Of all the pseudonymous writings, *Fear and Trembling* is closest to being auto-biographical, though in a manner so indirect that aside from his former fiancée Regine Olsen, who would most likely have under-stood those parts of his 'coded' message which were specifically for her, only informed readers with detailed 'insider information' on Kierkegaard's personal life will be in a position to understand and appreciate this aspect of his indirect communication.

Kierkegaard aptly chose the name 'Johannes *de silentio*' as the pseudonymous author of this book. This was also the name of a servant in a Grimm's fairy-tale, who – knowing the consequences – is turned into stone for warning his royal master of three dangers. The royal couple subsequently had two sons whom they sacrificed to bring Johannes back to life and, in return, Johannes brought the children back to life.

The primary objective of *Fear and Trembling*

Although Kierkegaard's pseudonymous author Johannes *de silentio* denies being a philosopher, and makes no claims to be a committed Christian, what he discusses is of great religious and philosophical significance; and though he speaks from an ethical standpoint, he clearly recognises the limitations of this mode of consciousness and is fascinated by the concept of faith even though he himself does not possess the quality. One has the clear impression that Johannes experiences towards this story the 'sympathetic antipathy and an antipathetic sympathy' that is Kierkegaard's description of dread – he is at the same time attracted and repulsed by Abraham's behaviour. 'Thus while Abraham arouses my admiration, he also appals me' (*FT h*, p. 89). Most of all he is disturbed by the fact that his rational mind finds faith utterly incomprehensible, for every interpretation he tries to make ends in complete failure until finally he cries out in despair, 'Abraham I cannot understand.'

This admission of defeat stands in stark contrast to both Hegelian and Kantian thinking, which claim to have 'rationally' assimilated and subordinated the notion of religious faith to ethical laws. For Kant, the essence of Christianity and God is captured and contained within morality, and the content of morality is embodied in ethical laws that are universally applicable and absolute – Goodness is only that which the powers of reasoning determine as being morally good. For Hegel, ethical laws are also universally applicable, but are historically and culturally determined and thus are local and provisional, so moral laws and the nature of Goodness are determined by the characteristic spirit of the culture prevailing in a society at a particular time in history.

Kant criticised Abraham for irrationality in taking it for granted that it was God who commanded him to sacrifice Isaac, whereas Hegel regarded the restrictive belief that the God of Abraham was the God of the Jewish people as a precursor of the more evolved religious notion (which would come much later) of a Lord of all heaven and earth. Hegel viewed Christian faith merely as a primitive, undeveloped expression of a quality which, thanks to Hegelian philosophy, would come to bear the stamp of Reason.

Common to both Kant and Hegel is the idea that God is Reason incarnate, consequently, if the powers of reasoning, based on what has been morally determined as right, tell a person that something is not good then it is definitely not good. According to this view there is no room for the thought that 'against God we are always in the wrong', and therefore there is no point in appealing to God independent of the moral code. Under such circumstances, as Kierkegaard's author Johannes asserts, 'the whole of human existence is entirely self-enclosed, as a sphere, and the ethical is at once the limit and completion' (*FT h*, p. 96).

It was the influence and authority of such beliefs that Kierkegaard strove to undermine, not only in *Fear and Trembling*, but also throughout his entire intellectual life. In *Fear and Trembling* he achieves this aim through discussions of the story that eventually will convince the vast majority of readers that defenders of Abraham must put aside ethics and discover a new 'category' of understanding in order to accept Abraham as the 'father of faith'. However, the reader is not told what this category is, only that existence within such a category is not limited by ethical codes of existence. This new category to which Kierkegaard refers is almost certainly the

Christian concept of faith – a quality that lies outside the realm of human understanding and which therefore requires a radical 'leap' motivated by a commitment to what is objectively uncertain and a paradox in every sense.

In sharp contrast to Hegelian and Kantian logic, faith is presented in *Fear and Trembling* as having an entirely independent status that lies beyond the grasp of rational thinking or social morality, and yet it requires a highly sensitive and morally mature individual to appreciate the true nature of its demands. Through his author Johannes *de silentio*, Kierkegaard skilfully constructs, in a manner typifying his indirect subtle style of communication, a vivid picture of the requirements and full implications of what he regards to be 'the highest passion of a person', a quality which for hundreds of years has been concealed beneath attractive, cheapened versions preached by worldly clergymen and misinterpreted by condescending rationalisations of faith offered by philosophers.

In Kierkegaard's time Hegelian thinking overshadowed every other philosophical outlook, thoroughly permeating theology, the Established Danish Lutheran Church and thus the lifestyle of Danish society. Consequently, perhaps the primary aim of *Fear and Trembling* was to expose simultaneously, the inadequacies of Hegelian thought, and the poor state of awareness in contemporary society, which Kierkegaard viewed as the everyday correlate of this philosophy. Most of all, Kierkegaard was concerned that Hegelianism had drastically damaged Christianity because it had emasculated the notion of faith and thus had ignored the fact that what Abraham did required 'nerves of steel'.

Even in the preface of the book it becomes clear that Kierkegaard's main attack was upon Hegel. In this short section his author Johannes mentions 'the system' around eight times, and to make sure that the reader is left in no doubt that he is referring to Hegelian thinking, he identifies the philosophy he is challenging as the attempt 'to transpose the whole content of faith into conceptual form' – Hegel's central claim concerning the relation of his system to religion is that the content is the same but that his philosophy perfectly replaces the inferior representational form of religion with his properly conceptual form. Johannes then goes on to say that his retelling of the Abraham story is directed at 'our age', ironically pointing out that in the present times, it is wrongly assumed that faith is easy, that it is the starting point of life rather than man's ultimate aspiration as it was in the past when man considered it 'a task for a whole lifetime' (as in the case of the early Christians).

Hegel also considered faith to be a provisional state of mind, merely a stepping stone on the path to personal maturity, that culminates in a higher rational explanation of reality provided by Hegelian philosophy, the highest manifestation of human evolution, where the true nature of religious faith can be experienced as it *really* is, and can be transcribed into rational words and concepts of a common language that can be shared with others. In the Hegelian state of consciousness, one has supposedly gone further than faith, and in so doing, faith has been placed in its proper place in the fundamentally rational scheme of things. So Hegel regarded faith as intelligible and subordinate to the rational mind. Kierkegaard believed this conclusion was erroneous and cheapened faith by dismissing it as an inferior stage of man's personal evolution – a state of immaturity transcended by Hegelian consciousness.

Kierkegaard's personal view was that ultimately all ethical laws are subordinate to the true Christian way of life defined by an individual's direct personal relation to God, based upon genuine Christian faith. His treatment of the story of Abraham and Isaac was specifically intended to bring this fact into unambiguous, sharp focus by demonstrating, through logical argument, that if one asserts that Abraham *is* the acknowledged father of faith then one *must* simultaneously accept the insufficiency of ethical principles as an all-encompassing determinant of man's conduct. Conversely, if one insists that ethical principles *are* the ultimate, universal determinant of 'right' conduct, then under these conditions one *must* condemn Abraham as a criminal with murderous intent, for there is no other way that ethical reasoning can interpret Abraham's actions.

In the epilogue, Kierkegaard's author Johannes asserts that Hegel's system provides society with a false sense of security, by presenting faith as something easy to attain, and by devaluing other human ideals, thus making the challenges they pose seemingly disappear. Then succeeding generations inherit Hegelian 'solutions' and thus also avoid facing up to the problems and challenges of existence. Johannes suggests that to counteract this tendency one needs to see what life's problems *really* are, whilst realising that they cannot be solved simply through the adoption of new forms of consciousness, but must be faced directly during each moment of one's existence.

Fear and Trembling is clearly a stinging critique of the spiritual lethargy of contemporary Christianity. Simultaneously, it acts as a reminder of the essential importance and true nature of genuine Christian faith, which was the ultimate challenge of early Christianity. The story of Abraham and Isaac is chosen by Kierkegaard's author Johannes as a form of theological shock treatment to awaken readers to a full awareness of the incredibly strenuous demands of faith, which had been ignored owing to the fact that the focus of religion had been on the 'results', the happy ending rather than the 'content' of faith, and thus the intense anxiety and suffering, the temptation and incomprehensible paradox and the single-minded spiritual commitment had been completely overlooked.

Johannes's attempt to shed some light on faith

Kierkegaard's author explains that whatever faith may be, it is certainly not something that can be comprehended by thought, for 'faith begins where thinking leaves off'. So Johannes concludes that if we are to speak of Abraham's greatness, we should first attain as much insight as possible into what it might have been like to have been in Abraham's position undergoing his trial of faith. Johannes attempts to do this in the first part of *Fear and Trembling*'s two divisions, in which we are tuned into the right frame of mind in a short section presenting four imaginary versions of the way that Abraham might have responded to God's command. In all of these variations, Abraham's actions and emotional responses are completely intelligible to the pseudonymous author Johannes's rational mind, but none of these responses to God's testing of his faith would have earned Abraham the title 'father of faith'. These four stories are presented by Johannes as imagined by someone in awe of Abraham's monumental achievement but increasingly confused about the nature of his actions. This person attempts to play the role of someone observing the events at the time, in order to grasp in *thought* what actually happened.

After this there follows another short section entitled 'Speech in Praise of Abraham'. The primary function of this chapter lies in its stark depiction of the nature of the choice facing Abraham. In order to obey God's will, Abraham needed to act not only against his natural inclinations as a loving, protective parent, but he also needed to violate deliberately a deeply rooted moral principle that forbids the killing of an innocent human being, in this case his own son – a fact which magnified to a maximum the horrifying nature of his choice. Johannes praises all the facets of the incredible faith that allowed him to do this, beginning from the moment Abraham receives his command from God to leave the land of his fathers, to the final event where, in obedience to God's will, he agrees to sacrifice Isaac. Johannes also points out that Abraham could have achieved greatness by sacrificing himself instead, or by sacrificing Isaac in a state of infinite resignation rather than faith, but his special greatness was that in submitting to God's command in a state of complete resignation he simultaneously had complete faith that either he would not lose his son or, if he did, that God would subsequently restore Isaac to him in this lifetime.

However, although Johannes admires Abraham, he raises the question as to whether or not those who glorify his memory really understand the full import of what they are admiring. In the second part of *Fear and Trembling*, which opens with a section entitled 'A Preamble from the Heart', he emphasises this point by ironically citing the hypothetical case of a preacher who during a Sunday sermon, completely ignoring the accepted moral standards of judgement, praises Abraham with his cliché-ridden, worldly piety. Moreover, upon being informed that one of his congregation intends to imitate Abraham, he hurries to the man and, calling him a loathsome creature who is the dregs of society, he chastises him violently for his murderous intent. Yet what justification does this preacher have for his righteous outburst? Had he not praised Abraham in his sermons for similar actions that he now condemned?

Johannes now asks why there is this discrepancy in people's attitudes – is it because Abraham has some special rights to greatness that provide him with immunity to sin, so that whatever he does he remains great? Johannes asks whether faith can make it a holy act to be willing to murder one's son – if not, then Abraham is doomed, owing to his murderous intent and probable insanity. So there is an irresolvable dilemma between the ethical view of Abraham's actions as *willingness to murder*, and the religious view as *willingness to sacrifice*. Johannes asserts that before one praises Abraham one should first deeply examine such questions.

The 'knight of resignation' and the 'knight of faith'

Johannes attempts to create a clearer picture of the nature of faith, by comparing and contrasting *resignation* and *faith*. To simplify this objective, he personifies these two qualities as the *knight of infinite resignation* and the *knight of infinite faith*. He explains that a person in the state of 'infinite resignation' has renounced their most treasured worldly hopes, completely convinced of the human impossibility of regaining again in this world what has been given up.

Faith encompasses this state, but simultaneously includes the belief – paradoxically, on the strength of the absurd – that nevertheless one's worldly hopes will again be realised. The word *absurd* as used in this context means *humanly impossible*. So a person with faith, according to Kierkegaard's explanation of the quality, is able to believe with certainty that the projects upon which their heart is set are possible even when they prove humanly impossible to achieve.

In Abraham's case, if he had only been a 'knight of resignation' he would have given up Isaac to God but would *not* have expected to get Isaac back because he would lack the belief that God fulfils humanly impossible hopes. In his resignation he would therefore simply understand that God wishes him to sacrifice Isaac, and that this will be the permanent end of Isaac. Having abandoned Isaac to God, he would now direct his love at God and away from the world, which now lacks everything he loves as a father. The act of infinite resignation in which one renounces everything entails complete surrender to God, as well as personal courage and discipline, but *not* faith; it is purely a rationally based movement that is made when a situation demands it, and all it requires is sufficient guts and self-control to overcome attachment to the finite world of form through submission to a love of God, which is the highest thing for a knight of resignation. In infinite resignation, one has become acutely aware of one's own complete dependence upon, and nothingness in the face of, the Eternal. One sees oneself merely as a product of the Creator and sustained and totally indebted to this Creator, so one renounces the temporal world of form in order to find God, but in doing this, one remains a permanent outsider to the world of form, and little or no pleasure is derived from worldly existence, which is now considered unimportant and meaningless.

As the 'knight of faith', Abraham, like the 'knight of resignation', accepts the *human impossibility* of a continued earthly love of Isaac, but because of his faith he simultaneously, on the strength of the absurd, believes in the divine possibility – which he anticipates as a certainty – that Isaac will be restored to him in this world. He trusted God's earlier promise that his son Isaac was going to become the ancestor of a new nation, and therefore believed that God would either retract his command or, if Isaac were sacrificed, Abraham believed by virtue of the absurd – the impossibility of it, humanly speaking – that God would subsequently return Isaac back to him alive, because of his faith that for God all things are possible. For ultimately, the movement of faith is putting one's utter trust in God to the test.

This characteristic of faith is what Kierkegaard's author Johannes describes as a 'double movement' – a movement of infinite resignation and, in the same instant, a movement of infinite faith. For Johannes, the paradox of faith is that these two movements are expressed, and happen simultaneously, in the same single action. When Abraham begins his journey with Isaac he has made the movement of infinite resignation by relinquishing, and accepting the loss of, absolutely everything that is of worldly value to him – his son, his wife, his social and family obligations and ethical principles and thus his societal rights. He has also given up his past and his future and he has even lost his self, because up until the moment of his infinite resignation, his self-concept was derived from existing as an ethical human being, which is now no longer the case; and yet he believes at the same time that all these things he has lost in this world will subsequently be returned to him *in this world* – that he will still be able to enjoy his son's presence in this life.

It is precisely this *double movement* characterising the knight of faith that Johannes finds completely absurd and utterly unintelligible – for Abraham places himself as a single individual in an absolute relation to God, and exists in state of consciousness where he simultaneously believes two mutually exclusive ideas. He then bases all his subsequent actions upon these contradictory, paradoxical beliefs! Johannes correctly surmises that from a human point of view he is crazy and cannot make himself intelligible to anyone.

However, the bare fact that Abraham is insane is not what astonishes Johannes – for there are numerous insane people in this world – what is completely incomprehensible to him is the fact that by virtue of his insanity, Abraham became the Father of Faith. Johannes, realising that it is his absolute relation with God that makes him great, calls Abraham's condition 'divine madness'. Johannes points out the fact that in his great act of faith, Abraham simultaneously demonstrated his love for God, his aspirations – which were to do God's will – and his confident belief in what is, rationally speaking, utterly impossible. Abraham's actions revealed that he had complete faith that all human life, his own, Isaac's and that of the rest of humanity, derives its value and significance from God, who is the source of creation, rather than from the forces and elements of creation in the finite world of form.

Johannes points out that the actions of a knight of faith are unintelligible even to another knight of faith – they cannot make their actions intelligible to one another, for only *God* is in a position to judge whether the knight's madness is divinely inspired and not demoniacal, because from a behavioural viewpoint both types of madness appear identical. Consequently the knight of faith exists alone in his being, in total isolation.

This 'double movement' of faith, which Johannes finds so unintelligible, might perhaps be partly clarified in the following way. Although Abraham's consciousness is in a surrendered state of faith, this does not mean that his powers of reasoning have simply shut down – indeed, the practical survival demands of his journey, suggest that this is definitely not the case. Abraham's perception of reality, however, unlike those living in the ethical state of consciousness, is no longer exclusively constructed by the rational mind, for he now 'sees' and believes, primarily through the eyes of faith. Reasoning has become merely his tool, not his master –

though he uses his rational mind for matters of everyday survival, he does not heed its opinions regarding his faith-based beliefs.

Unlike other human beings, Abraham and all 'knights of faith' occupy two states of consciousness simultaneously – 'rational-consciousness' of the *finite* world of form with its *finite possibilities*, and 'faith-consciousness' of the *infinite* with its *infinite possibilities*. So the 'renouncement' made by the 'knight of faith' is in a sense illusory – within the dimension of consciousness upon which the person of faith bases their apparently absurd convictions and their belief in personal salvation, nothing is actually renounced or considered absurd or impossible; on the contrary, all is embraced and yet – though they remain completely uninfluenced by it – there is still a full acceptance of the *finite impossibility* of their beliefs. As Johannes points out: 'for it is only in the finite world that understanding rules and there it was and remains an impossibility' (*FT h*, p. 75).

So what Johannes finds incomprehensible – that Abraham can simultaneously possess two mutually exclusive beliefs – is due to the erroneous assumption that these two 'movements' take place within the same dimension of consciousness. This happens because Johannes experiences reality only through one dimension, the rational mind, and the idea of mutually exclusive beliefs occurring in this mode of consciousness is of course ridiculous. Abraham's continuous state of *infinite resignation* in which he always understands that his hopes are '*humanly impossible*' is enclosed entirely within his rational mind, whereas his constant utter certainty of regaining Isaac (as well as his other signs of faith) exists exclusively in his consciousness state of *infinite faith*. So although the two beliefs occur simultaneously, they do not take place in the same mode of consciousness, and it is this fact which, in a sense, resolves the dilemma of 'mutual exclusivity'.

So for a man of faith, from the point of view of his rational mind his faith-based beliefs will always appear absurd and remain an impossibility. But since he now lives in a fundamentally 'faith-based reality', the opinions of his rational mind cannot undermine his faith – for Abraham 'faith rules.' So if such a man of genuine faith is questioned, he will always be prepared to admit the impossibility of his beliefs and will nevertheless still have utter faith in them; indeed

Johannes points out that *infinite resignation* is a prerequisite to faith. 'Infinite resignation is the last stage before faith, so that anyone who has not made this movement does not have faith; for only then does my eternal validity become transparent to me, and only then can there be talk of grasping existence on the strength of faith' (*FT h*, p. 75). So in infinite resignation one becomes aware of an infinite relation to reality which in turn opens the doors to the possibility of receiving the grace of faith. If a person does not utterly realise and acknowledge the human impossibility of their faith-based beliefs, then this indicates clearly that they have not yet reached the stage of infinite resignation which always recognises the humanly impossible nature of absurd beliefs of faith. Such individuals are therefore living not in *faith* but in *illusion* fuelled by intense desire and wishful thinking, which makes them 'convinced' that their dreams will come true, whilst they live in complete denial of the truth that what they believe in is humanly impossible. A belief of genuine faith exists *in spite of* and not *in denial of* the human impossibility and paradoxical nature of such a belief. Only *illusory* faith is *blind* faith – genuine faith has clear vision.

It seems that the state of infinite resignation in a 'knight of faith' contains an additional action of renunciation that does not occur in the 'knight of infinite resignation'. Aside from renouncing his worldly hopes, it seems very evident that the 'knight of faith' also renounces his trust in the rational mind as the final judge of what he should believe and what existential choices he should make in his life – instead he chooses to heed the advice of his 'faith-mind' on such matters. So it would seem that in order to open the doors of consciousness to the dimension of 'infinite reality' with its 'infinite possibilities' one first needs to renounce one's total trust in, and attachment to, the rational mind. To faith, the belief in infinite possibility is not absurd, because the notion of impossibility or absurdity only exists in the finite world of form which is ruled by human reason, whereas in the state of faith one has been liberated from the thinking mind and thus from all concepts, including the concept of absurdity.

The knight of faith's 'ordinary' experience and involvement with daily reality with its simultaneous awareness of 'infinite reality' is a state also attributed to 'Zen enlightenment', in which a person is described as 'being in the world, but not of it'. Kierkegaard's conception of the transition from a normal state of consciousness to the state of infinite resignation and then beyond this, to faith, is reflected in the well-known Zen Buddhist description of the stages of enlightenment: 'Before enlightenment occurs, mountains are mountains' (in other words, one is fully immersed in the finite world of form and in a 'normal' state of consciousness); 'at the moment of enlightenment, mountains cease being mountains' (that is, everything in the finite world has been renounced by the state of infinite resignation – one feels a deep connection with the infinite but *alienated* from the world of form which now has lost all its attraction); 'but then mountains become mountains again' (this is characteristic of the state of faith in which there is once again a sense of connection with, and interest in, the finite world of everyday life whilst remaining perfectly in touch with the formless realm of infinity). So prior to becoming a knight of resignation one lives in normal everyday existence fully immersed in the world of form. Renouncing the world, one no longer feels part of it and everything in the finite world of existence appears unimportant. As a knight of faith, one again becomes fully immersed in the ordinary world but with one foot remaining in eternity. With the courage of faith one can immerse oneself fully in the finite world of form whilst simultaneously remaining aware of the absurd, paradoxical nature of one's existence.

The modern knight of faith

Though he has never personally met one, Johannes hypothesises that the knight of faith in our time belongs entirely to the world, blending in with the rest of society, indistinguishable from everyone else. For they completely transform their life *inwardly* – they put their humanity and daily existence in their proper place, simultaneously maintaining a *relative* relationship to the world and an *absolute* relationship to the Eternal. This is why there exists no *essential* outward expression of their inner state, no behaviour which 'proves' that a person has true faith. In contrast, knights of infinite resignation tend to be recognisable, for in order to remain in constant contact with the infinite, they renounce permanently all worldly hopes but in the absence of any belief that they will 'regain' in this life what has been relinquished, thus they live conspicuously apart from normal existence which tends to make them outwardly easily distinguishable from the average human being. In *denying* their humanity, their secularity, their actions are, in a sense, still a *worldly expression* – one might find this type living an ascetic lifestyle, separated from normal existence, in a monastery or perhaps in the Hare Krishna movement.

In contrast to this, Kierkegaard's emphasis on the normality of modern-day 'knights of faith' indicates that the story of Abraham and Isaac is not meant to be an illustration of the sort of behaviour expected from a person of faith, but as an allegory in which Abraham's actions reflect or symbolise some general characteristics of genuine religious faith – true faith is not restricted to 'great men' such as Abraham, or saints, but is available to every human being.

To illustrate this point, Johannes hypothesises the existence of a knight of faith living in Copenhagen and asks 'who is he?' Johannes answers that the man of faith is visibly at home in the world and in his job – it could be a 'postman', 'shopkeeper' or 'tax collector'. Their behaviour is perfectly ordinary. The difference is that 'inwardly' this man has made, and at every moment is making, the 'movement of infinity'. He can feel the deep existential pain and sadness of infinite resignation that comes from realising the impermanent nature of everyone and everything they have relinquished; yet at the same time he feels the blessedness of infinity.

He has felt the pain of renouncing everything in the world that is precious to him, and yet the finite experiences of worldly existence still taste just as good to him as to the average worldly man who never knew anything higher, because the inner security derived from faith liberates him from all anxiety, allowing him to appreciate fully all the temporal pleasures of existence as if they would last forever. But his experience of the finite world is not that of the ordinary man. Because the knight of faith has permanently relinquished his attachment to worldly things, even though he simultaneously 'gets back' the world, he now experiences worldly life only by virtue of the absurd. Consequently, this person lives his existence in a state of selfless care. He lets things take care of themselves, and yet at all times he seizes the moment and makes the best of it, for he does not do even the slightest thing except by virtue of the absurd. The knight of faith demonstrates in his very being that renouncing all attachment to worldly things does not mean that one is simultaneously renouncing all *care* for these things. He feels at home and thoroughly enjoys the pleasures of the finite world *because* he cares. There is no indication that he has given up his hopes for this world, nor any sign of the silent resolution of Abraham, and yet he too at every moment is 'making the movement of faith' against his established certainty that 'humanly speaking' it is absurd that the things he enthuses over should have the value he seems to ascribe to them.

Throughout everything they do, however, the knights of faith remain permanently in touch with the Absolute, with the Infinite – thus they are very much *in the world*, but not *of it*. Only the knight of faith can express perfectly the sublime in the pedestrian – this is their primary achievement. Perhaps Søren felt when he wrote this work that he was one of them – that he gave up his attachment to Regine Olsen through infinite resignation, and by virtue of the absurd, through absolute faith he believed that she would be restored to him. Even if this was the case, later he certainly did not feel this way, as he said that he would have remained with Regine if he had possessed true faith.

The Problemata – three crucial questions

In *Fear and Trembling* the core of the text is found under the heading 'Problemata'. This poses in turn three questions, whose answers are an examination of the story of Abraham's willingness to sacrifice Isaac. The most obvious objective of this section is to demonstrate that if Abraham does indeed deserve the praise attributed to him in the section of the book entitled 'Speech in Praise of Abraham', then several central principles of Hegelian thought are invalidated. If, however, these Hegelian principles are indeed valid, then Hegelians should certainly *not* be endorsing Abraham's greatness.

These Hegelian principles are discussed and challenged in the discussion following each of the three problematical questions. The answers to each of the three questions have the same structure. Though some readers of Kierkegaard (e.g. Andrew Cross) have disputed the following idea, Professor Alastair Hannay (who is an acknowledged world authority and translator of Kierkegaard's writings) has suggested that the type of argument Kierkegaard uses is what logicians call *modus tollens* – 'if A then B. If not B, therefore not A.' In this situation A is a general definition of ethics (which is clearly intended as a statement of the Hegelian ethics prevailing in Kierkegaard's time) and B represents a specific conclusion about ethics logically derived from the former definition.

In each case, the ethical is defined as the universal – for both Hegel and Kierkegaard 'universal' indicates 'the society as a whole', and according to Hegel's concept of what he terms 'the ethical life', behaviour is moral or ethical only when it is linked by intention and/or fact to the well-being of the whole society. So the measure of a person's morality is determined by the degree to which their behaviour conforms to the ethical principles and expectations determined by the society to which they belong.

After defining ethical as universal, the *problemata* discussion proceeds by presenting a logically deduced conclusion or answer to the question that can be drawn from an analysis of various features of ethical existence that are implied by this primary definition. The reasoning which follows this is that if one accepts the validity of this conclusion about ethical life then one must concede that Hegel's account of the ethical is correct.

At this point, the author Johannes points out that if Hegel's account is indeed right, then Hegelians have no right to talk of faith or to give credit to Abraham as the father of faith, because from the perspective of this Hegelian conclusion about ethical existence, Abraham must stand morally and criminally condemned for his intention to commit murder.

The three questions are: 'Is there a teleological suspension of the ethical?', 'Is there an absolute duty to God?' and 'Was it ethically defensible of Abraham to conceal his purpose from Sarah, from Eleazar, from Isaac?' The three conclusions or answers, drawn on the basis of the assumption that the ethical is 'the universal', are: 1) that a person's moral behaviour must be evaluated in terms of its underlying social intention; 2) that there are no duties to God other than duties that are in the first instance to the universal (to the ethical requirements of the society as a whole); 3) that it is a moral obligation not to conceal one's moral projects or the reasons one has for not carrying them out (in other words, Abraham should have revealed his intentions to his wife Sarah, his son Isaac and his servant Eleazar).

In the responses to each of these *problemata* it is demonstrated that Abraham is *definitely* violating the principle of the ethical as universal, through his breach of the requirements designated by the corresponding conclusion that was based on this principle. Through effectively demonstrating that the very *essence* of Abraham's heroism lies in the *complete absence* of ethical justification for his actions, Kierkegaard effectively illuminates a significant flaw in Hegel's system. For if Abraham is to remain the hero that he is believed to be, then one has to accept that the individual must take precedence over the universal – the society as a whole. The devastating implication that this premise has for the whole field of ethics (and for philosophy) is obvious.

Problema I: 'Is there a teleological suspension of the ethical?'

Johannes points out that the ethical realm, which is social morality, is universally and always applicable – its morals or laws apply to everyone at all times, so all actions and every part of a person's being are subordinate to this ethical realm. Since ethical principles are supposed to apply equally to everyone, this means that there can be no such thing as individual morality – according to ethics, if something is right for me, then it must also be right for anyone else who finds themselves in the same situation. From the ethical standpoint, there is nothing outside itself that it regards as a higher purpose, or final goal for which it is striving – there is nothing that supersedes it and therefore it represents the final goal for all human consciousness that lies outside its realm.

Therefore, the life purpose of the individual living in the ethical realm of consciousness is to abide continually by its demands, and this requires the subordination of individuality to ethical obligations. Actions undertaken by the individual on his own behalf are only moral if they can be linked in intention and/or fact to the sustenance of the society as a whole. The assertion of one's own individuality for personal purposes only, is regarded a sin. An ethical individual who feels the impulse to assert this type of individuality is thus faced with a spiritual trial that can only be successfully passed through surrendering this urge to the requirements of the ethical realm.

If one assumes therefore that social morality represents man's highest potential and highest goal, then, as such, it must also be man's eternal salvation. Therefore it would be a contradiction in terms to suggest that this can goal can be surrendered, for there is apparently nothing higher outside of itself to which it can be surrendered. Under these circumstances, teleological suspension could lead only to the state of nihilism. One can only surrender something if there is something higher to which it can be surrendered, and if there is, then that which is surrendered is not lost but merely assimilated.

Johannes points out that Abraham's faith is the paradox that demonstrates that a person's individuality – the single individual – is of greater importance than the ethical realm. If this is not the case, then Abraham is lost.

To clarify Abraham's relation to the ethical, Johannes compares and contrasts his behaviour with that of the tragic hero. If one observed the actions of a tragic hero in isolation, without any knowledge of their purpose, one would be forced to conclude, quite correctly, that there has been a serious violation of moral conduct. In spite of such appearances, however, there is a clearly intelligible ethical justification to their actions.

The tragic hero always adheres to the requirements of social morality as the highest purpose of existence. His actions remain ethical because they are motivated, even demanded, by his allegiance to ideals of the ethical life that are of far greater importance than those which have been breached. In this context, the act of violating one set of ethical values in order to fulfill the requirements of higher ethical values, redeems and transforms the act into heroic sacrifice. This process can be viewed as a teleological suspension of one ethical value for the sake of satisfying another superseding ethical value. Jephtha and Agamemnon killed their daughters, but the success of the invasion of Troy depended upon Agamemnon's sacrifice of his daughter Iphigenia, and if Jephtha – who led Israel to victory over the Amorites – had not kept his promise to sacrifice the first being to greet him on his return (his daughter), the victory would have been taken away from him. Brutus actually killed his son, but as consul he was responsible for enforcing the law, which in this case meant condemning his son to death.

So although all these three are certainly blameworthy on account of the suffering they caused to themselves and their families, they are in another sense completely vindicated in their own eyes and by the State because their terrible deeds are for a greater cause, and thus they become tragic heroes who remain at all times entirely within the ethical realm. According to the social morality of their time – the laws and customs not only *of* their people but also *by* their people and most important of all *for* their people – the highest require-ments are the needs of the nation, the State and society, and these needs prevail over the otherwise protected needs of the family. Consequently, in spite of the feelings of intense pain, deep personal loss and moral scruples that tragic heroes obviously experience due to the collision between their personal duties and desires and their higher duty to the state, they at least derive some comfort and reas-surance not only from the sympathy and respect of those around them – even perhaps from their victims – but also, and primarily, from the knowledge that their actions are undeniably justifiable due to the fact that they are conforming to the requirements of supreme ethical principles, with which they fully identify, and which take precedence over all personal considerations.

Abraham's situation is entirely different. Unlike the tragic hero, his 'collision' is not an ethical collision, in the sense of a tragic conflict between ethical duties; instead, it is a collision *with ethics* itself. He has an allegiance *outside* the ethical realm and his actions also transgress the ethical domain – he temporarily suspends the influence of all ethical obligations for the sake of this higher purpose. Abraham's task is not eased by any comforting support or respect from his society – he stands isolated and alone with no possibility of justifying his actions to others. He has placed himself in an 'absolute relation to the absolute' – his relationship with God is entirely personal, independent from, and unrelated to, society and all other worldly concerns. God's command is addressed to him alone, and Abraham's actions cannot be rendered intelligible by any human standards. Also, since his task entails an absolute duty to God that transcends ethical reasoning and which must be fulfilled in spite of powerful temptations to the contrary – if Abraham attempted to vindicate himself in humanly understandable terms he would fail, and his attempt would be in conflict with his absolute duty to God.

Unlike the tragic hero who kills his family but is deemed ethical because he did it to save an entire society – for a higher ethical purpose – Abraham can make no such claims. His actions were not for the purpose of saving a nation, or upholding the values of the state or to appease angry gods. The unethical nature of his actions are ironically further accentuated by the fact that in killing Isaac he would be wiping out the chances of the future nations that would have arisen through Isaac's children. So we can see that he does not even have any *selfish* interest that could explain his behaviour, for all his hopes for the future were invested in his son.

So what was the motivation behind Abraham's actions? The answer is that his intention was to satisfy God's demand that he should prove his utter faith in God. He simultaneously does it for his own sake, in order to prove this to himself. God's demand presents Abraham with a powerful temptation. A temptation is normally understood as being that which potentially can cause a person to ignore the call of duty. From an ethical standpoint, it is *the desire to obey God's will* that is tempting Abraham to breach *his ethical obligations as a father*. However, Abraham regards God as the highest authority, and thus from his perspective God is using *Abraham's love for Isaac*, combined with his desire to satisfy his ethical responsibilities as Isaac's father, in order to tempt him into violating *God's command and his faith*. So it is clear that Abraham feels his duty is to God, whereas social morals represent to him, under these circumstances, merely a temptation that could prevent him from doing his duty that is equivalent to God's will.

So, unlike the tragic hero who is great because of his ethical or moral virtue, Abraham is merely a potential murderer unless he is vindicated by his faith. For Isaac's life represents the promised continuance of his people and therefore Abraham's intention to kill him clearly violates his two principal social role responsibilities: as a father, and as a leader of his people. In subordinating both these vitally important social responsibilities to his own spiritual salvation, Abraham steps entirely out of the ethical domain of conduct.

If Abraham's conduct is nevertheless exonerated, then one is simultaneously defending and affirming the priority of individual rights and undermining the validity of Hegel's ethical view that the individual must subordinate himself to the nation state. Thus one must also accept that the laws and customs of Abraham's people are ultimately subordinate to a higher law. Therefore, faith requires a 'teleological suspension of the ethical'.

This, however, does not imply that religious faith is in conflict with the moral law or with my duty to my neighbour and myself – it merely shows that faith requires a higher allegiance, than to society and its moral conception of right and wrong. What is at issue here is the ultimate source of the moral law, including my duties to God, neighbour and self. Is it society or God? Johannes makes this point by distinguishing the universal from the absolute:

> Then faith's paradox is this, that the single individual is higher than the universal, that the single individual determines his relation to the universal through his relation to the absolute, not his relation to the absolute through his relation to the universal. The paradox can also be put by saying that there is an absolute duty to God (*FT h*, pp. 97–8).

So it seems reasonable to conclude that Abraham's actions definitely contain, and require, a teleological suspension of the ethical – a temporary setting aside of social morals. As a single individual in direct relation with the divine he superseded the ethical realm of values, and this is the irresolvable paradox. How he reached this state, or remained in it, is inexplicable, but if one disagrees that this was his situation, then that makes him neither the father of faith nor even a tragic hero, but a potential murderer. Therefore Hegelians have no right to speak condescendingly of faith as something they understand and can move beyond, for according to Hegelian philosophy Abraham must be judged as morally evil to the highest degree because of his complete willingness to murder.

From this conclusion it seems clear that Kierkegaard is fully justifying the possibility – if it is required – of a temporary suspension of all ethical obligations by anyone involved in a direct personal relation to God whose actions are in allegiance to God's will. This central thesis of *Fear and Trembling*, which has been a source of much controversy, has been stigmatised as amounting to the advocacy of 'moral nihilism', and for those taking this position, none of the persuasive arguments in favour of the thesis is of any relevance whatsoever. One does not need to enlarge upon the obvious dangers of justifying morally abhorrent conduct on the basis of a rationally absurd belief that is supported by total trust in God and an allegiance to carrying out God's will. To begin with, how can anyone be certain, when receiving a command from God, that one is not experiencing an auditory hallucination based upon a mental illness such as schizophrenia, or, alternatively, if it *were* somehow possible to be certain that one has genuinely received an external command, how can one be sure that it is the voice of *God* and not the devil in disguise?

As Kant points out when discussing the story of Abraham, 'it is at least possible in this instance a mistake has prevailed'. Kant would enthusiastically support the view that in Abraham's case, since his presumed divine command required the violation of man's most important and fundamental moral law, 'thou shall not kill', Abraham therefore had the option of refusing to believe that the command actually came from God, and thus could have ignored it without feeling that he had betrayed God. According to Kant, a morally conscientious individual would naturally and correctly have chosen this option.

So it seems that Abraham can only be justified if one believes it is defensible to suspend morality for the sake of obedience to an overriding authority whose decrees demand utter obedience. However, since there is no valid line of logic which says that morality *can* or *should* be suspended, it seems clear that ethical reasoning and faith are mutually exclusive states of consciousness and thus the reader is ultimately left with a profound existential either/or decision: to live an exclusively religious existence in the 'divine world' with Abraham 'the father of faith' or to live in the 'human world' without access to the category of consciousness known as faith.

Problema II: 'Is there an absolute duty to God?'

According to ethics, the complete goodness of God is contained within it, and therefore ethics is divine morality and thus the highest duty. Thus ethics would claim that duty to the moral law is ultimately duty to God. This, however, is a false assumption. To base one's whole existence upon the premise that ethical laws are final and all-inclusive, transmutes the notion of God into purely an abstract intellectual concept. Consequently, when people under these circumstances speak of the ethical duty to love and obey God, what they are really saying is that it is their duty to obey the moral law, since God in this context has been absorbed in, and is subordinate to, the moral law. Duty to ethics is at most duty to that which has its source in God, so the ethical duty is not an absolute duty to God.

Under these conditions, it would be considered impossible for someone to enter into an individual personal relationship with God, and since an attempt to do so would require individual self-assertion with no ethical justification, it would be regarded as a sin, according to Hegelian social morality. So from an ethical viewpoint there can be no absolute duty to God, and thus Abraham's actions must be judged as lying outside ethical boundaries, for he exhibits a total obedience to God only. If, however, one decides that Abraham *is* considered the true father of faith, then one must accept that God's will must take precedence over all morality.

However, since the realm of ethics cannot comprehend Abraham's private relationship with God, and if Abraham is truly to be regarded as a noble father of faith, another definition of faith is required in order to understand him. There is a problem, however, because this category of faith cannot be expressed through words because thinking lies within the *finite world of form*, which cannot comprehend the *infinite realm* in which faith operates. Therefore since faith cannot be expressed, it cannot be understood. So we are left with this: either Abraham is a potential murderer or we stand before the enormous paradox of faith – the individual in direct relation to the absolute – that can never be resolved.

The paradox of faith is that social morality is subordinate to the individual who has an absolute duty to God, because their direct personal relation to God now determines their compliance with the demands of social morality. In contrast to this, those who live exclusively within the ethical realm allow *social morality* to determine their relationship to God.

In adopting this position, Kierkegaard was not denying the essential significance of ethical laws within a society, nor the tremendous importance of the moral commandments attributed to God. He merely wished to point out that for those living within a *religious* state of consciousness, the ethical realm *cannot* possess absolute sovereignty over one's existence, since from the perspective of religious consciousness, the obligation to conform to ethical laws ultimately depends upon the nature of an individual's commitments to God – a God who *transcends* human reason and who is the ultimate source of *all* moral law. However, using a similar type of argument, one could equally defend the reverse situation, namely, that the sovereignty of God's will over a person's existence *cannot* be justified from within an *ethical* state of consciousness.

Problema III: 'Was it ethically defensible of Abraham to conceal his purpose from Sarah, from Eleazar, from Isaac?'

According to Hegelian ethics, ethical behaviour must always be disclosed so that others are always in a position to judge the moral worth of your actions. True moral behaviour is transparent, and wilful attempts to conceal one's motives are regarded as sinful according to these principles of social morality. The question here is whether or not Abraham's failure to reveal his intentions to Sarah, his son Isaac and his servant Eleazar can be justified on the basis of his faith as a single individual in direct personal communication with God. If it can be justified on this basis then once again we are dealing with a paradox that lies outside the domain of social morality.

Abraham was silent because all his actions were rooted in faith, and this state of consciousness exists exclusively within the infinite realm of being, whereas words exist exclusively within the finite world of form. Consequently Abraham had at his disposal no means whatsoever to communicate verbally the reason behind his actions either to himself or to anyone else, which is one good reason why he did not attempt to do so. Additionally, it may also have been clear to Abraham that if God is the highest authority in the universe, it would therefore be impossible for anyone to pass judgement on

God's command, which was the motivation behind all Abraham's actions. When involved in a direct personal relationship with God, one's personal moral state cannot be judged by any finite mind. In answering the call of faith, Abraham would have realised that his actions needed justification *only* in God's eyes, for his pact was with *God* and with no one else.

So Abraham believes that his absolute duty to God's will – upon which he bases his actions – overrides the relevance of the principle of the ethical as universal, and he also is physically, intellectually and emotionally unable to reveal his intentions to the people involved in this drama. Even if he had attempted to explain his actions as being a test of his faith by God, his explanation would not be ethically acceptable because according to the definition of ethics as universal, God could only test him by tempting him *away* from his familial and social obligations – there could not possibly exist a duty to God that lay *outside* this conception of ethics. In addition, any attempt on Abraham's part to explain his actions would be a violation of his faith towards God because, assuming he does have total faith, then his complete trust would exclude any inclination even to attempt an ethically intelligible explanation.

So if we accept the conclusion that Abraham's actions are justifiable, then once more, Kantian and Hegelian ethical requirements are rendered null and void, because Abraham's silence *violates* social morality and can only be justified if one accepts that the paradox of his faith, as an individual in direct relation to God, supersedes the ethical realm.

Further interpretations

So each answer to these three questions confirms the central theme of *Fear and Trembling* – the incompatibility of Hegelian thinking with biblical faith, as represented by Abraham on behalf of both the Jewish and Christian Bibles. The final conclusion Johannes obviously expects the reader to draw at the end of this whole section is that, contrary to Hegel's central claim, the Hegelian *system* is not the *perfection* of Christian faith but its *abolition*, for ultimately all ethical laws are subordinate to the 'author' of the law – God. On this basis, one must assume that social morals (universal moral laws) are to be obeyed under all circumstances with two exceptions: 1) a universal moral law may be breached for the sake of satisfying a higher universal moral law; 2) universal moral laws – the entire ethical realm – may be teleologically suspended under the special circumstances in which a person's duty to God requires this, because universal moral laws arise from and are subordinate to the infinitely larger realm of the divine law of God, who is the source of all universal moral laws and the entirety of existence.

This view has led to interpretations of *Fear and Trembling* which support a 'divine command' law of ethics that suggests it is the duty of every deeply committed religious individual to be prepared for the event of a direct command from God that must take precedence over all rational and moral obligations. And perhaps total unconditional obedience to God's will can in some sense be viewed as a morally justifiable action on the basis of the conviction that 'God is love'. For instance, in the case of Abraham, due to his very special personal relationship with God, one might reasonably surmise that he has reliable 'insider information' regarding God's nature, which has utterly convinced him that God is completely benevolent, all-powerful and entirely trustworthy. Therefore he has complete faith that whatsoever God might ask of him must be the right thing to do no matter how incomprehensible or horrific it may seem, because obedience to God cannot possibly have any negative consequences for him or anyone else. For this reason Abraham, certainly from his own point of view, is still maintaining his ethical integrity and moral resolve when he agrees to sacrifice his son. This outlook fits with Kierkegaard's own religious position, for at various points in his authorship and in his private journals, he insists on God's unwavering goodness and believes that our duty is first and foremost to God. 'This is all I have known for certain, that God is love. Even if I have been mistaken on this point or that point, God is nevertheless love.... Like spring-water which keeps the same temperature summer and winter – so is God's love. His love is a spring that never runs dry' (*The Journals of Kierkegaard*, p. 394, ed. and trans. Alexander Dru, Oxford University Press, London, 1938).

In *Fear and Trembling*, however, Kierkegaard does *not* emphasise this view – on the contrary, there is an emphasis on the horrifying nature of Abraham's actions and the necessity for a knight of faith to be able to *transcend* ethics. One valid potential reason for this tactic, however, is that a primary objective of this work is to undermine the control over religion imposed by Hegelian ethics, and therefore to suggest the possibility that there *may* have been an *ethically* justifiable basis for Abraham's actions would clearly be counterproductive to this endeavour. Also, perhaps Kierkegaard did not wish to put the idea into anyone's head that murdering one's own child could be considered morally justifiable.

Another important and obvious overall implication contained in the story of Abraham and Isaac is the fact that it is possible for someone to be an evolved, noble-minded human being, even if their behaviour lies outside the boundaries of the social morality of the society they inhabit.

This idea is completely unthinkable to Hegelians, who believe there is an inseparable link between an individual's personal evolution and the degree to which they accept and comply with the laws of social morality. If one probes even deeper into this story, one can also reasonably conclude that if Abraham's behaviour is regarded as praiseworthy, this strongly implies that a person can be an evolved, virtuous human being even *before* they have expressed such qualities in a socially moral manner, that benefits their community. Therefore, when such a person outwardly manifests moral behaviour, it must be regarded as an indication or *consequence* – at the level of the individual – of a pre-established or prior virtuous nature, rather than a *causal* factor of their evolved consciousness. In examples such as this, universal moral law has become a natural, organic expression of an individual's pre-existing humanity.

The reader should also keep in mind, however, that throughout *Fear and Trembling*, the judgement of Abraham's actions as having taken place outside the realm of the ethics is based upon 'valid' analysis of Abraham's behaviour from an objective vantage point that assesses the situation through the eyes of social morality – it is not a judgement that is based upon Abraham's *subjective* experience. What Abraham himself would assert regarding his faith-motivated conduct is that he is *preserving* or *re-affirming* his ability to express himself ethically, for he is certain – no matter how crazy or illogical it may seem to others – that Isaac will be returned to him *in this life*, even if he actually sacrifices him.

Therefore, he believes that his willingness to sacrifice Isaac is compatible with the laws of social morality because since he is certain, in his faith, that he will not actually lose Isaac, he is also certain that he can fulfil his ethical duty, which is to exercise his fatherly love and care for Isaac. In Hegelian language, one could say that he believes that these ethical ideals will be preserved even if he acts in a manner that directly violates those ideals. Abraham believes this on the strength of the absurd, that for God all things are possible.

From Abraham's perspective, he is simply demonstrating his faith to God by handing over to God the responsibility of allowing him to continue exercising his duty as a father. In his actions Abraham is proving to God that because of his faith in him, he is willing and able to surrender totally all dependence on human reason and thus live an ethical existence merely on the strength of the absurd – in other words, Abraham's utter faith in God means that his conception of what is possible in life is no longer limited by his knowledge of what is *humanly* impossible. Moreover, Abraham's act of faith shows that he does not require any proof of the eternal justice of God in order to be utterly convinced of it in the depths of his being, in the here and now. He already experiences utter security in God's eternal justice, prior to the event that could provide him with concrete evidence of this justice.

Thus Abraham is also demonstrating that a person's belief in the essential importance of the dictates of social morality can be founded upon principles that are the diametrical opposite of the principles upon which those living in the ethical realm base their moral beliefs – for instance, Abraham's belief in the primary importance of the single individual, and faith (trusting that what is humanly impossible *is possible*) versus the belief of Hegelian ethics that the society as a whole is of primary importance with its well-being based upon the dictates of human reason.

One can also interpret in the story of Abraham and Isaac, on a much deeper and more subtle level, the Christian theme of sin and forgiveness; for we learn from Abraham's experiences on Mount Moriah that God has the power to transcend the ethical and interact with the lives of those who have broken ethical laws. *Fear and Trembling* tells us that without God, Abraham is lost, but because of

God's role in the story, Abraham, who intended to commit murder, is transformed into 'the father of faith'. Since God can transform Abraham's potential sins into a virtue, perhaps Kierkegaard intends an analogy between Abraham and the rest of humanity in order to let us realise that we too have the potential to establish an absolute relationship to God that suspends the ethical, and therefore, on this basis, God's grace can also forgive us our sins.

This potential interpretation is supported by comments in Kierkegaard's papers in a draft for the manuscript of *Fear and Trembling*: Kierkegaard considers the possibility of presenting Abraham's previous life 'as not devoid of guilt', so that Abraham is led to 'perceive the divine command as God's punishment' (*Pap.*, IV A 77; *JP*, §5641; cf. *Pap.*, IV B 66). Another obvious indication of this theme is seen in the discussion of the third *Problema* in which Johannes points out, in reference to the story of 'Agnes and the merman' in which the merman has sinned by seducing and falling in love with an innocent young woman, 'For when through his own guilt the individual has come out of the universal, he can only return to it on the strength of having come, as the particular, into an absolute relation to the absolute' (*FT h*, p. 124). It is no coincidence that his choice of the words 'as the particular, into an absolute relation to the absolute' are identical to the words Johannes uses earlier to describe Abraham's movement of faith, for Kierkegaard means the reader to draw a parallel between the fact that though the stories are different, both the merman and Abraham are saved only by a direct relationship with God that transcends ethical considerations.

Finally, Abraham's obedience to God can also legitimately be viewed as representing a call from the infinite part of the self (the part of us that is related to God or infinity) to identify oneself as an individual standing on the threshold of infinity rather than as merely a finite component of society with no individual freedom of choice. Kierkegaard saw the 'knight of faith' as the highest expression of the self. In this state of consciousness one grasps the uncertainty and absurdity of all existence and there is the deep realisation that ultimately we are alone and in a state of absolute isolation, but through faith this is experienced as aloneness before God.

Autobiographical reflections in *Fear and Trembling*

Kierkegaard's broken engagement with Regine, which obsessed him throughout his life, provided the primary autobiographical inspiration for the book. Aside from the other literary objectives of this book, Kierkegaard also uses the story of Abraham and Isaac as a covert means of explaining to Regine his motives for breaking their engagement. The fact that Regine is meant to detect this intention is clear from the motto which Kierkegaard chose for the title page of the book, a quotation from Hamann: 'What Tarquin the Proud said in his garden with the poppy blooms was understood by the son but not by the messenger.' These lines allude to an old Roman story in which Tarquinius, not wishing to trust the messenger who had come from his son to ask what should be done with the people of Gabii, took the messenger into the garden and chopped the heads off the tallest poppies – this successfully signalled to his son that the most eminent men in the city should be executed.

Kierkegaard explains to Regine the good intentions behind his cruel treatment of her in the first version of the four intelligible variations of the Abraham story presented by Johannes in the opening section of *Fear and Trembling*. In this version, Isaac *knew* that Abraham intended to sacrifice him and Abraham tries to comfort him in vain. Abraham then adopts a cruel, harsh approach and claims to be a ruthless idolater and murderer. Isaac falls to his knees in fear asking for God's mercy and Abraham says to himself that it is better that Isaac regards him as a monster than he should know that Abraham's actions are due to the temptation of God's divine will, for such knowledge could cost Isaac his mind and perhaps make him curse God. The autobiographical connotations are clear. If Regine is made to believe that Kierkegaard is a scoundrel this can prevent her from losing faith in existence and from losing her mind – because she might be unable to make sense of a world which justifies the breaking off of an engagement. Kierkegaard wrote in his diary that his act of assuming complete responsibility for the separation would free Regine so that she could fall in love with someone else. In spite of his honourable motives, when he returned from a trip to Berlin to discover that Regine had become engaged to Fritz Schlegel (who later became governor of the Danish Virgin Islands), Kierkegaard experienced what seemed to be a mixture of surprise, disappointment, regret and bitterness.

A different message is concealed in the traditional version of the story. Just as Abraham had been commanded by God to sacrifice what he most valued in the world, Kierkegaard felt he had sacrificed *his* greatest worldly love, for reasons that included his belief that divine guidance had other plans for him. In his journal he wrote that if he had had faith for *this* life he would have stayed with Regine, but that also would have necessitated the sacrifice of his career as a writer and everything else for which his life had prepared him.

Kierkegaard, like Abraham, could neither explain nor justify his apparently immoral actions, so in this sense, their acts of sacrifice were simultaneously self-sacrifice because of society's rejection of such behaviour. Also, just as Abraham, in the face of absurdity, believed he would not lose Isaac, so Kierkegaard felt – in a spiritual sense – that in spite of his broken engagement he would not lose Regine.

Prior to the actual writing of *Fear and Trembling*, Kierkegaard had described Abraham's conduct in his private journals as being more noble-minded than anything he had read about in tragedies. Perhaps in showing that in spite of his actions Abraham was a noble individual, Kierkegaard also wished, by analogy, to indicate that an eternal justice might also attribute nobility to his own actions.

Kierkegaard's obsession with his unhappy love life is also reflected in numerous stories of frustrated love, as well as marriages prevented by fate, which are spread throughout the text of *Fear and Trembling*. These include Aristotle's failed relationship; the tale of a young man whose marriage threatens to 'destroy a whole family'; and the stories of 'Sarah and Tobias' and 'Agnes and the merman'. The latter story examines the painful choices facing the merman who has seduced and then fallen in love with an innocent young woman – the biographical parallels with Kierkegaard and Regine are obvious. All of these stories contain either the theme of marriage prevented by past sins or the issue of family lines that are plagued by a curse. It seems very likely that Kierkegaard intended Regine to realise that breaking his engagement had saved her from being a victim of his family's sad fate.

Finally, there is also abundant evidence to support the claim that the conduct of Kierkegaard's father influenced many of the themes chosen for this book. There are numerous tragic heroes whose conduct endangers their offspring, and of course the primary story of Abraham's intended sacrifice of Isaac, which Kierkegaard saw as a metaphor for his own life. He felt that in a sense he had almost been 'sacrificed' on the altar of his father's morbid religiosity, but that at the last minute God had saved him through the death of his father, whom he had always felt would outlive him. He believed that his father, through his stern and cruel religious upbringing, had sacrificed his normality, thus preventing him from leading a normal existence as a family man with a respectable career like other people. Thus his life precluded a career, marriage, parenthood and normal family life.

Chapter Five

Kierkegaard's attack on Hegel's Philosophy

One of Kierkegaard's greatest contributions to philosophy was his critique of G. W. F. Hegel (1770–1831), who was considered the most important German idealist philosopher of the nineteenth century. Kierkegaard's involvement and battle with Hegel's thought catalysed the development of many of the insights and themes of his own work. This is why an understanding of the fundamental concepts behind Hegel's philosophy is crucial to an intelligent reading of Kierkegaard's works.

His fundamental dispute with Hegel was based around Hegel's claim to have developed a fully comprehensive system that could explain the whole of reality. Kierkegaard responded to this with the assertion that reality may well be a system for God, but that it cannot be so for any human being, because both reality and humans are *incomplete* and all philosophical *systems* imply *completeness*. He was equally critical of the Hegelian belief that God is an inherent part of human society and social morality. Kierkegaard saw God as being 'absolutely different' or 'wholly other' – that which any human institution or achievement can never capture.

Though Kierkegaard attacked all systematic, speculative philosophies, he was primarily concerned with Hegelianism, because it overshadowed every other philosophical outlook, thoroughly permeating theology, the

Established Danish Lutheran Church and thus the lifestyle of Danish society, including the intellectual élite. Kierkegaard acknowledged the magnitude and brilliance of Hegel's intellectual accomplishments and the fact that there is a valid sphere within which speculative thought holds true (e.g. science, mathematics, etc.), but because Hegel seriously believed he had reached *ultimate* truth, this rendered his claims comical – whilst Hegel sought to contain all of reality in the conceptual net of his system, the actual *process of existence* simply slipped through its meshes.

What most disturbed Kierkegaard, however, was the negative influence of Hegelianism upon the Christian religion.

> For a man to prefer paganism to Christianity is by no means confusing, but to discover paganism as a highest development within Christianity is to work injustice both to paganism and to Christianity…. The speculative movement which plumes itself on having completely understood Christianity, and explains itself at the same time as the highest development within Christianity, has strangely enough made the discovery that there is no 'beyond.' The notions of a future life, of another world, and similar ideas are described as arising out of the dialectical limitations of the finite understanding (*CUP (S.L.)*, p. 323).

Unlike Kierkegaard, Hegel did not believe that self-realisation and ultimate truth was dependent upon the 'outside assistance' of divine grace – Hegel's view, which he expressed in the third part of his *Encyclopaedia*, was 'God is only God in so far as he knows himself and he can only know himself through man'.

According to Kierkegaard, these basic assumptions of Hegel's thought undermined the validity of his entire philosophy as a means of understanding the central values intrinsic to *concrete* human existence.

The story begins with the fundamental assumption of Hegel's entire System.

Hegel's universe

From the viewpoint of Hegelian logic, the logical beginnings of creation could be presented in the following way: in the beginning, God, who is pure Mind and therefore pure Being, tried to *think of himself*. However, since it is impossible to think of pure Being, God thought *nothing*, which is the *opposite* of Being. However, according to Hegel, God *is* God's thought, so his failure to 'think' pure Being led to a distancing of himself from his own essence – Hegel termed this 'God's *self-alienation*'. Biblical symbolism reflects Hegel's insight in its explanation of the relation between God and Satan – Satan is an angel who has 'fallen away' from divinity, which according to Hegel's manner of thinking is symbolic of divinity that has become self-alienated.

Another apparent biblical confirmation of Hegel's 'truth' of self-alienation is evidenced in the story of the 'burning bush'. When Moses asks 'Who art thou?', God answers, 'I am what am' ('I am that which is'). God is unable to answer in words the question Moses poses, without 'dividing' his essence into a subject–object relationship: 'I am' = subject; 'that which is' = object. So, logically speaking, if a subject is the object then it is not itself as subject. In other words God, in Hegel's manner of understanding, is in a sense experiencing an identity crisis at this stage of his evolution, and this simultaneously means that humans are also experiencing an identity crisis because, in Hegel's view, *the human mind is merely a manifestation of the divine mind*. Hegel asserted, 'Man is God self-alienated.'

Hegel called his philosophy 'absolute idealism', and he equates 'the rational mind' (Hegel uses the German *Geist*, which can mean both mind and spirit) with 'absolute mind', or 'divine mind'. For Hegel, mind or spirit = the divine mind = the Absolute = God = Nature = World = the Universe = Man. Thus Hegel's beliefs were *pantheistic*, for he regarded everything in existence as divine. For Hegel, that which God *creates* is *identical* with God. According to his belief, therefore, the structure of the universe is the same as the structure of God's mind, so if one reaches an ultimate understanding of the logical structure of the world or universe one has simultaneously reached an ultimate understanding of the logical structure of God's mind.

Hegel was convinced he had achieved this with his system – he asserted that he had attained a complete, rational understanding of human life and history and that anyone capable of following his methodical progression of logical concepts would automatically attain ultimate, rational understanding of God's mind.

Hegel believed his system represented 'absolute knowledge' based upon an absolute science of logic, and he saw existence, God and the rational mind as identical – he asserted, *'the Rational is the Real and the Real is the Rational'* (taken from *Grundlinien der Philosophie des Rechts*, in *Samtliche Werke*, vol. 7, ed. Hermann Glockner). It should be noted here that when Hegel uses the German word 'Wirklichkeit', meaning 'the Real', he intends it to communicate a synthesis of 'essence' and 'existence'.

Kierkegaard flatly disputes this assertion, which eliminates the clear distinction between ontology and epistemology. He emphasises that existence and thought are *not* identical and one cannot possibly *think* 'existence'. Kierkegaard points out that thought is always a form of *abstraction*, and thus not only is pure existence impossible to *think* but all forms in existence are *unthinkable*; thought depends upon language, which merely abstracts from experience, thus separating us from *lived* experience and the *living essence* of all beings. Kierkegaard also vehemently disagrees with *all* views of existence in which 'the qualitative distinction between god and man is pantheistically abolished' (*SUD (L)*, p. 192).

He vigorously attacks Hegel's belief in the supremacy of the rational mind by pointing out the fact that our *mortal* nature places definite *limits* on our understanding of reality. Because we are *finite* beings, we cannot possibly *know* or *understand* anything that is *universal* or *infinite* such as God, so we cannot *know* God exists, since that which transcends time simultaneously transcends human understanding. So even if there is such a thing as *timeless* or *infinite* 'truth', or God, we are not in a position to comprehend this because we ourselves are *not* timeless or infinite. This is why Kierkegaard asserts that all attempts to explain, find evidence or offer rational proofs for God's existence are unconvincing, irrelevant and doomed to failure. He writes, 'When a rich man goes driving at night with lights on his carriage, he sees a small area better than the poor man who drives in the dark – but he does not see the stars. The lights prevent that. It is the same with all intellectual understanding. It sees well close at hand but takes away the infinite outlook' (*JP*, I, p. 534).

Kierkegaard does, however, admit the attractiveness of Hegel's approach, describing it as 'an illusory land, which to a mortal eye might appear to yield a certainty higher than that of faith' (*CUP (S.L.)*, p. 213).

Hegel's triadic dialectic process

Hegel based his entire philosophical system upon the beginning of creation, in which *Being* (God) gave rise to the antithesis *Nothing*. Although Being and Nothing cannot be *thought*, since they represent the absolute limitation of all thinking and all reality, Hegel asserts that this transcendental partnership started a process that gave birth to the entire universe. For he claims that the tension between these extreme polar opposites gave rise to a third event, 'Becoming' – the beginning of all creation. He asserts that the momentum and *structure* of this process – 'Being', creating its *antithesis* 'Nothing', with the tension between these two *resulting in the creation* of 'Becoming' – has continued unceasingly since it began. He called this three-stage process the *dialectic* (a term he borrowed from Plato). He termed the first stage of the process *immediate (unreflective) unity*, the second stage *reflective disunity*, and the third *reflective unity*. It should be noted that the secondary literature on Hegel frequently refers to these three stages as *thesis*, *antithesis* and *synthesis*, in spite of the fact that these were not terms that Hegel used to explain his theory. (These rather mechanical notions were invented in 1837 by a less-than-sensitive Hegel expositor Heinrich Moritz Chalybaus).

The fundamental presupposition of Hegel's entire philosophy is based upon his belief that this 'dialectic process' is a natural and *necessary* law of nature that governs *all* patterns of development in the world *and* in the entire universe. He sees it as a *logical process* of evolution, a built-in plan – analogous to the genetic blueprint that determines all life. Hegel asserted that we could explain and understand the entirety of world history in the light of this dialectic process.

For instance, as any particular nation develops, it naturally produces opposition to itself (its *antithesis – reflective disunity*). This opposition then enters into direct conflict with it (the *tension between opposing forces*) and out of the struggle emerges a new civilisation that is of a higher order than either of the previous ones, because it

137

incorporates what is of most value in each (the *synthesis – reflective unity*). After a while there will arise opposition to this new civilisation and the ensuing conflict will lead to the establishment of yet another even more evolved civilisation which incorporates and synthesises elements of the earlier ones. Each time a particular conflict is resolved, it is because man has taken a step forward in consciousness from the state of *reflective disunity* to the state of *reflective unity*. So Hegel sees history as making steady progress on account of this continuous process, and each historical moment is an advance that is born of the conflict and tension between mutually dependent, opposing forces. Even when we view certain periods in history as a regression rather than evolution, according to Hegel this is only because our faculty of understanding is not yet sufficiently developed to perceive the 'cunning of Reason', which uses what only *appears* to be retrograde movements in order to make hidden progress.

We can see this same process at work within the abstract world of ideas. In an example presented in Plato's *Republic*, Cephalus suggests that 'justice' means 'telling the truth and paying one's debts'. Socrates, in response, offers a contrary case (the *antithesis – reflective disunity*): If you borrowed a weapon from a friend who later demanded it back, but you noticed he had become insane, you would sense that it would be wrong to return it, so justice under *these circumstances* would require you *not* to pay your debt. Therefore, the original assertion that 'justice' means 'paying one's debts' is not always true. A new definition is required (which will result from these opposing definitions) that will embrace both the original assertion as well as the objection to it. This new definition (the *synthesis – reflective unity*) will also elicit an opposition to it, which will result in yet another definition embracing both the new definition and its opposition – and thus consciousness continually evolves, on both an individual and a communal level. The entire course of history has been determined by this dialectic, and nothing can alter this course.

Consequently, those involved in social action who believe they are instrumental in changing the course of history are in fact, in Hegel's view, merely pawns controlled by this omnipotent dialectic process. Hegel regarded the State as a separate entity with an independent existence, more important than any individual citizen, because its continued existence guarantees the continuance of the culture, though individual members die. In other words, each individual is to the State what a bee is to the beehive.

Hegel strongly opposed the Romantic view that one should reject the external prohibitions of society and live as a free, independent-minded individual relying upon the call of personal conscience in determining right and wrong. He felt that this would be just as likely to result in evil as good, for he was convinced that if one left humans to the dictates of conscience the result would be evil, anarchy and perversion. He believed instead that the best solution is to surrender one's life of individuality to the concrete, social duties and customs of bourgeois life, identifying right and wrong with the prevailing bourgeois morality. Although this approach may be far less than satisfactory, according to Hegel this is not because the *approach* is wrong, but is due to bourgeois society being still at the stage of 'reflective disunity'. Eventually, however, society will reach its final, perfect stage of development, 'reflective unity'. For Hegel, this will be manifested by the State, in which *individual human will* coincides perfectly with the *will of the Nation* – personal desires and feelings of personal significance and fulfilment will be rooted in, and perfectly compatible with, one's social existence and duty to the nation – according to Hegel, to submit to this State is to lose one's bourgeois freedom, but gain a higher freedom.

Kierkegaard vigorously attacks Hegel's suppression of individuality by pointing out that it is impossible to create a valid system or set of rules in any society which can adequately interpret existence or define how we all should live, for each person's experience is individual to them, and existence is incomplete and constantly developing and changing. The human situation is filled with ambiguity and paradox, and the fundamental problems of life defy rational objective explanation. Individuals create their own natures through their own choices, which must be made in the absence of universal objective standards – the validity of a choice can only be determined subjectively. Kierkegaard asserts that obedience to the State discourages people from working life out for themselves. The individual is thus deprived of personal choice and responsibility for their existence whilst living under the delusion that things have already been adequately worked out for them.

139

A conviction which became one of the cornerstones in Kierkegaard's defence of individual human freedom of choice against the determinism of Hegel's dialectic was that all great historical figures must make their first step one of opposition, because in real life it does not hold true that something new simply emerges as a necessary consequence of a previous condition. Lenin, Marx and all practical revolutionists held this same conviction.

The universe discovers its true identity

Hegel claims that each stage in the dialectic process is ultimately an expression of the inner struggle of the universe/God/man towards complete self-understanding – history is a record of this. This pattern will continue until the universe/God/man finally achieves complete self-realisation in one all-encompassing truth that includes all partial truths. At this point, according to Hegel, both the dialectic process and world history will have come to an end. The universe/God/man will now be an entirely unified logical entity that can be completely understood – it will understand itself. At this point *thought* and *being* have realised a state of oneness. Hegel asserted that his 'system' would speed up the evolution of human understanding and thus hasten the birth of this final stage of universal harmony when all *triadic dialectical processes* would be subsumed in an ultimate state of *reflective unity* in which the unity of man/universe/God is fully conscious.

So Hegel believed that the entirety of existence is composed of only *one* Being – God, the universe, the absolute, pure Being, the divine are merely different names for this one Being. So the universe and everything in it is simply a manifestation of this one Being. So when Isaac Newton asserted that between any two masses there is a force of attraction directly related to the quantity of the masses and inversely related to the square of the distance between them, Hegel viewed this as an example of the universe/God expressing *knowledge of itself*. Isaac Newton's insight did not belong to an independent being as it might have seemed, but was a spark of awareness within the infinite universal brain. In 1687, however, when Newton made this statement, Newton (e.g. the universe/God) was unaware of this fact, so Newton had no idea when he made this observation about a universal force that the universe was not merely the 'object' of his knowledge, but also the 'knower' of this knowledge.

This situation is rather similar to someone inspecting a set of eyes in a mirror without realising that the eyes making the inspection are the same as the eyes being inspected. When the person finally realises 'those eyes in the mirror are my eyes', this brings an end to the imagined separation between the inspecting eyes and the eyes being inspected and the person now understands that subject and object are one and the same. In the same way, when a human being systematically develops the understanding that the universe is both the *object that is known* and the *subject that knows*, then the universe will have reached the final stage of knowledge of itself as Subject, God's identity crisis will now be over.

So Hegel believed that the goal of all history is the evolution of understanding in the universe/God/man entity to the point where it realises itself as the *only Being* in existence, and this process of evolution is therefore completed once this understanding is reached. According to Hegel, he achieved this understanding in his greatest work entitled *The Phenomenology of Mind*, which he claims is the culmination of all knowledge since finite minds first appeared on this planet. Hegel asserted that as part of the dialectic process it is our destiny to progress to the stage where we no longer experience the world as alien or hostile, for we realise that the world is a part of us because only the Rational Mind is real and all human minds are a part of this Rational Mind, which is also God or the universe.

Ironically, Kierkegaard's attitude to Hegel's philosophy was, in a sense, an example of the dialectical process. Although he deeply admired Hegel's achievements he simultaneously strongly opposed his conclusions and in opposition to Hegel's ideas developed his own ruthlessly anti-Hegelian philosophy, but this was suffused with Hegelian concepts – a prime example being Kierkegaard's own version of the dialectic.

Kierkegaard crucifies 'Hegelian Christianity'

The following passage by Hegel sums up what Kierkegaard found most disturbing regarding Hegel's attitude towards Christianity:

> The principle of the Christian Religion should be worked out for
> thought, and be taken up into thinking knowledge, and realised in
> this ... and it should attain to reconciliation ... and the riches of
> thought and culture belonging to the philosophic Idea should
> become united to the Christian principle. For the philosophic Idea is
> the Idea of God, and thought has the absolute right of reconciliation,
> or the right to claim that the Christian principle should correspond
> with thought (G. W. F. Hegel, *Lectures on the History of Philosophy*,
> trans. E. S. Haldane and Frances H. Simon, London: Routledge &
> Kegan Paul, 1968, pp. 10–11).

Hegel was convinced that philosophy – when it has reached its final
stage of evolution, which is Hegel's system – subsumes and supersedes religion. Hegel regarded Christianity as the 'absolute religion'
whose true insights had been formulated in a rationally incomprehensible primitive mode of expression, but claimed that through his
system the fundamental tenets of Christianity had been decoded and
expressed as rationally acceptable objective truths. Hegel considered
the truth of various key Christian doctrines to be *indirect truth*
expressed via *pictorial* or *symbolic* and *metaphorical language* – for
example, the truth of the central Christian doctrine, that God
became man in the form of Jesus, is simply a metaphorical means of
revealing the truth that the finite world, man and God (the Absolute)
are one and the same. The God/man becomes aware of this truth, at a
metaphorical level, through its creation of Christianity. Hegel
believed that the Christian religion uses a symbolic transmission of
truth because it is still at the *reflective disunity* stage of the dialectic
process. Thanks to Hegel, God or the 'Absolute' can now be experienced *as it is*, in the non-pictorial, conceptual language of philosophy
as represented by Hegel's system – which is the highest stage of experience of the truth of the Absolute, the stage of *reflective unity*.
Consequently, belief in Christianity no longer requires subjective
faith – the rational mind and religion can now harmoniously coexist.
Hegel regarded even the Christian paradox of faith as entirely intelligible and subordinate to the rational mind.

In *Fear and Trembling*, using the biblical story of Abraham and
Isaac, Kierkegaard seeks to undermine Hegel's philosophical system
and his conception of religion. Ironically, he uses pure Hegelian
logical argument to prove conclusively that if Abraham does indeed

deserve the title 'father of faith', then the fundamental principle of Hegelian ethics is invalidated. This principle states clearly that nothing supersedes social morality which is universally and always applicable – its morals or laws apply to everyone at all times. This means that there is no such thing as 'individual morality' because, according to Hegelian ethical principles, something that is morally right for me must also be right for anyone else in the same situation. Kierkegaard clearly demonstrates that Abraham's actions utterly violate all ethical premises and that the very *essence* of Abraham's greatness lies in the *complete absence* of ethical justification for his actions, for his actions clearly transgressed all ethical, religious, civil and family law. Consequently, if Hegelians claim that their principles *are* valid, then instead of praising his greatness, as they do, they should be condemning Abraham as a criminal with murderous intent. Alternatively, if they still choose to honour him as the 'true father of faith', then they have to accept that the *individual* must take precedence over the *universal* – the society as a whole.

Kierkegaard's dialectic self versus Hegel's dialectic self

Kierkegaard completely refutes Hegel's assertion that the contradictory or opposing forces within the dialectical process are eventually and naturally resolved because the dialectical process constantly and automatically moves towards a state of harmonious completion.

A child's first experience of its parents is what Hegel would describe as a state of *immediate (unreflective) unity* characterised by a spontaneous feeling of harmony with the parents. In adolescence, they may reject their parents as narrow-minded and oppressive. The previous state has now been replaced by *reflective disunity* – their conflict, or *disunity*, stems from *reflection*, their negative appraisal of their parents. As mature adults, the state of *reflective disunity* might be transcended by a third stage – *reflective unity*, where increased understanding and compassion arising from *evolved* conscious reflection enables them once again to love and accept their parents.

Hegel would regard the state of harmonious communication between parents and child that takes place at the *reflective unity* stage

143

of the dialectic as being the result of a natural process of *mediation* or reconciliation between opposites in conflict, which are automatically resolved at the third stage of the dialectic process.

Kierkegaard, however, would assert that the solution to the conflict between a child's desire for independence and the achievement of a state of union with its parents is reached only by the ongoing effort made by the child's spirit, or will, which struggles constantly to hold together in balance the opposing or competing tendencies of self-assertion and the desire for union. This state of balance is not a *reconciliation* between two opposing forces within a state of harmony, but a tenuous 'holding-together' of the self, which is simultaneously being pulled in opposite directions by a desire for perfect union with the parents – which would entail a suppression of self-assertion and genuine individuality – and a desire to exist as a completely independent, autonomous self – which would require a rejection of the parents.

Kierkegaard emphatically refutes Hegel's assertion that these contradictory tendencies eventually will be overcome. Instead he believes that the task requires a continual confrontation with the tension caused by the contradictory demands of maintaining independence and individuality whilst simultaneously upholding a harmonious relationship with the parents. This same pattern of conflict can be seen within human society, where there can never be a harmonious tension-free reconciliation between a person's need to express their unique individuality and their need to be part of a community.

According to Kierkegaard, the maintenance of true selfhood requires a continuous effort to 'hold together', in some sort of balance or synthesis, the multitude of opposing tendencies that exist within the personal self – this is Kierkegaard's conception of the dialectic of selfhood. The effort to do this always causes anxiety, and there is no permanent solution to this paradoxical existential demand that is an unavoidable part of being one's true self. The tension and anxiety arising from this human predicament can only be escaped when you cease being a complete person – through self-deception, insanity or death.

So Kierkegaard, like Hegel, regards the self as a synthesis of contradictory impulses but he strongly refutes Hegel's assumption that these opposing forces within the psyche eventually and naturally evolve or make a transition to a harmonious state of self. Kierkegaard emphasises that the development of the self is not a natural process and that these contradictory forces will never be reconciled or annulled. Instead, the true self is constituted by a synthesis or composite of various opposing or competing impulses, desires and needs which always remain in opposition, but which are 'held together' through the sustained efforts of the will or spirit. 'While a genuine human being, as a synthesis of the finite and the infinite, finds his reality in holding these two factors together, infinitely interested in existence' (*CUP (S.L.)*, p. 268).

Kierkegaard, therefore, strongly contests the fundamental premise of Hegel's concept of the dialectic process – the concepts of 'mediation', 'transition', and 'negation' ('negation' in this context refers to the idea that the conflict between opposing forces within the self can be annulled). Kierkegaard states,

> Negation, transition, mediation, are the three masked men of suspicious appearance, the secret agents, which provoke all movements.... In the sphere of historical freedom transition is a state. However, in order to understand this affirmation one must not forget that the new situation comes about by the leap. For if this is not kept in mind, transition acquires a quantitative preponderance over the elasticity of the leap (*Concept of Dread*, trans. Walter Lowrie, Princeton University Press, 1962, pp. 73–6).

Hegel's disregard of the 'either/or' factor of existence

Kierkegaard's book *Either/Or* is a parody on a key characteristic of Hegel's philosophy, rooted in Hegel's reinterpretation of Aristotelian logic. In choosing this title for his book, Kierkegaard was implying that this aspect of Hegel's philosophy encouraged the current type of alienation from selfhood implicit in the lifestyle which Kierkegaard termed 'aestheticism'.

Hegel claimed that he had discovered a fundamental error in the three foundational principles of logic that had been presented by Aristotle in the third century BC, and he replaced this logic with his 'dialectical logic'. Aristotle's *Law of Identity* (A = A) means that a thing is identical to itself. For example, 'It is snowing here' equals 'It is snowing here'. Aristotle's *Law of Non-Contradiction* (*not* both A and not A) means that something cannot be both true and not true at the same time. For example, it cannot be the case that 'It is snowing here' and 'It is not snowing here' in the same instant. Aristotle's *Law of the Excluded Middle* (either A or not A) means that 'Either it is snowing here' *or* 'It is not snowing here' – there is no third possibility that exists. Hegel asserted that these three principles all misinterpreted reality by implying that everything in existence is static and black and white. Hegel asserted that in fact reality was a constantly changing process comprised of continually shifting hues of grey. Hegel's new dialectic logic subverted Aristotle's traditional laws of logic. So the *Law of Identity* was inaccurate because every single thing is always *more* than itself. The *Law of Non-Contradiction* is inaccurate because every single thing in existence is both itself and *not* itself. And, finally, the *Law of the Excluded Middle* is inaccurate – Hegel replaces Aristotle's *Either/Or* with a *Both/And*, which allows a multitude of possibilities excluded by Aristotelian logic. Kierkegaard felt that Hegel had committed a serious mistake in eliminating the principles of logic – especially the *Law of the Excluded Middle*, because it was a direct attack on subjectivity – the essence of individual human experience.

Kierkegaard saw this aspect of Hegel's philosophy as dehumanising life through its disregard of the true nature of the oppositions within the dialectic of the self. He saw this facet of Hegel's thought as leading to an attitude of indifference and demoralisation, because it denies humans personal freedom, through its neutralisation of the significance of the 'either/or' factor, which is essential for making individual free choices between the various possible ways one can live – without free choice, the attainment of true selfhood becomes an impossibility.

Kierkegaard also realised that the acceptance of Hegel's conception of the dialectic structure of the self renders human existence, *in theory*, far too easy because *in theory*, conflicts or oppositions eventually are mediated and disappear automatically as part of a natural process that requires no individual choice or effort other than the submission of one's personal will to the will of the State. Kierkegaard regarded Hegel's system as a comprehensive theoretical foundation and defence of bourgeois ideals, and regarded the application of his principles to society as being equivalent to a mass lobotomy which is epitomised by the bourgeois life. This way of existence is polluted by compromises that create an easier existence by robbing a person of their individuality and thus personal freedom. So, according to Kierkegaard, Hegelianism in one sense appears to offer a theoretical justification for the cowardly denial of true selfhood.

In the following passage from *Either/Or*, he mocks what he saw as perhaps the fundamental flaw in Hegel's philosophy:

> Marry, and you will regret it. Do not marry, and you will also regret it. Marry or do not marry, you will regret it either way. Whether you marry or you do not marry, you will regret it either way.... Hang yourself, and you will regret it. Do not hang yourself, and you will also regret it. Hang yourself or do not hang yourself, you will regret it either way. This, gentlemen, is the quintessence of all the wisdom of life (*EO 1 (E)*, pp. 22–3).

Kierkegaard accused Hegel of developing a 'both/and' philosophy – a philosophy of reconciliation and synthesis – whereas Kierkegaard stressed the necessity of an 'either/or' philosophy which emphasised the importance of personal responsibility and choice-making, which are essential components of living as one's true self in the constantly unfolding process of existence.

Chapter Six

Kierkegaard's attack on 'counterfeit Christianity'

Kierkegaard's notorious assault on official religion appears to have been carefully planned and calculated, for his private journals prior to the attack record a long period of introspection and debate concerning the risks involved, and his *Edifying Discourses* provided clear signals to his contemporaries that a crisis was on the horizon.

As Kierkegaard saw it, the evasion of the requirements of a genuinely religious Christian existence, which had been going on for centuries, was now greatly amplified in his time because Hegelian philosophy had permeated the intellectual leadership and the scholarship of Christianity. Consequently, pseudo-Christianity had become virulent in society. This had influenced the intellectual élite and scholarly teachers of Christianity condescendingly to examine various doctrines of the Gospel, from a supposedly objective and higher vantage point, in order to demonstrate how correct reasoning and understanding could reveal their truth. Consequently, only revelations which can be justified by reason were considered acceptable. Kierkegaard regarded this presentation of 'the reasonableness of Christianity' as a form of treason because it dared to presuppose that an infinite God and his infinite wisdom could be grasped by finite human understanding. Since, as finite beings, we cannot *know* God exists, Kierkegaard asserts that one can accept Christianity solely by making a 'leap to faith', and if we are unable to live in true faith then we should give up Christianity altogether. This point of view is extreme, but the extent to which Kierkegaard personally would have supported this and the various other radical opinions he offered is not entirely clear, for he later admitted that many of his viewpoints were designed to be provocative in order to supply a much needed 'corrective'.

In addition, he observed that in keeping with the Hegelian fashion of 'going farther' than the last generation, the theologians even had the audacity to submit the most sacred of Christian dogma to the Hegelian dialectical process, which claims that early stages of religion or philosophy are superseded by higher syntheses through the passage of time. As a result, matters such as faith and incarnation were divorced from the historical context upon which their true significance depends, and thus original Christian truths were altered beyond recognition. In an entry in Kierkegaard's journal whilst he was vacationing in Gilleleje in the summer of 1835, he clearly indicates this immense disappointment with contemporary Christianity: 'When I look at a fair number of individual samples of the Christian life, what strikes me is that instead of bestowing strength on them – yes that, in contrast to the pagan, Christianity deprives such people of their manhood and they are like the gelding in relation to the stallion' (*Pap.*, I A 96, from 1835; *Papers and Journals: A Selection*, p. 43). In the final year of his life, Kierkegaard's criticism of the Church was to intensify dramatically – in a journal entry the year before he died he writes, 'Christianity is on such a high level that even humanity of the best-intentioned kind is not just a misunderstanding, a false view, but is of Satan…', and, later, he describes Christendom as 'Satan's invention' (*Pap.*, XI A 375, from 1854; *Papers and Journals: A Selection*, p. 602).

At the heart of Kierkegaard's campaign against Christendom was his assertion that the Established Church had become fundamentally a secular institution in the hands of the State, controlled by a bureaucracy whose main concern was to increase the material well-being of its members. As Kierkegaard saw it, this gigantic confidence trick being played upon those whom the Church professed to serve had been concealed behind a screen of hypocritical religious verbosity. 'One *cannot* live of nothing. This one hears so often, especially from priests ... and precisely the priests perform this trick: Christianity actually does not exist – yet they live off it' (*JP*, I, p. 158).

Kierkegaard claimed that to fathom the true intentions hidden behind the religious language of his day, one needed to adopt a reverse interpretation of the terms being used – for instance, 'preaching the word in poverty' should be understood as really meaning 'pursuing a profitable career', and the statement 'renunciation of earthly goods' was to be interpreted as 'the acquisition of earthly goods'. He ironically compared the situation with one in which a man regularly uses the word 'farewell' to indicate that he had arrived – Kierkegaard remarks, 'how could it occur to anyone on hearing the word "farewell" that a person is arriving?' He thus implored his readers to cease official worship completely in order to avoid participating in practices that amounted to making a fool of God: 'Whoever you are, whatever in other respects your life may be, by refusing to take part in all this public worship of God as it is now, you have one sin the less, and that a great one' (*KAUC*, p. 211).

Although in his youth he had supported the Church, he now felt in his later years that God had entrusted him with the task of destroying the Established Church. Consequently, in his religious writings, he considers it his mission to expose the colossal deception and falseness of official Christianity. He writes, 'For many different reasons, and prompted by many different factors, I originally had the idea of defending the Established Church. Divine Guidance has surely had the idea that I was precisely the person who was to be used to overturn the Establishment' (*JP*, XI B, p. 110). He hopes that his work will open the doors to a true understanding of the nature of faith and the essence of *genuine* Christianity and Christian truth. He claims that although people may accept the validity of Christian doctrine, 'the lives people live demonstrate that there is really no Christianity – or very little.' He also acknowledges his own lack of true Christianity. He writes that part of his task – in the service of Christianity – is 'to disabuse people of the illusion that they are Christians'. In the spirit of Socrates who claimed to his contemporaries that he knew nothing, Kierkegaard states, 'For my part I do not call myself a "Christian" but I am able to make it evident that the others are still less than I.'

Fundamental flaws in modern Christianity

Kierkegaard saw several fundamental flaws. He accuses the contemporary Christian of having forgotten the original meaning and challenge of genuine Christian faith. He criticises so-called 'Christians' for blindly accepting Christianity without first acknowledging the 'offence' it presents to our intellect, aesthetic nature, 'herd' instinct and natural commonsense. He states: 'When Christianity came into the world, it did not need to call attention to the fact that it was contrary to human nature and human understanding' (*Works of Love: Some Christian Reflections in the Form of Discourses*, p. 199, trans. Howard V. Hong and Edna H. Hong, Harper Torchbooks, New York: Harper and Row, 1962). As Kierkegaard saw it, true Christianity is the deliberate and resolute refusal to be offended – it requires achieving a state of mind where that which is potentially offensive is embraced as the Truth, *in spite of* its offensiveness. He criticises the fact that most people now have 'faith' in the Gospel simply because it is presented in a manner which renders it attractive and acceptable to human reason. According to Kierkegaard, however, faith that is rooted in *understanding* is not *true* faith, but merely an intellectual acceptance of doctrines containing dogmatic truths. Genuine faith, which lies at the heart of Christianity, *cannot* be sanctioned by human reason.

He observes that the general absence of true faith in contemporary Christianity is connected with, and reinforced by, the fact that virtually anyone can 'become' a 'Christian' – people now call themselves Christian merely because they are born to Christian parents in a Christian nation – and this has reduced Christianity to a mere fashionable tradition adhered to by swarms of unbelieving 'believers'. Kierkegaard points out that that 'any determinant which applies to *all* cannot enter into existence but must lie outside as meaningless'. For instance, good can only exist if there is also evil – if everyone is good then the idea of goodness ceases to have any meaning. He writes, 'when all are that, then to be that = 0'. Therefore, 'If we are all Christians, the concept is annulled' (*JP*, IV, p. 478). He states that God's formula for Christianity is 'the individual in opposition to the others'. Mankind, however, driven by its herd instinct, has cunningly succeeded in abolishing Christianity by making it readily available to everyone.

Epitomising this whole problem is the existence of the Church congregation, which Kierkegaard absolutely abhors – he describes the idea of having people become Christians by the thousands as fraudulent – in his words, 'The concept of congregation has been Christianity's ruination.' 'With Christ, Christianity is the individual, here the single individual.' He describes the congregation as a system that is responsible for keeping the lives of ordinary people in a type of 'prolonged state of childhood' since it deprives them of the initiative to take responsibility for their own lives. He passionately believes that Church and State should be completely separate. 'If the clergy unreservedly and in self-denial had been willing to consult the New Testament, it would have seen that the New Testament unconditionally requires the separation of Church and State' (*Søren Kierkegaard's Papers*, XI A IV, p. 414, trans. Howard V. Hong and Edna H. Hong). Kierkegaard notes that Christian doctrine merely serves to collect followers, thus providing power to the clergy, which is why the clergy encourage virtually anyone to call himself or herself a Christian – irrespective of the lifestyle. In his words: 'it is in the interest of the clergyman's trade that there be as many Christians as possible.' Kierkegaard believed that the Established Church emphasised the light, cheerful, festive and communal aspects of Christianity in order to attract as many members as it can, and as a consequence religious rituals have degenerated into mere entertaining social functions.

Consequently, the idea of being or becoming a Christian has been completely emptied of the significance it originally possessed. 'The Gospel no longer benefits the poor essentially. In fact, Christianity has now even become a downright injustice to those who suffer' (*Søren Kierkegaard's Papers*, IV, p. 411, trans. Howard V. Hong and Edna H. Hong). Kierkegaard accuses the clergy of the Established Church of being hypocrites who do not practise what they preach – in his work *Attack upon 'Christendom'* he says that they are simply actors in disguise, and caustically remarks that the only difference between Church and theatre is that the Church doesn't allow you to claim your money back if you don't like the show! He even accuses the clergy of being a bunch of effeminate men in women's clothing – 'Beware of those who wear long gowns … it is of course women's attire. There is of course something ambiguous and risqué about men in women's clothing, and ambiguity is precisely the most fitting expression for official Christianity' (*Samlaede Vaerker*, XIV, 212–14, trans. Howard V. Hong and Edna H. Hong). Over and over again he insists that he wants the Church to admit its failings, its mediocrity, in order that it might then 'take refuge in Grace' and thus gain the strength to take some steps in the right direction.

On the grounds of simple human integrity he had implored Church officials to acknowledge publicly the discrepancy between the Christian ideal and what they were preaching to their congregations. He wished them to confess that they were no longer preaching the real essence of New Testament Christianity, which requires the unconditional surrender to living in the way of Jesus Christ. He saw that modern Danish Christianity had completely erased the distinction between the way of the world and the way of the Lord. Danish Lutheranism had completely integrated the religious life with the bourgeois way of existence, in spite of the fact that Luther himself had emphatically protested against the subordination of the holy way of life to secular interests. In addition, though Luther had accentuated the necessity of genuine Christian faith, official Christianity had made asceticism and Christian altruism unnecessary.

In direct contrast to this, Kierkegaard pointed out that God educates the individual through the *experience* of suffering, not its exclusion.

> Only when a person suffers and wills to learn from what he suffers does he come to know something about himself and about his relationship to God. The key to finding rest in suffering is: let God rule in everything. As soon as unrest begins, the cause for it is due to your unwillingness to surrender yourself to God (*Upbuilding Discourses in Various Spirits*, pp. 252–61, trans. Howard V. Hong and Edna H. Hong, Princeton University Press, 1993).

Consequently, the renunciation of the world required by true Christianity cannot possibly mean the same as coming to easy terms with the world, which modern Christianity condones. He asserted that the godly man is one who is passionately committed to suffer whatever is required in the process of carrying out God's will on earth. Therefore a faith that does not inspire one to carry out the works of love is sterile and hypocritical. In December 1854, following the death of his father's friend Bishop Mynster, Kierkegaard made it quite clear that anyone professing to be a Christian was required unconditionally and fully to follow the way of Christ. 'This is Christianity: Let a person begin seriously to realise his need for Christ. Let him literally give all his fortune away to the poor, literally love his neighbour, and so forth, and he will soon learn to need Christ' (*JP*, I, p. 206). Kierkegaard referred to the early days of true Christianity when becoming Christian required effort and sacrifice – a difficult way of living entailing suffering, sin and guilt, in which one separates oneself from the crowd to live an ascetic existence. For Kierkegaard true Christianity calls not for the admiration but for the imitation of Christ – a following of the way of Jesus in self-denial, sacrifice, suffering and a direct relationship with God. He writes: 'What is Christianity? Simple: to be like Christ.'

He stresses that each individual must discover their own relationship with God directly, rather than attempting to communicate via priests or any other human 'authority' that claims to represent God: 'When the individual relates himself to God through the race, through an abstraction, through a third party, Christianity is abolished…. Every call from God is always addressed to one person, the single individual' (*JP*, II, p. 282).

The concept of anxiety

Kierkegaard's *The Concept of Anxiety* (written in 1844), published under the pseudonym Vigilius Haufniensis, has exercised an enormous influence on philosophers such as Jean-Paul Sartre and Martin Heidegger, and it has been a primary source for existential psychology and psycho-analysis. Kierkegaard makes it clear from the beginning that the anxiety (or dread, as it is sometimes translated) he refers to has nothing to do with our instinctive fear of something specific which we consider to be a real future threat or an immediate danger. (In this chapter the author uses both *anxiety* and *dread* depending upon which seems to best fit the context.)

In this work, which purports to be a psychological study of 'original sin', Kierkegaard uses the context of the Genesis story as a backdrop to his discussion of anxiety and the nature of freedom in relation to the idea of sin, because he observed structural similarities between the questions of how sin first arises and how freedom first arises. He begins his investigation by reconstructing Adam's mental state prior to the fall.

The 'pre-human' anxiety of 'innocence'

Kierkegaard asserts that in the beginning, when man was first created, he was in a state of innocent ignorance. His existence was characterised by inner harmony and perfect union with his environment; man was 'in immediate unity with his natural condition' (*CA (E)*, IV, p. 313). In this state, man's consciousness was in many respects similar to that of the animal kingdom, completely absorbed in its immediate surroundings, oblivious of the past and future. So this peaceful condition arose from a state of ignorance, unconscious of individual freedom.

In this condition, allegorically described in the myth of the Garden of Eden, mankind is not yet fully human because, according to Kierkegaard, 'the spirit in man is dreaming' (*CA (E)*, IV, p. 313). But Adam continually senses the existence of his dreaming 'spirit', which projects itself – perhaps through Adam's imagination – as a 'nothingness' outside of him, and this 'presence' of nothing – the 'phantom' relation between Adam and his dreaming spirit – creates anxiety in him. This anxiety, in one sense, is literally about '*nothing*', and in another sense, it is about a not-yet-discovered latent '*something*'.

Kierkegaard explains that this 'innocent' anxiety experienced by Adam contains no guilt, nor is the discomfort it produces disruptive to peace of mind. 'The anxiety that is posited in innocence is in the first place no guilt, and in the second place it is no troublesome burden, no suffering that cannot be brought into harmony with the blessedness of innocence' (*CA (E)*, IV, p. 314).

The birth of human anxiety

Then a prohibition and threat of punishment (death) is introduced, which destroys Adam's inner harmony – he is warned by God not to eat fruit from the 'Tree of the knowledge of good and evil.'

> What passed by innocence as the nothing of anxiety has now entered into Adam, and here again it is a nothing – the anxious possibility of *being able*. He has no conception of what he is able to do; otherwise – and this is what usually happens – that which comes later, the difference between good and evil, would have to be presupposed. Only the possibility of being able is present as a higher form of ignorance, as a higher expression of anxiety, because in a higher sense it both is and is not, because in a higher sense he both loves it and flees from it (*CA (E)*, IV, p. 316).

In other words, God's prohibition 'you may not' triggers in Adam the realisation 'I can', and he sees his inner freedom for the first time, reflected back, mirrored in the realm of possibilities opened up by God's warning: 'anxiety is freedom's disclosure to itself in possibility'. Although he realises that he is *free* – that he has the freedom to act – he does not yet have any idea what he can do.

Kierkegaard frequently asserts that 'Anxiety is the *possibility* of freedom' (*CA*, p. 155), but this is only half the story, for once a person realises that they have this *possibility* of freedom (that they are potentially free) they *simultaneously* understand that they *are* free; 'freedom is never possible, as soon as it is, it is actual' (*CA*, p. 22). Freedom only remains a potential, or *possibility*, whilst a person is *unaware* of its existence, but in the exact same instant that a person (as in the case of Adam) recognises this possibility of their own freedom, the *possibility* is transformed into a '*fact*'. Since the transformation is *instant*, what the person actually recognises is not the *possibility*, but the *fact* of their own freedom. For freedom, like God, is *always* present. What is not always present is our *awareness* of its existence. Kierkegaard also asserts that 'Anxiety is entangled freedom, where freedom is not free in itself but entangled, not by necessity, but in itself' (*CA*, p. 49). In other words, in the grip of anxiety, our freedom of choice is being used to choose non-freedom and, as a consequence, we are free but do not yet *use* our freedom.

Kierkegaard also claims that, psychologically understood, a key feature of anxiety is symmetrical emotional ambivalence – 'anxiety is a *sympathetic antipathy* and an *antipathetic sympathy*' (*CA (E)*, IV, p. 313). Anxiety is characterised by a desire for what one fears, and a dread of what one desires – the possibilities of one's freedom are experienced as attractive and desirable and also, at the same time, as undesirable and terrifying, and these conflicting emotions are felt with a similar intensity. Therefore, when Adam realises he *can* disobey God, in his anxiety he feels the impulse or desire to do this, but he is also repelled by the realisation that his freedom means that there is nothing to stop him. Kierkegaard states 'in a higher sense he both loves it and flees from it'. In his private journals he adds to this description, 'Anxiety is a desire for what one fears, a sympathetic antipathy, anxiety is an alien power which grips the individual, and yet one cannot tear himself free from it and does not want to, for one fears, but what he fears he desires. Anxiety makes the individual powerless' (*Kierkegaard's Journals and Papers*, I, p. 39; **Pap.**, III A, 233).

One of several reason why humans want to 'flee' from anxiety and yet 'really love' it, is because freedom has always been man's greatest desire, and since anxiety is the manifestation of our freedom, whatever negative feelings it may produce, it nevertheless reminds us of this condition of being that we so much yearn for and which is ultimately life's greatest gift.

However, due to the fact that most human beings tend to use various escape strategies to block from their mind this awareness of freedom, most people do not walk around constantly plagued by anxiety, for they lose themselves in their work or in other activities that allow them to deny this crucially important truth of existence. There is a clear motive for this denial – human consciousness, existence or reality, always entails a collision between *actuality* and *possibility*, between what *is* and what *is not* (but which *could be*) and everything arising in reality also contains its antithesis as a possibility. Therefore every moment of our existence, confronted with an unknown future and our freedom of choice between all the possibilities facing us, we are standing on a precipice and before us lies a gaping abyss of uncertainty and utter insecurity; the resulting anxiety that arises if we face up to this fact is not really so surprising.

In this state of consciousness we realise that our moment-by-moment existence is not characterised by 'being' but is a constant process of 'becoming'. The conscious awareness that we are not a definable, fixed entity, but simply a continuously changing uncertain process that could end at any moment, is the root source of this dread or terror that so often surfaces in human consciousness. The tremendous feeling of insecurity and hopelessness that arises with this realisation of our utterly precarious human existence is, according to Kierkegaard, the state of consciousness that can also inspire us to take the irrational leap to faith – after all, when the mind realises that its current condition is completely hopeless then what has it got to lose by taking an 'irrational' leap into the unknown, even if this holds no actual guarantee of salvation?

However, the normal and understandable response of most people to their anxiety is to push it into the back of their mind or to escape into various activities that drown it out altogether; for the pain of anxiety, if experienced in its *full intensity*, is unbearable for most people. There are, however, times when one becomes caught in the grip of anxiety and one just cannot seem to escape it, 'neither through amusement, nor by noise, nor during work, neither by day nor by night' (*CA (E)*, IV, p. 422). Under such circumstances, as Kierkegaard states, anxiety can become *the* most torturous experience known to man, 'And no Grand Inquisitor has such dreadful torments in readiness as anxiety has, and not secret agent knows as cunningly as anxiety how to attack his suspect in his weakest moment' (*CA (E)*, IV, p. 422).

Such anxiety can arise anytime, anywhere, without warning. For instance, I may be taking a quiet walk in the countryside when out of the blue, as if from nowhere, the suffocating feeling of the pointlessness of everything overwhelms me. Life suddenly appears utterly senseless – all ambition seems futile and achievements shrink into insignificance as I am confronted with the unlimited possibilities facing me, including my own demise. I find myself staring directly into the void of nothingness – the inevitability of my death, the 'terrible perdition, and annihilation live next door to every man'. It is not however the *experience of dying* that is dreaded in the mood of anxiety, but our *being able not to be* – the fact that our finite form becomes *nothing*. This strange feeling of anxiety, or dread, that one's consciousness will one day be completely and permanently terminated – that one will entirely cease *to be* – cannot be compared to any other form of human experience. Any security I normally derive from my everyday existence, material possessions and personal relationships is instantly shattered. The whole experience could be summarised as a *crisis of meaning*. I now feel alienated from everything that formerly mattered to me and my existence and surroundings now seem strange and inhospitable.

Anxiety – the terror of our monstrous freedom

Even if a person's escape strategies have effectively prevented them from such unexpected attacks of anxiety, there are sometimes certain situations familiar to most of us in which the anxiety of freedom *cannot* be ignored. Most people standing at the verge of a tall cliff or building and looking over the edge have experienced a perfectly normal instinctive fear of falling, but this is sometimes accompanied by the terrifying impulse to throw oneself *intentionally* off the edge – this strange feeling, usually felt in the pit of one's stomach, simultaneously *draws us towards* and *repels us* from the edge. What we are experiencing is the dread or anxiety of our complete freedom to choose – even such an unpleasant possibility. Not everyone has looked downwards from a high place, but almost everyone has experienced the same sensation of dread in some form or another. Sometimes, and quite commonly, it can express itself in a pathological way – driving along a narrow road, late at night in the pouring rain, furious at an oncoming car's blinding headlights, the thought darts through one's mind, 'I *could* steer right into him.' This '*I could*' – my freedom – triggers in me an immense feeling of dread. I am horrified by the enormity of my unrestricted freedom of choice that includes even the most terrifying of possibilities. There is absolutely *nothing* to stop me from driving my car head-on into the other vehicle – nothing but *myself*, my own *will*.

Kierkegaard felt a sense of anxiety or dread towards Christianity.

It is terrible when I think, even for a single moment, over the dark background which, from the very earliest time, was part of my life. The dread with which my father filled my soul, his own frightful melancholy, and all the things in this connection which I do not even note down. I felt a dread of Christianity and yet felt myself so strongly drawn towards it (*Journals of Kierkegaard 1834–1854*, p. 274).

The nature of Adam's anxiety – the birth of guilt

In Adam's case, the anxiety he experiences following God's prohibition has an added dimension to it as compared with what he previously felt. Whereas formerly Adam's anxiety had been related to an *outside* 'nothing', after God's prohibition awakens in him the realisation that he is free, his anxiety becomes internalised and intensified, and is now experienced as an anxiety relating to an *inside* 'nothing' – his inner freedom. Additionally, in spite of the fact that he has no concept of death or punishment, he nevertheless feels an instinctive foreboding of danger in God's warning. The sense of there being a 'consequence' were he to exercise his freedom – 'the possibility of a possibility' – that which *is not* but which *may be* – has accentuated to Adam the significance and closeness of his freedom, thus intensifying his anxiety further.

Though previously his anxiety had been connected with a 'pure nothing', Adam's present anxiety is now related to a more '*specified*' nothing – his knowledge of *being able*, of having the *freedom*, to commit an *unknown forbidden act* that will result in an *unknown unpleasant consequence*. In other words, Adam's innocence is standing on the precipice of sin, just one step away from sin, and Adam does not have a clue as to what on earth is going on. Although Adam is still innocent at this point, his *anxiety* is guilt-ridden – even though he knows he has *not yet* violated God's prohibition, his anxiety makes him feel as if he already had: 'Innocence is not guilty, yet there is anxiety as though it were lost' (*CA (E)*, IV, p. 316).

Kierkegaard asserts that 'psychology' can comprehend Adam's reactions up to and including this point *immediately preceding* his act of 'sin', but it *cannot* go further – it is outside the scope of psychology to offer explanations as to *why* Adam would now choose to disobey God. However, since Adam's innocent condition is already polluted by guilt-ridden anxiety, Kierkegaard suggests that it is *this factor* that *enables* him to sin. Therefore Kierkegaard hypothesises 'anxiety as the presupposition for hereditary sin' (*CA (E)*, IV, p. 319). He concludes that anxiety is the psychological state that *precedes* the basic human fall into sin.

The innocence and the guilt of anxiety

Kierkegaard's assumption here is suggesting that in spite of the fact that we cannot *rationally* explain *why* we sin, it seems probable that guilt-ridden anxiety is the *motivating* and *enabling* force behind human sin. He also explains, 'But he who becomes guilty through anxiety is indeed innocent, for it was not he himself but anxiety, a foreign power that laid hold of him, a power that he did not love but about which he was anxious. And yet he is guilty for he sank in anxiety, which he nevertheless loved even as he feared it' (*CA (E)*, IV, p. 314).

In other words, if I do something bad, commit a sin, in one sense I am completely innocent, because my sin was a consequence of my anxiety, which I *did not create*, since it is part of my human condition. And yet I am also guilty, because although I am not responsible for the *presence* of anxiety I do have the freedom to choose *not to allow* the magnetic pull of anxiety to engulf and control me. Kierkegaard suggests that to be anxious about freedom's possibilities is to be anxious about what one will do with one's freedom, and part of this anxiety is a fear of committing sin. But Kierkegaard warns us that just as fear of illness can produce illness, so can anxiety about sin can lead to sin – he explains that anxiety often conceals a *desire to sin* – so those who are frightened or anxious about sinning are often also attracted to sin, which frequently leads them to sin. So anxiety enables us to do wrong (sin), which in turn intensifies our anxiety thus further predisposing us to further wrongdoing, and so it continues in an endless circle. Anxiety about sin can also lead us to the sin of being dishonest with ourselves about sinfulness so that when a person claims that their act of succumbing to a sin was due to their *incapacity* to resist desire, according to Kierkegaard, this is simply the cunning of desire providing them with an legitimate excuse to indulge themselves in what they know is wrong. In other words, the apparent powerlessness we experience that leads to sin is in fact *self-created weakness* – those who lack self-control are not *unable* but *unwilling*.

It is interesting to note at this point in the discussion that Kierkegaard may possibly have intended some irony in his choice of the title *The Concept of Anxiety* – in view of the central role of the 'Concept' or 'Notion' in Hegel's philosophy. Alternatively, perhaps he was ironically emphasising people's *misconception* of anxiety, for according to Kierkegaard's explanation of it, it is clear that 'anxiety' is quite definitely *not* a concept, rather it is the *non-conceptual* foundation of *all concepts*. For if the very first experience of anxiety and the very first impulse to sin are inseparably connected as Kierkegaard asserts, and if the sin Adam committed was his disobedient action of eating from the tree of knowledge, then *all knowledge*, in other words, *all conceptual thought*, is *grounded in anxiety* because anxiety is the necessary *enabling* condition of sin, the presupposition of hereditary sin.

The different faces of anxiety

Much later, in his *Christian Discourses*, Kierkegaard wrote, 'anxiety is about tomorrow'. Our awareness of the future triggers in us a feeling of anxiety. The object of this anxiety is still 'nothing', since the future does not exist and never will. When the future 'arrives' it is no longer the future but the *present*. Nevertheless, with every choice or decision I make, I am creating my 'future circumstances' as well as my 'future *self*' in the sense that my future is my *not-yet-arrived present*.

Each time I choose, it is with the knowledge that I can never know whether the choices I make are right or wrong. This makes me realise the utter uncertainty that lies at the heart of existence – the nothingness of existence.

I can only escape this feeling – run away from my freedom – by living a superficial existence that ignores this freedom, but ultimately, all attempts to escape my freedom are mere illusion, for, as Kierkegaard points out, freedom is my unavoidable destiny – for *not to choose freedom* is *also* an expression of our *freedom of choice*. This relation of anxiety to the future is supported by discussions in *The Concept of Anxiety*, which often associate anxiety with the experience of foreboding or presentiment. Since anxiety arises with the awareness of our freedom of choice, and any choice I make now has unknown consequences for me in the future, it is reasonable to assume that the sense of the 'foreboding' of anxiety that Kierkegaard speaks of might be related to the 'unknown nothing' of my future self and circumstances.

In Kierkegaard's conception of anxiety, he also describes a type of anxiety that potentially can arise in relation to the possibility of goodness. An example of this might be seen in the case of a man whose life is locked into a vicious circle of immoral living. If he suddenly becomes aware of the fact that he could, if he chose to, break this cycle of immoral living, even though this idea might attract him, he may at the same time be repelled by it – he dreads the possibility of freedom from the enslaving grip of sin which simultaneously *attracts* and *repels* him. Thus, in this sense, he is experiencing anxiety related to the *possibility of a good existence*.

Anxiety – the gateway to salvation

Kierkegaard interpreted anxiety as a kind of homesickness of earthly life for something higher than the finite world of form, and the ultimate reason why Kierkegaard investigates the story of Adam's fall is that he sees it as an excellent mythical illustration of the manner in which the experience of anxiety precipitates the transition from a state of 'unselfconscious immediacy' (undeveloped consciousness) towards self-awareness and personal responsibility for one's life.

When a person's consciousness is undeveloped, even though consciously they may be completely unaware of their spiritual potential, they nevertheless can sense an indeterminate presentiment of their potential freedom to shape who they are and what they become. But it seems an individual only becomes truly aware of their potentialities through the experience of sin. Anxiety is the precondition for sin. According to Kierkegaard, however, anxiety does not merely foreshadow the possibility of sin – more importantly it manifests in a person a vague subliminal recognition of the fact that the key to realising their true identity, their individual spiritual self, lies in devoting the resources of their finite worldly existence to a constant striving towards the eternal, the divine.

'Whoever has learned to be anxious in the right way has learned the ultimate' (*CA (E)*, IV, p. 421). Kierkegaard asserts that a most important task of existence is to learn how to be anxious in the *right way*, otherwise 'we perish by never having been in anxiety or by succumbing to anxiety' (*CA*, p. 155). The first 'death' refers to the spiritless rejection of our potential to evolve spiritually. The second 'death' is due to giving way to our sinful inclinations.

Kierkegaard disregards as beneficial all forms of anxiety that are about external or worldly matters. In contrast, in 'right anxiety' the person has learned to look at his past finite sins and this makes him realise that he is also infinitely guilty. But at this point he needs to make the leap to faith, for Kierkegaard suggests that if an individual without faith in the infinite realm of existence realises in his anxiety the full depth of his wrongful way of life and the utter fragility of his finite existence, then this is likely to trigger in him a downward spiral of self-destructive behaviour. 'In order that an individual may thus be educated absolutely and infinitely by the possibility, he must be honest toward possibility and have faith' (*CA*, p. 157).

The ambivalence of the fall and the dialectic nature of selfhood

So man's loss of innocence clearly has highly ambivalent consequences – in one sense it can be viewed as a 'fall', due to the resulting dissatisfaction and anxiety that are the inevitable consequences of being alienated from the state of immediate (unreflective) unity. In another sense, this fall also marks the birth of man as a *human*, separate from the rest of the animal world, for the fall bestowed upon mankind knowledge and freedom. Man's fall is thus both a 'descent' into restlessness and anxiety, and an 'ascent' to freedom and, potentially, true selfhood.

Once the fall has occurred, man is free, but *not free* to return as a human being to the earlier state of innocent ignorance and harmony. The consequence of the fall, therefore, is that humans are destined to search for a state of being analogous to the pre-fallen condition, but one that also includes the uniquely human qualities of freedom and knowledge. In other words, mankind is alienated from his condition of immediate and unreflective unity by the opposing force of knowledge and freedom, and though one cannot *overcome* the resulting state of reflective disunity, one can, according to Kierkegaard, use the sustained effort of the will of the human spirit to hold together in synthesis or balance the various opposing or competing impulses and desires. In this way, ultimately through faith, true selfhood can be reached.

Anxiety, however, is not only the ambivalent response to freedom, but it is also the continued response to this effort of holding together the opposing elements of the dialectic structure of the self. It is only because man is made up of both animal nature *and* spirit that he can experience anxiety. 'If a human being were a beast or an angel, he could not be in anxiety. Because he is a synthesis, he can be in anxiety' (*CA (E)*, IV, p. 421). For, according to Kierkegaard, from one perspective a human can be described as a 'synthesis of the psychical and the physical' – a soul/body synthesis of instincts, impulses and awareness that defines an individual's worldly attributes and status – but he also has the capacity to transcend this definition of himself through the will of his 'spirit'. Kierkegaard emphasises in *The Concept of Anxiety* and in other texts that human beings *are* spirit – that there is an *infinite* component to our existence. He repeatedly reminds us that if this were not the case then anxiety, despair, sin and faith would be impossible.

Kierkegaard observed that although a person's spirit holds the key to their true self, few people relate to this aspect of their being. Some people do not even know of its existence, and others, for various reasons, reject their spirit – the source of their potential 'selfhood' – for the sake of adopting a worldly identity – a false self. According to Kierkegaard, to be a human being is to exist in a state of *becoming*, and I have free will to choose *what* I become, even if I deceive myself with all sorts of clever excuses that this is not the case. Therefore ultimately I am entirely responsible for who I am.

However, the elements which compose the self are, and always will be, in opposition with one another and it is an act of a person's *will* or *spirit* which holds together these conflicting components of the self. This *holding together* always produces significant tension and anxiety which tempts the person to give up their constant effort in order to escape. Consequently, rather than being something that needs to be *cured* or avoided, *existential* anxiety (anxiety arising from the dialectical nature of the structure of the true self, rather than *pathological anxiety* of emotional disturbance) is part of our human predicament, an unavoidable companion on our journey towards selfhood – the pathway to genuine selfhood is paved with dread.

Ignoring the 'self' is the only sin of the self

Kierkegaard asserts that anxiety is not only the *predisposition* to sin and is *intensified* by sin, but *more importantly* it is a manifestation of man's potential to achieve perfection. For Kierkegaard, ultimately there is only one fundamental sin, in the sense that all other sins *arise* from this sin, and *depend* upon this sin for their continued existence. In Kierkegaard's eyes my only sin as a human is being aware of the cost of not benefiting from the advantages of being 'spirit', and in spite of this, being willing to sacrifice this opportunity to live as my true spiritual self in relation to the infinite, for the sake of a *false identity* that is entirely defined by the values of a finite worldly existence.

The reasons for ignoring one's potential selfhood become clearer if we use the analogy of friendship. Suppose I had only one honest friend whom I could always trust in a time of need, but this friend leads an existence characterised by personal commitment to the spiritual path and a lack of attachment to worldly pleasures. In addition, they see through my act, so in their presence my ego is undermined rather than boosted. Under such circumstances I might well choose to turn my back on this friend (my true spiritual self) and instead spend my time with 'fair weather' friends who praise my success and love having fun (finite worldly existence). In other words, I reject my spiritual self because this part of my being sees the shallowness of my finite worldly concerns and it notices all my faults and negative behaviour.

Although anxiety enables us to sin – to ignore the call of spirit and turn our back on our 'infinite potential' for the sake of fulfilling worldly desires – if instead we do not attempt to escape it, according to Kierkegaard, it can also inspire us to make (with God's grace) the leap to faith which Kierkegaard believes is the antithesis to sin. He also asserts that the greater a person's anxiety, the more evolved is his spirit, and if it were possible to remove anxiety, one would cease to be fully human.

'Anxiety is the dizziness of freedom, which emerges when the spirit wants to posit the synthesis and freedom looks down into its own possibility, laying hold of finiteness to support itself. Freedom succumbs in this dizziness … freedom, when it again rises, sees that it is guilty' (*CA*, p. 61). In this passage Kierkegaard seems to be suggesting that anxiety arises when there is an inner pull to unify one's finite self with one's infinite spiritual self. The finite self pulls away from this, holding tight to its connection with finite world of form, dizzy from its glimpse into its infinite spiritual potential.

Kierkegaard is also suggesting here that from the moment a person first denies their opportunity to be free, their whole existence is changed, for when they come face to face with their potential freedom again, they realise that they have been guilty of denying themselves this freedom. To bridge the gap between the state of guilt and freedom requires a leap that can only be made by faith, and Kierkegaard describes how anxiety makes this possible.

> Anxiety is freedom's possibility, and only such anxiety is through faith absolutely educative, because it consumes all finite ends and discovers all their deceptiveness…. Whoever is educated by anxiety is educated by possibility, and only he who is educated by possibility is educated according to his infinitude. Therefore possibility is the weightiest of all categories (*CA (E)*, IV, p. 422).

Kierkegaard is pointing out how anxiety – the Nothing that surrounds us at all times – makes a person realise the pointlessness of relying on, or expecting anything from, finite existence – it thus serves to free us from our self-deception and illusions about life by severing our attachment to the finite world of form in which 'terrible perdition, and annihilation live next door to every man'. This sense of the futility of all finite endeavours can cleanse our vision and potentially allow us to view our existence in relation to the 'big picture' – infinity. It thus causes a person to re-evaluate their life in relation to *infinite* values rather than finite values. Former attachments to the world melt away, and a new perspective on existence provides the opportunity for making dramatic changes in the direction of one's life. So anxiety can reveal the shallowness of a self that is founded entirely upon worldly values and can potentially inspire a person to become 'a single individual', a self grounded in its relation to the infinite. However, this full healing potential of anxiety only occurs if the insights of anxiety catalyse a leap to faith which brings back meaning again to finite existence, this time a sense of meaning that is based upon a relation to the infinite.

In spite of the insight provided by anxiety, this leap to faith is still no easy matter, for even at this stage a person is faced with a task that requires making a total self-commitment to an *objective uncertainty* – a leap into the mystery of the unknown. He experiences a feeling similar to someone standing on a precipice who is aware of the possibility of jumping over the edge and who simultaneously feels strangely drawn and repelled by this possibility, though in the former example the 'leap' (of faith) appears to offer the *possibility* of salvation, rather than certain death. Kierkegaard observes, 'The dread of possibility holds him as its prey, until it can deliver him saved into the hands of faith. In no other place does he find repose' (Kierkegaard, *The Concept of Dread*, trans. W. Lowrie, Princeton and London, 1944, p. 141).

Although this statement appears to imply that the feeling of anxiety will be overcome permanently if he makes the leap to faith, this is not likely to be the case, since the maintenance of true faith (according to Kierkegaard) involves *repeated*, or continued, leaps of self-commitment to this objective uncertainty. This suggests that the release from the grip of dread that occurs after the leap is perhaps only a state of 'temporary remission' and that the dread arises again and is present prior to each repeated leap because, as Kierkegaard has already clearly explained, dread is always at hand in an individual who is on the verge of making a leap to faith.

The final antidote

So it is clear that Kierkegaard sees anxiety not as something to be 'cured' by psychotherapy or suppressed by medication, but as a crucial resource for our spiritual education – for the evolution of human consciousness towards an understanding of its true nature. For similar to the situation whereby great works of art often emerge from an artist's great suffering, the overwhelming pain of anxiety potentially can expand our consciousness into an illuminated perception of existence. Normally, absorbed in our false sense of self, we identify with, and hide behind, the seemingly 'stable' universe of our habitual thoughts, feelings, attitudes and worldly values. This creates a superficial sense of permanence, an escape from acknowledging the truth that we are living a superficial existence founded on the finite world, which came from nothing and which returns to nothing. Meanwhile, we are ignoring our true self that is grounded in the infinite – anxiety, however, can serve to bring us 'home'.

Unfortunately, however, because the 'nothingness at the heart of our existence' revealed by anxiety is so disturbing, most people spend their lives, consciously or unconsciously, trying to block out this uneasy, indistinct background feeling through their absorption in the numerous escapes that society provides. This removal of anxiety, however, is a 'pyrrhic' victory, a manifestation of *despair*, since it simultaneously removes one's potential for reaching genuine individuality and true selfhood. For despair in all its forms (the subject of the next chapter) is the avoidance of the task of becoming a true self.

Despair – the fatal sickness

Despair is a central concept in several of Kierkegaard's works, but the most comprehensive and advanced treatment of it appears in his book *The Sickness unto Death*.

In this chapter, as in previous chapters, I am attributing what is said to *Kierkegaard* rather than to his *pseudonyms* as he would have wished, firstly because it is less confusing and more pleasant to read, and secondly because I have chosen only pseudonymously written material which I believe does in fact closely reflect Kierkegaard's personal opinions. Kierkegaard also stated in his journals that because of its Foreword, *The Sickness unto Death* is *not* indirect communication.

According to the notion of despair as described in *The Sickness unto Death*, everyone is always already in a state of despair, whether they know it or not, for despair is regarded as a characteristic of the human spirit, a sickness of the spirit – a conflict within the psyche that has existed and which always will exist as part of mankind's predicament.

Not many people are consciously aware of their despair *all the time*; most humans become aware of it only periodically, and some individuals are *never* conscious of its existence and thus only experience it subliminally. Everyone who chooses to, can become fully aware of this inner sickness. The more intensely conscious one becomes of the fact that one is in despair, the closer one is to the potential cure. Whilst a person is unaware of, or denies, being in despair there is no hope they will find freedom from it, for there will be no motivation to take the action necessary to eliminate it.

The nature of despair – its source and function

Kierkegaard saw the true self as constituted by a composite of opposing or competing impulses and desires which are held together in balance or synthesis through the continual effort of the 'will' or spirit.

> A human being is spirit. But what is spirit? Spirit is the self. But what is the self? The self is a relation that relates itself to itself … the self is not the relation but is the relation's relating itself to itself. A human being is a synthesis of the infinite and the finite, of the temporal and the eternal, of freedom and necessity, in short a synthesis. A synthesis is a relation between two. Considered in this way, a human being is still not a self (*SUD (E)*, XI, p. 127).

According to Kierkegaard, to become one's true self, to maintain the balance of an integrated, true self, requires the harmonisation or synthesis of the soul/body which occurs when the soul/body identifies itself as being spirit, and this happens when the soul/body relation relates to itself, since this relation it has to itself *is* spirit. At this stage, the soul/body relation, which now realises itself as spirit, must also relate itself to, and identify itself with, the power that made this entire process possible – the power that established it. So the true self subsumes the entire *relation* of the body/soul relation relating to itself (as spirit), relating to God. 'The self is a relation that relates itself to itself … and in relating itself to itself relates itself to another … the relation relates itself to that which established the entire relation' (*SUD (E)*, XI, p. 128). If in the final part of this process, instead of relating to 'the power that established it', the self commits itself to the laws of social morality, then the result will be only an 'ethical self', which eventually must be transcended to reach genuine selfhood.

This complex *action* of holding the true self together is not something that remains once it is 'achieved', rather it is an ongoing activity that requires continuous effort by a person's spirit, or will, which struggles constantly to hold together in balance numerous opposing or competing tendencies in the psyche. Without this constant exertion of the will, genuine selfhood cannot be maintained, and the effort required to hold together the self is accompanied by constant and intense anxiety which can only be escaped when one ceases being a complete person – through self-deception, insanity or death. The path *towards* true selfhood also entails this same anxiety, which is why most people don't even *begin* the journey. Those who do usually give up the struggle after a while, and the few who *are* actually living as their true self are under continual temptation to quit.

When a person escapes from this anxiety and the task of genuine selfhood, there will always be an unhealthy relationship or balance between the opposing elements of the self – Kierkegaard describes this as 'the misrelation in the relation of a synthesis that relates itself to itself' (*SUD (E)*, XI, p. 130). It is this that forms the roots of despair. So a very general broad definition of Kierkegaard's view of despair is: *an unwillingness to live up to the expectations of selfhood.*

So Kierkegaard believed that in all forms of despair there is a corresponding imbalance in the synthesis between the opposing elements of the self. Not relating to the power that established the synthesis is also a form of despair and imbalance. From a moral standpoint he regarded the state 'despair' as a sin because it is a choosing (either consciously or subconsciously) not to be what God destines us to be. 'Sin is: before God in despair not to will to be oneself, or before God in despair to will to be oneself' (*SUD (E)*, XI, p. 193).

Apart from the case of *despair* as open *defiance*, Kierkegaard regards the various manifestations of despair as a fundamental condition of self-deception which is experienced by all human beings who have not yet achieved genuine selfhood.

In Kierkegaard's discussion of this *existential* despair, to be in a state of despair does not mean the complete loss or absence of hope as the etymology of the word suggests. It also does not necessarily mean to be 'depressed'. In fact, there is no unique feeling associated with despair. As a structural disrelationship in the dialectical structure of the self, Kierkegaard compares it to tuberculosis, a structural physiological condition which in its early stages might not be felt at all, and when it does become apparent may be experienced as fatigue or elation, depression or contentment – in other words, there is no actual 'feeling of tuberculosis'. Similarly, Kierkegaard asserts that there is no 'feeling of despair' in its earlier stages, and if or when despair increases in intensity, the feelings it produces can vary greatly from person to person.

Kierkegaard sees despair as an advantageous and essential characteristic, one of the key features of human existence that differentiate us from the realm of nature and the rest of the animal kingdom.

> Is despair an excellence or a defect? Purely dialectically it is both....
> The possibility of this sickness is man's superiority over the animal
> ... for it indicates infinite erectness or sublimity, that he is spirit....
> Consequently, to be able to despair is an infinite advantage, and yet to
> be in despair is not only the worst misfortune and misery – no it is
> ruination (*SUD (E)*, XI, p. 129).

The potential to experience despair that arose as a consequence of the 'fall' opened up for man the possibility/opportunity of having a self since, as we have said, despair is a symptom or result of the failure to become one's true self.

But despair not only functions as a signal or reminder of this failure to live as the true self, but it is also absolutely essential for the purpose of providing man with the necessary motivation, inspiration and passion to rectify this failure. When a person becomes fully aware of the pain and suffering of their underlying despair, which is 'the worst misfortune and misery', this acts as a punitive measure or negative reinforcement (dished out by existence/God) that can inspire a person to embark on life's ultimate journey – the path to genuine selfhood.

According to Kierkegaard, the eternal element in me is my true self that I can and should identify with, and become, for the worst failure as a human being is not to become who I am – my eternal self. This failure is the source of all spiritual corruption. 'For despair is precisely to have lost the eternal and oneself' (*SUD (L)*, p. 195). He also states: 'to have a self, to be a self, is the greatest concession, an infinite concession, given to man but it is also eternity's claim upon him' (*SUD (E)*, XI, p. 135). So, in this sense, it would be accurate to say that despair is the most precious sickness known to man, and so there is no reason to despair (in the etymological sense of the word) if you are suffering from 'existential despair', since this is potentially your 'ticket' to freedom.

Kierkegaard asserts that despair is a sickness for which the person is continually responsible, because it is freely chosen, the motive/cause being the cowardly attempt to escape the anxiety that necessarily exists in the act of striving towards or holding together the contradictory elements of the true self. 'Every moment he is in despair he is bringing his despair upon himself' (*SUD (E)*, XI, p. 131). Kierkegaard asserts that most people who feel despair secretly hope that there *is* nothing to hope for, for if this is not the case then they must consciously acknowledge that their lives are being wasted.

He also asserts that the reason it is possible for a person to 'choose to be sick' is because humans have the capacity to use *denial* to maintain a half obscurity about their own condition.

> At one moment it has almost become clear to him that he is in despair; but then at another moment it appears to him after all as though his indisposition might have another ground ... something outside of himself, and if this were to be changed, he would not be in despair. Or perhaps, by diversions, or in other ways, e.g., by work and busy occupations as means of distraction, he seeks by his own effort to preserve an obscurity about his condition ... or perhaps he is even conscious that he labours thus in order to sink the soul into obscurity.... For in fact there is in all obscurity a dialectical interplay of knowledge and will (*SUD (L)*, p. 181).

This is an extremely important passage, for it illuminates a theory of despair as being a form of *intentional self-corruption*, or sin, which removes any sense of paradox from the idea that a person is capable of *knowingly* corrupting themselves. Although this activity only takes place whilst a person is under the influence of a kind of igno-rance or 'half obscurity about their own condition', this state is nevertheless *willed* by the person, and thus they are not only fully responsible for their 'pseudo-ignorance' but they are also sublimi-nally conscious of it. So despair is a psychological corruption of the self for which a person is *entirely responsible* even if they seem to be ignorant of their condition.

But if a person is making a conscious effort to remain ignorant, then they must also *know* that they are making an effort to remain ignorant, so one would assume that the whole endeavour would fail. Kierkegaard says that their success relies upon 'double-mindedness', 'self-deceit' and cleverness.

So, either subliminally or consciously, everyone knows if their manner of living is an avoidance of true selfhood, and the greater their conscious awareness of this dishonesty to themselves, the more despair they consciously experience. Even someone who seems to be completely caught up in worldly affairs senses, at least subliminally, the pointlessness of it all. In avoiding the reality of my true self, through attempting to live as a worldly self, I am a self divided against itself – this is what Kierkegaard means when he speaks of the 'double-mindedness' of despair.

Whether despair is avoidance of an ethical self or of the genuinely spiritual self, the underlying structure is the same – 'to want to be rid of oneself' (*SUD h*, p. 50). In *The Sickness unto Death*, despair is described as a *not* wanting to be a self other than the self one most enjoys being – the self that is absorbed in the finite world. This self does not want there to exist any higher conception of the self that it *ought to be*, and refuses even to think about the possibility that the despairer is one who backs off from the notion that there is anything 'eternal' to measure up to.

This tactic, however, is futile, for according to Kierkegaard in *The Sickness unto Death*, all human beings are 'primitively organised as a self', and everyone is 'characteristically determined to become himself' (*SUD h*, p. 63). Later Kierkegaard, through his author Anti-Climacus, suggests that even if a person does not want to journey towards true selfhood, because of the difficulties involved in the process, an outside 'power' 'compels him to be the self he does not want to be' (*SUD h*, p. 50).

The different faces of despair

The Sickness unto Death describes various *forms* of despair as well as degrees of despair, ranging from completely unconscious despair to the most intense consciousness of despair. In its simplest sense, despair is the consequence of not 'willing to be the self which one truly is' (*SUD*, p. 151). The person in despair despairs because he *is not*, and does not think he can become, the *true* self he potentially is, and he also wishes to be rid of the self he is now, and despairs 'because he cannot consume himself, cannot get rid of himself, cannot become nothing' (*SUD*, p. 151). Kierkegaard implies that in despair one is therefore consumed by an unconscious death wish – this is why he describes despair as 'the sickness unto death' – not because it *causes* death but because there is a longing for the death of the self one is. According to Kierkegaard, 'the more consciousness, the more intense the despair'. However, the more intense one's experience of despair, the greater chance one has of being inspired to overcome despair. Those who are completely unconscious of their existential despair have no hope of finding salvation from their suffering.

The despair of weakness

Kierkegaard regards any self that exists in relation *to the world* rather than *God* as suffering from a despair of *weakness*. One could define this weakness as being an *addiction* to the world (see Alastair Hannay, *Kierkegaard*, p. 379). In all types of *despair of weakness* the person is attempting to escape from the fact that he has an eternal self, a fact of which he is aware, either consciously or subliminally. Despair that is due to *weakness* is defined by any way of life in which one fails to live as a 'single individual', free from the influence of what the rest of society thinks of one. This failure might stem from a lack of awareness that one has the potential to live as a free individual, or more often it is due to consciously attempting to escape this responsibility or to obscure it from one's awareness so that one forgets about it. In such situations one believes that the despair arises from unfulfilled worldly expectations or loss of worldly 'possessions', which may be material or human. So this despair that in reality stems from the failure to be one's true self, is displaced to despair over worldly things. In this mode of despair it is common for a person to look with longing at the lives of other people who represent what they would like to be and what they would like to have. Any misfortune provides this individual with the opportunity to blame their despair upon bad luck instead of the real source, which stems from the avoidance of selfhood and the desire to be rid of the false self that they are at the moment.

One of the most popular forms of escape from despair is self-forgetfulness through sensual experiences – this is the escape of the 'sexaholic' or the gourmet. Some people, though conscious of their despair, have a false conception of the condition. They mistakenly believe that there are others who are not in despair – that their despair could potentially have been avoided – and this misconception causes them further despair. The true conception of despair knows that despair is a human condition and recognises the self as being in that condition. *Concluding Unscientific Postscript* describes this despair as the response to misfortune that brings one out of one's present limited understanding, so that 'the transition to another understanding of misfortune is made possible' (*CUP*, p. 434). This new understanding of misfortune allows a person to 'comprehend suffering' (*CUP*, p. 434), an insight that allows one to see that despair is an essential part of life rather than avoidable intrusion.

Conscious despair *incorrectly* conceived is the despair of introversion in which the normal tactics for escaping despair via various diversions in the outer world become ineffective. Kierkegaard calls this the despair of 'reserve'. In this despair the person 'sits as it were the self and watches itself employed in filling up time with willing not to be itself' (*SUD*, p. 196). Shakespeare's Hamlet appears to be suffering from the despair of introversion – feeling helpless and incapable of action, he hires the services of actors to perform the action that he himself should carry out. This example is also appropriate because Kierkegaard claims that there is a danger of suicide at this stage, because in the despair of introversion, the person has become consciously aware of their death-wish, but they seem to avoid looking at its 'source', which is their avoidance of the task of true selfhood. On a positive note, however, the despair also becomes more *passionate,* which is an indicator that there is also a will to live. If the person gets through this suicidal crisis this means they have rejected suicide and *willed* existence. However, they still despair because they have only *willed* their *own* conception of self, for they have no belief in the possibility of achieving true selfhood.

Many highly successful people in society suffer from various forms of the despair of weakness. They work incessantly to maintain their conception of a secure material existence and/or social status. But the moment this is taken away from them through illness or misfortune they invariably fall to pieces, for their sense of self rests entirely upon externals – a worldly existence devoid of any sense of their true self, their inner spirit. Consequently, when the 'externals' are no longer acceptable, neither is their life.

And yet, if one were to ask them 'What are you so busy for? What is the point of all your hard work if without warning you become ill or drop dead?', they would offer some material justification or angrily dismiss the question. For these types escape despair, their spirit-lessness, by working themselves frantically into the ground. This prevents them from thinking too much about the deeper meaning of existence, for to do so would mean acknowledging that they are rejecting their true self, thus rendering their life meaningless. Even if there are moments when they realise the nature of their condition, usually they will retreat again to the illusory sanctuary of their self-deception, rather than endure the excruciating pains of anxiety that are essential for shattering worldly illusions, thus clearing the pathway towards genuine selfhood. According to *The Sickness unto Death*, the self we become when preferring the worldly option, the self that develops in an outward rather than an inward direction and whose outward direction does not express an inward direction, must be 'broken down' in order to become itself' (*SUD h*, p. 96).

Most people in this category, even if they become aware of the possibility of true selfhood – the highest mode of human existence – are most likely to choose to remain where they are, in the 'basement' of life – indeed it is likely that they will vigorously justify their lifestyle, taking offence at anyone who suggests that they should give it up for a more evolved existence.

The despair of unconsciousness

The majority of people are unaware of, or in denial of, their spiritual self, their connection to the infinite realm of existence, and thus they do not fulfil, and have no chance of fulfilling, this essential requirement of genuine human existence. For this reason their lives are wasted, because all their 'security' and all their modes of pleasure or contentment are in fact disguised forms of despair. In *The Sickness unto Death*, the most common despair in the world is cited as being the despair of those people who as yet are not conscious of themselves *as spirit*. A person lacking 'consciousness of an infinite self' (*SUD h*, p. 100) cannot yet see what their task of selfhood actually is. Kierkegaard regards this as an inauthentic form of despair: 'Being unconscious in despair of having a self' (*SUD h*, p. 51).

In the despair of unconsciousness the individual blames his despair on *something*, when in fact he is despairing over *himself*. For example, if an actor in this category fails to get a much desired film role, he will despair over this. In fact, however, it is not the *lost film role* over which he is despairing. His despair is over *himself* – because he did not get the film role, he now hates and can no longer tolerate the *self which failed* and it is *this self* over which he despairs and which he wishes *to be rid of*. Even before he was refused the role, he wanted to be rid of this self and would have temporarily succeeded if he had got the part. He would still have been in despair beneath his fleeting happiness, for the real root of his despair is his failure to live as his *true self*. The formula for despair is always the same – 'To despair over oneself, in despair to will to be rid of oneself' (*SUD (E)*, XI, p. 133). This self that people wish to be rid of is the true spiritual self. For example, in the above case when a person is despairingly willing to be himself – that is, to be a self that fits his image of himself – he in fact wishes to be rid of the self he really is (his true self) in order to be the self he dreams of being. Ultimately, all his despair stems from torment caused by the failure to become his true self (of which he is not even aware).

In describing unconscious despair in comparison with other modes of despair, Kierkegaard says, 'an even more horrible expression of this most terrible sickness and misery is that it is hidden ... that it can be so hidden in a man that he himself is not aware of it' (*SUD (E)*, XI, p. 141).

In unconscious despair, the individual has no sense of their inner spirit, potential selfhood or their existential despair – they identify themselves totally with things outside of themselves and therefore their sense of self is entirely at the mercy of fate, and subliminally they feel a deep sense of emptiness. 'There is a blind door in the background of his soul, behind which there is nothing' (*SUD*, p. 189). This despair is extremely widespread amongst people in whom the self is 'entirely finitized, by having become, instead of a self, a number, just one man more, one more repetition ... and while it is true that every self as such is angular, the logical consequence of this merely is that it has to be polished, not that it has to be ground smooth' (*SUD (L)*, p. 166).

In other words, unconscious despair is most commonly found amongst people who are completely absorbed in one of the multitude of ready-made identities provided by society. Thus they willingly adopt and conform to the cultural customs, expectations and interpretations of life offered by the culture or social group to which they belong. The majority of human beings suffer from this type of despair because human civilisation clamps a straitjacket of conformity on every child that is born, so there is an almost overwhelming pressure for people to adapt to the understanding, behaviour and basic mode of survival which is shaped by the ready-made explanations, evaluations and standards of the particular society, and period in time, which they inhabit. This is a highly effective strategy of self-deception for avoiding the full force of the truth of one's inner despair, for just as 'there are insects that protect themselves against attackers by raising a cloud of dust. Likewise man instinctively protects himself against the truth and spirit by raising a cloud of numbers' (*JP*, II, p. 373).

Consequently, the way of living and self-understanding of the person unconscious of their inner spirit is often deeply rooted in, and compliant with, the anonymous public – they behave, speak and possess the same values as the general public or 'crowd' (Kierkegaard's term for the general public). The crowd pressures individuals into conformity through the *levelling off* of distinctions and the *levelling down* of possibilities – for instance, at school, children who are 'different' are rejected until they learn to conform with their peers – learn the 'way of the crowd'.

Even those who believe they are independent-minded 'individuals' belonging to the world of counter-culture – whether it be the hell's angels or the 'hip-hop' generation who truly believe they are escaping the influence of 'the crowd', by 'doing their *own* thing', with their supposedly 'different' or 'cool' style of dress, hairstyle, body-piercing or tattooing – are deluding themselves. These types too are merely conforming to the particular 'crowd' of the counter-culture. As Kierkegaard points out, a person who is part of the crowd finds 'it too venturesome a thing to be himself, far easier to be an imitation, a number, a cipher in the crowd' (*SUD (L)*, p. 167).

Defiant despair

According to Kierkegaard defiant despair arises when a person has genuinely realised that they are an independent individual with full freedom and responsibility of choice, alone in the world before the vastness of infinity. However, they refuse to acknowledge the fact that their existence is 'grounded in the power that established it'. They deny their relation to and dependence on God. Instead, free of all influence from the expectations of their background and their peers, they independently strive to determine all aspects of their existence; they 'want to be themselves', to be utterly self-reliant. This is a futile desire that is a form of despair because it exists in complete denial of their debt to, and reliance upon, the infinite creative force of the universe.

Defiant despair is typically seen in strong-minded individuals who use this awareness of their unique individuality and personal freedom as a basis for shaping their very own conception of self. They 'invent themselves' independently of any spiritual or divine support, using the personal power of their individuality and inner freedom to make their own unique mark on the world by devoting their energy and talents entirely to the satisfaction of their own personal worldly ambitions. These types are offended by any sense of despair in themselves, and their passion for life turns to rage when problems or misfortune strike. They become indignant and resentful and use such events as an excuse to curse the whole of existence. In response to hardship they expect and ask no one for help and simply intensify their battle against the opposing forces of existence – they would rather suffer increased hardship than lose their sense of self-reliance by asking God or anyone else for help. 'He rages most of all at the thought that eternity might get it into its head to take his misery from him' (*SUD*, p. 206). Whatever the outcome of this war, he loses. If he 'wins', he solidifies an empty, false sense of self and loses any chance of achieving genuine selfhood. If he 'loses', then in his eyes he is a pathetic failure – however, if in his disappointment his conscious despair is sufficiently intensified, he may be pushed to the edge of the 'precipice', close to the possibility of making a leap to faith and genuine selfhood.

The lives of those in society who are classified as super-successful often fall into this category of defiant despair. This exploitation of their individuality and freedom of choice purely for worldly purposes is regarded by Kierkegaard as one of the worst forms of weakness – it is a weakness of presuming that one cannot escape the demands of the world, because there is nothing else (eternal) to live up to in existence; at the same time, however, deep down this person knows very well that ultimately fulfilment is not derived from worldly pursuits. In this situation, despair does not arise from the *weakness itself*; instead, the despair is the refusal to acknowledge this *as a weakness*. In the case of *passively defiant despair*, instead of putting their weakness out of mind, this person makes a point of parading their weakness as a decisive reason for claiming that the project of spiritual selfhood, based on faith in an outside power, is not worth striving for.

Transcending despair

'Who thinks of hitching Pegasus and an old nag together to one carriage for a ride? And yet this is what it is to exist for one compounded of finitude and infinitude!' (*JP*, I, p. 55). This apt metaphor describes very well Kierkegaard's view of our human dilemma, but in spite of this predicament he is optimistic that we simultaneously possess a solution to this dilemma – our personal freedom of choice.

> The most tremendous thing conceded to man is – choice, freedom. If you want to rescue and keep it, there is only one way – in the very same second unconditionally in full attachment give it back to God and yourself along with it. If the sight of what is conceded to you tempts you, if you surrender to the temptation and look with selfish craving at freedom of choice, then you lose your (true) freedom. And your punishment then is to go around in a kind of confusion and brag about having – freedom of choice (*JP*, II, p. 69).

The reason Kierkegaard believes that being bound to God is the true source of personal power is because only then is one freed from despair to participate in the life of true Love that is the basis and stabilising factor of finite human existence. 'The greater the conception of God, the more self there is; the more self, the greater the conception of God. Not until a self as this specific single individual is

185

conscious of existing before God, not until then is it the infinite self' (*SUD (E)*, XI, p. 192).

To turn one's back on this possibility and to attempt to utilise one's freedom of choice for *finite* purposes results in despair, which Kierkegaard views as sin. Freedom of choice is the ontological prerequisite for true freedom and in this sense a genuine good.

However, Kierkegaard claims that freedom *in itself* is only *good* if it is *correctly used*. He asserts that the supreme challenge of existence is to realise *true* freedom, by transcending the *normal* use of freedom of choice as a mere tool of *worldly aspiration*, in order to commit oneself freely to *one single choice* that excludes all others, and which is the guiding force of one's life – a life now defined by total commitment to this one purpose. 'With complete decisive determination he impresses upon his action the inner necessity which excludes the thought of another possibility. Then freedom of choice or the "agony" of choice comes to an end' (*JP*, II, p. 74). This last line indicates Kierkegaard's view that being faced with a wide variety of possibilities is a form of 'agony' that fuels despair, because having numerous choices is a sign that one is still not truly committed to becoming one's true self.

In this state, freedom is often experienced as *agony*, because any choice one makes requires the exclusion of numerous other choices that may be equally attractive, and there is always a fear that what one chooses might turn out to be the *wrong* choice. Most people are very conscious of this 'agony' of choice, even in mundane situations. For instance any 'bibliophile' will frequently have experienced terrible indecision when financial resources dictate the exclusion of some interesting books from a selection they have chosen in a bookshop. Imagine how much larger the agony is when the choices concern one's way of life – often, however, the pain is repressed from conscious awareness, felt as a background sense of deep dissatisfaction with life – despair.

To reach and maintain true selfhood, therefore, not only requires constant effort but also great courage and personal commitment. Kierkegaard describes this task in *The Sickness unto Death*: 'The formula that describes the state of the self when despair is completely rooted out is this: in relating itself to itself and in willing to be itself, the self rests transparently in the power that established it … existing in the light of God, and answerable to God' (*SUD (E)*, XI, p. 128).

Anxiety is an unavoidable companion in this endeavour, and those who strive to escape it are choosing to live instead in a state of despair. To let go of the effort required to be one's true self – to allow the 'held-together' synthesis of the self to fall apart – in order to escape this tension and anxiety is considered by Kierkegaard to be a cowardly human act. Unfortunately, however, Kierkegaard observes that most humans choose to live in a diversity of ways in which they fail to answer 'the call of the infinite'.

Kierkegaard asserts that *all worldly preoccupations* serve only to divert a person away from the only true, worthwhile goal of existence; for human fulfilment lies beyond all earthly ambitions and can only be realised if we choose to commit ourselves to our creator. What Kierkegaard considers to be the key to developing the strength to make this commitment to God is summed up perfectly in the following passage.

> As a Christian he has acquired a courage unknown to the natural man, a courage he acquired by learning to fear something even more horrifying. That is always how a person acquires courage: when he fears a greater danger he always has the courage to face a lesser. When one fears a danger infinitely, it is as if the others weren't there at all (*SUD*, p. 39).

The single purpose of existence

Kierkegaard suggests that the first crucial step on the path towards personal freedom is to establish oneself as a 'single individual'. 'Every call from God is always addressed to one person, the single individual. Precisely in this lies the difficulty and the examination, that the one who is called must stand alone, walk alone, alone with God' (*JP*, I, p. 100). This means turning *inward*, away from the world, by exercising one's freedom of choice uninfluenced by the expectations of others. The next task is to expose all cowardly forms of escape from despair, what Kierkegaard calls strategies of self-deception, such as rationalisation, vanity, weak excuses and procrastination.

The journey to genuine selfhood also requires a clear understanding of the nature of self, beginning with the self one is at the moment. For

Kierkegaard, the notion of self is linked with a 'standard' or 'goal' that determines the requirements for becoming a particular self, whether that be an aesthetic self, an ethical self or a religious self – this defines the ideal version of the self. 'Everything is qualitatively what it is measured by' and with regard to the self this means its 'standard … is always that directly in the face of which it is a self' (*SUD h*, p. 111). In other words, a child judges itself by taking its parents as setting the standard against which it measures itself to see if it is meeting the requirements of its sense of self. Later on it may measure itself against the standards of social morality within its culture.

Although in Part One of *The Sickness unto Death* Kierkegaard refers to the 'standard' of true selfhood only *indirectly* as 'that which has established the entire relation', later, in Part Two, *God* is presented as the measure of the self, so now an 'infinite accent is laid upon the self when it acquires God as its standard' (*SUD h*, p. 111). 'The self is the conscious synthesis of infinitude and finitude, which relates to itself, whose task it is to become itself, which can only be done in the relationship to God' (*SUD h*, p. 87). Finally, towards the end of *The Sickness unto Death*, Christ, through whom God has revealed 'what stupendous reality a self has', is presented as the *ultimate* measure. But unlike all other standards of self, such as the *ethical* self, which can be 'chosen' simply by following the laws and expectations defined by social morality, this highest selfhood is no longer something one can *choose* to be purely on an independent basis. For *genuine selfhood* one also needs divine help, assistance through God's grace.

So, finally, it seems that we have travelled a complete circle to return once again to the recurrent theme underlying Kierkegaard's entire authorship and life, namely that the *one and only* panacea for *all ills* – which in this case means the cure for our 'sickness unto death' – is found in the act of faith. 'The absurd is an expression of despair: humanly it is impossible – but despair is just the negative mark of faith' (*Papers and Journals: A Selection*, p. 459). So the bottom line is that Kierkegaard sees despair as the essential consequence of a wide variety of ways of living that *exclude* the presence of *faith*. Rather dogmatically, he assumes that human nature is specifically constructed so that only one particular brand of faith – Christian faith – is effective, and gaining of access to this faith essentially requires embracing the Christian message.

Chapter Nine

The three spheres of human existence (aesthetic/ethical/ religious)

In his works *Concluding Unscientific Postcript* and *Stages on Life's Way*, Kierkegaard's pseudonyms describe humans as living on one or more of three different planes of existence, each of which corresponds to a different lifestyle – 'the aesthetic', followed by 'the ethical' and finally 'the religious'. Kierkegaard sometimes calls these 'the stages on life's way' and at other times he refers to them as 'spheres of existence'. In his later (post-*Postscript*) writings, he reduces these three main stages to the 'aesthetic' and the 'religious', with the latter now including ethics (with God).

Each different mode of existence has its source in a corresponding state of consciousness that determines the particular outlook or 'world view' responsible for the values, ideals, motivations and behaviour of that mode of existence. They are 'stages' in the sense that what Kierkegaard is presenting can be seen as a developmental theory of human existence.

As a person continues to evolve in consciousness there tends to be a progression from the aesthetic to the ethical and then onwards to the religious stage. There is also a hier-archical arrangement *within* each sphere – some humans will express a particular mode of existence in an unde-veloped manner, whereas others are exemplary of more evolved versions of that way of life. Since the development through the stages of existence has a spiritual character, it is *not* automatic, like *physical* growth, but requires a *conscious choice* by the individual. These different stages therefore can also be viewed as self-contained *spheres* in which a person might spend their entire life.

However, very few individuals fall *entirely* within just one category. Those living according to the ethical way of life naturally enjoy values of the aesthetic domain but they are not *ruled* by their desire for pleasure. Similarly, the religious mode of consciousness includes both the ethical and aesthetic spheres but their *religious values* are dominant.

Kierkegaard sees those living in the aesthetic sphere as basing their existence upon an individual search for personal satisfaction or fulfilment that depends entirely upon *external contingencies* of the *everyday world*, which means they are confined to one dimension of existence – the finite world of form. He also views the ethical way of life as being confined to only *one* dimension of the everyday world, but this time personal fulfilment is sought through one's *inner* development, as *part of a group* – it is based upon devoted commitment to family, friends and the values of social institutions.

Kierkegaard was convinced that both these ways of life, even in their highest, most ideal versions, ultimately lead to an experience of despair that stems from a structural dysfunctional relationship within the self. Neither way of life is worthy of a person's total commitment because only a *two-dimensional* life – the religious life – which embraces both the finite world *and* the *infinite* aspect of our existence, encompasses the full scope of human potential.

The examination of the aesthetic realm is conducted through Kierkegaard's pseudonymous characters. Most of these are 'refined aesthetes', some of whom have an awareness of their predicament; others are unconscious of their own failings but full of insight into the weaknesses of those around them. Kierkegaard observed that in contrast to the ethical and religious sphere of existence, the aesthetical outlook on life does not provide a person with any *stable* sense of identity or self. Instead it *alienates* humans from selfhood. It is also the sphere which the majority of people occupy. This is why he devoted a great deal of his writing to identifying, describing and prescribing *existential* remedies for this way of life.

If Kierkegaard were alive today, it seems likely that he would view emotions such as anxiety, despair, failure and a sense of emptiness not as feelings which should be removed by therapy, but as valuable warning signs that one's *lifestyle* is unhealthy. For if one were to remove such feelings through therapeutic treatment this would destroy a major incentive for changing one's unsatisfactory mode of existence.

In masterfully stripping away and exposing the multiple layers of self-delusion that cloud the awareness of those trapped in an aesthetic lifestyle, Kierkegaard motivates us to find our *own* way out of the abyss of despair by taking full responsibility for the choices we make in our life.

His thoughts on the aesthetic way of life were quite obviously based upon direct personal experience, for not only did he go through a highly self-indulgent period at university, but he also made substantial use of his inheritance to ensure that his working environment and lifestyle were as comfortable as possible. First-class cuisine and fine wine were regularly delivered to his stylishly furnished residence, and in the summer-time he hired carriages to take him on relaxing drives through the countryside. What is perhaps a little surprising, however, is that not only did he openly admit that his manner of living was extravagant, but he also insisted that his agreeable lifestyle was a *necessity* – an essential precondition for his writing.

Kierkegaard closely examines the aesthetic and the ethical sphere in his work *Either/Or*. His main discussion of the core of the religious sphere, faith, is most fully covered in *Fear and Trembling*.

Either/Or exemplifies Kierkegaard's typically indirect approach. He presents the different stages of life in a highly imaginative and empathetic manner that allows the reader to 'step inside' and see various contrasting perspectives on existence, through the eyes of different characters he portrays. And because he speaks to his readers through the medium of various pseudonyms, the life-views are allowed to 'speak for themselves', leaving the *reader* to draw his or her *own* conclusions. His intention is to encourage readers to look at themselves honestly – to see in the text a reflection of their own lives as the expression of a *set of values* that *rules* their way of living and to *evaluate* those values in comparison with other values that might offer a more satisfying, fulfilling existence.

There are also autobiographical reflections throughout, and he even used his private journals to provide some of the material. One can therefore discern in the texts his personal hardships, psycho-logical troubles and dissatisfaction with his student years. In addition there are frequent echoes of his complex relationship with his father and his traumatic broken engagement with Regine, for whom he wrote some of the material – in particular, the section 'Diary of a seducer'.

Kierkegaard also chooses to focus primarily upon the *best* that each mode of existence has to offer. So for the aesthetic sphere he devotes most of his discussion to the lifestyle and views of the 'refined aesthete' (the ironist, the romantic), in the ethical sphere he portrays the ultimate in bourgeois virtue by revealing how an extremely ethical judge thinks one should live, and in the religious sphere he chooses the ideal of Abraham, the paragon of religious faith. This tactic is logical – if the absolute *best* that a particular approach to existence has to offer is insufficient, this automatically invalidates less evolved versions of that perspective on life and demonstrates that the *very essence* of that life-view is deficient. The experience of reading Kierkegaard's literary presentation of the spheres of existence will sometimes feel rather uncomfortable – like looking in a mirror and seeing aspects of one's own behaviour and way of living that one might often prefer to ignore.

The aesthetic sphere of life

The aesthetic life-view encompasses the numerous levels of consciousness and sophistication that span society. The most unde-veloped aesthetic lifestyle is defined by a coarse, instinct-driven pursuit of personal pleasure. In sharp contrast is refined aestheticism, inhabited by cultured individuals who enjoy sophisti-cated intellectual and artistic forms of pleasure.

According to Kierkegaard, every level of aestheticism is defined by *immediacy*. Typical of *all* forms of 'immediacy' is the failure to reflect seriously upon the nature of one's way of living. The person whose relation to existence is defined by immediacy is seldom deeply committed to anything in life, for when they lose interest in something or see a more attractive alternative, they simply change direction. Consequently their life lacks continuity, stability and genuine focus. Instead, existence is viewed in terms of possibilities that can be contemplated or briefly 'tasted', rather than in terms of long-term projects or ideals that are to be fulfilled.

The person with an aesthetic worldview tends to accept passively the life that was 'given' to him by the random forces of chance or destiny that also determined his nationality, country of birth, race, religion, family and social identity.

Because he lives in 'immediacy' he does not subject his lifestyle, given attributes and behaviour to *critical reflection* – his existence and level of contentment are determined and governed entirely by factors not of his choice and not under his control. The aesthetic person's life is based upon external contingencies of reality – purely worldly values that are at the mercy of the changes of time, and because of this, when things go wrong with his external world he can feel as if deprived of everything that makes life worth living. 'Before me is continually an empty space, and I am propelled by a consequence that lies behind me' (*EO 1 (E)*, p. 8). So the immediate person pursues what he takes to be 'the good' without reflecting upon, or calling into question, its goodness; he lives a life whose content is determined by his instinctive desires and by the norms of his society, and he does *not* reflect upon whether or not his conception of the good has any genuine merit, whether his desires and ideals should be transformed or modified, or whether his society's norms have any *genuine* authority or value for him. He does not ask himself whether there is any other way of living available to him than the one he is living now.

A young child's unreflective trust in its parents is also an expression of *immediacy* – a pointer to the fact that adults who relate to the world through immediacy are, like children, in a state of *emotional immaturity*. Similar to a young child, when things are going well, this person sees this as due to 'going through a good patch', and the bad times are considered to be mainly the result of *misfortune*, so existence is experienced as being the result of factors *beyond* one's control rather than something that *could* be controlled. Instead, life is taken as it comes, as if it were merely a *happening* in which one finds oneself. It does not occur to this person that he is responsible for the way his life is: 'Fortune, misfortune, fate, immediate enthusiasm, despair – these are what the aesthetic life-view has at its disposal' (*CUP*, p. 434). So those who live an aesthetic existence regard the *self* as something *given* rather than something *chosen*.

Undeveloped aestheticism exists in *unrefined immediacy*, characterised by a craving for *immediate* desire-satisfaction through enjoyments that require neither personal cultivation nor effort – drugs, alcohol, one-night stands, sunbathing on the beach, and so on. The person who lives in unrefined immediacy is usually socially unselective – prepared to accept passively the company even of those to whom he feels indifferent. One example of this type of unrefined immediacy would be the self-indulgent beer-drinking, cigarette-smoking 'couch potato' who sits in front of the 'box' every evening watching football after his regular night out with the 'lads' at the local pub. One of Kierkegaard's more cultured 'aesthetes' condescendingly describes this type of person.

> Certainly this class of animals is not the fruit of man's appetite and woman's desire. Like all lower classes of animals, it is distinguished by a high level of fecundity and propagates beyond belief. It is incomprehensible, too, that nature should need nine months to produce such creatures, which presumably could rather be produced by the score (*EO 1 (E)*, p. 260).

Being trapped in a life of 'unrefined immediacy' is also the dilemma of many young adults who, in spite of being highly intelligent, talented and well-educated, choose to waste their potential by living on unemployment benefit so that they can sleep late, and live a self-indulgent lifestyle involving drinking and drugs.

Not much higher up on the evolutionary scale of consciousness is the aesthetic life-view in which health and beauty are prized above all else. Those who attempt to gain control over these fragile, temporary features of existence are similar to a child at the seaside who desperately fights to save his sandcastle against the force of the incoming tide. Nowadays the tremendous popularity of this 'keep healthy and young' view of life is mirrored in society's obsession with fashion, dieting, health clubs, face lifts, and so on. Kierkegaard sees this approach to life as tragic, for when someone's sense of self is based largely upon on these values, they are surely destined for a life of despair when their health or looks decay, for theirs is an utterly spiritless existence without *inner* substance.

A little further up the hierarchy of aestheticism are those who inhabit the business world – their entire life consists simply of chasing superficial forms of pleasure, the main one being the immense satisfaction they derive from closing a profitable business deal. Kierkegaard obviously has contempt for this type of aestheticism.

> The most ludicrous of all ludicrous things, it seems to me, is to be busy in the world, to be a man who is brisk at his meals and brisk at his work. Therefore, when I see a fly settle on the nose of one of those men of business in a decisive moment, or if he is splashed by a carriage that passes him in even greater haste ... I laugh from the bottom of my heart. And who could keep from laughing? What, after all, do these busy bustlers achieve? Are they not just like that woman who, in a flurry because the house was on fire, rescued the fire tongs? What more, after all, do they salvage from life's huge conflagration? (*EO 1 (E)*, p. 9).

Kierkegaard, however, mainly discusses the 'refined aesthete' who lives through the most *evolved* form of immediacy. In the manner with which Kierkegaard describes this view of life it is sometimes reminiscent of nineteenth-century Romantic attitudes. This person *consciously* chooses their aesthetic way of life and is socially highly selective. He or she disdainfully rejects those of 'unrefined immediacy', as well as those who epitomise 'passionless bourgeois banality'.

Although the sophisticated aesthete's relation to life is also characterised by *immediacy*, instead of an *unreflective* pursuit of desire-satisfaction, this type contemplates and calculates *how* best to enjoy life – rather than mindlessly 'latching on' to whatever opportunity for pleasure might cross his path, *his* enjoyments are the products of *cultivation*. As with *unrefined immediacy*, however, he still lacks the detachment required for *critical* reflection upon his attitudes and behaviour. The *quality* of his reflection is shallow, for it is directed either towards superficial aspects of his *external* reality or used to enhance his self-indulgent absorption in or introspection of his changing moods. In other words, he does not deeply question the validity of his lifestyle and his devotion to enjoyment. His pursuit of enjoyment is merely a more developed derivative of the *primitive* version of *immediate* pleasure-pursuit. Just like those living in the state of *unrefined* immediacy, the refined aesthete *unreflectively* accepts the fundamental *given* conditions of life as determining his existence, thus he, too, denies responsibility for the fundamental direction of his life.

When things go wrong, he simply blames *existence* rather than considering the possibility that his *attitude* and *behaviour* might be at fault. Instead of assuming responsibility for his condition he sees it as an unavoidable consequence of the tragic, unalterable conditions of the human predicament and thus wrongly assumes that life is inescapably meaningless. 'How empty and meaningless life is.... My life is utterly meaningless' (*EO 1 (E)*, pp. 13 and 20).

He may decide that he is 'doomed' or 'fated', ascribing his suffering to something *unalterable* in his physical or psychological make-up or life situation – that he has 'a naturally depressed nature' or that 'he is a victim of childhood abuse'. Some aesthetes, perversely, choose to view *sorrow* and *despair* as the *purpose of existence* – in other words, their conception of 'pleasure' is *suffering*. Perhaps, like the tragic hero, this person might even take *comfort* in the thought that he is 'fated by nature' to such despair and take pride in his heroic capacity to endure despair without complaint. He may even gain a perverse satisfaction from the thought that *at least* his *suffering* is 'something in life' which cannot be taken away from him.

Kierkegaard, who is an expert at detecting all the subtle subterfuges of self-delusion, sees this 'seductive fatalism' as seriously flawed because in accepting and perversely deriving *pleasure* from our despair and the conditions that cause it, we place ourselves at the mercy of fate and enter the psychological state of 'learned helplessness', thus excluding from our awareness even the *possibility* of personal responsibility or freedom.

What all aestheticism has in common, from the most primitive to the most refined, is a life that is dominated by what Sigmund Freud called 'the pleasure principle' – the pursuit of pleasure and the avoidance of pain (though one person's idea of *pleasure* may be another's conception of *pain*). Hence, 'aestheticism' falls at least partially into the category of hedonism, even though this fact might not be so clearly visible in some of the more intellectual versions of aestheticism.

Ultimately, though, whether one's conception of pleasure is fresh chocolate truffles, perverse forms of pain, fine wine, winning a lucrative business contract or discussing philosophy and 'new age' concepts, the same applies. So, whether aware of the fact or not, *all* individuals in the aesthetic sphere of existence are controlled by the *pleasure principle* and thus they lack any real *inner life* or solid *sense of self* – happiness is sought primarily through externals, so life is at the mercy of uncontrollable and unpredictable factors. Consequently, a person who is living an aesthetic existence never develops fully their potential humanity, because in their obsession with pleasure and avoidance of pain they share in a primitive biological principle that motivates all lower forms of life from garden slugs to chimpanzees.

Using the emperor Nero as an example of someone who had no impediments to the satisfaction of all his desires, Kierkegaard illustrates that even when a life of perfect hedonism is possible, ultimately it becomes boring, meaningless and empty, filled with feelings of dread that are only briefly escaped during the experience of new pleasures. Eventually no pleasure can drown the anguish and melancholy that become constant companions to this existence that submerges the human spirit in a multitude of diversions, a spirit that is thirsting for a higher form of existence.

The only real difference between primitive and sophisticated aestheticism is that the *latter* has realised that, ultimately, repetitive forms of *sensual* gratification become boring, whereas the intensity of *all* pleasure increases significantly when it involves the *consciousness* and not *just* the physical senses.

By developing a spiritual/intellectual basis for one's enjoyments, sensual pleasures become intensified and more enduring, one opens the door to exotic, sensual delights of the mind, heart and spirit. The refined aesthete develops these sophisticated means of entertainment because he regards boredom as the number one enemy in existence that must be defeated at all costs.

> Boredom is the root of all evil, no wonder, then, that the world goes backwards, that evil spreads. This can be traced back to the very beginning of the world. The gods were bored; therefore they created human beings. Adam was bored because he was alone; therefore Eve was created. Since that moment, boredom entered the world and grew in quantity in exact proportion to the growth of the population. Adam was bored alone; then Adam and Eve were bored together; then Adam and Eve and Cain and Abel were bored *en famille*. After

that, the population of the world increased and the nations were bored *en masse* (*EO 1 (E)*, p. 258).

To overcome his boredom, one of Kierkegaard's highly eccentric sophisticated aesthetes develops what he calls 'the Rotation Method', which allows one to create one's own personalised world of pleasure. This requires avoiding all commitments including love, marriage and even friendship. Then one does unusual things like attending the theatre, but only the middle of the play. One reads only the third section of a book, one irritates sensitive people and one falls in love but only with the *idea* of the lover, so that if anything happens to this person, one won't be affected. In other words, one remains merely a spectator and manipulator of life, which will allow one to remain free and to escape boredom.

This approach, however, eventually fails and Kierkegaard's refined aesthete reaches a state of desperate despair.

I don't feel like doing anything. I don't feel like riding – the motion is too powerful; I don't feel like walking – it is too tiring; I don't feel like lying down, for either I would have to stay down, and I don't feel like doing that, or I would have to get up again, and I don't feel like doing that, either. *Summa Summarium:* I don't feel like doing anything (*EO 1 (E)*, p. 4).

The aesthete has now reached the stage where it is possible that he may acknowledge to himself the inadequacies of aestheticism and realise that his inner spirit craves for a more meaningful existence. If this spiritual need is repressed his life will become intolerable. Kierkegaard observes that between the aesthetic mode of living, in which the *given self* (immediate nature) is the *fundamental* determinant of one's way of life, and the ethical mode of living, which uses *freedom of choice* to override the influence of the given self, there is an *intermediate stage*, characterised by complete detachment and disidentification from the *given self*, but *not yet* any identification with the *ethical self*.

Instead the person identifies with their activity of detachment – their *ironical self*. Kierkegaard believes that once someone has 'seen through' the shallowness of their aesthetic way of life but has not yet committed himself or herself to the ethical way of life, this interim state of consciousness, characterised by detached cynicism, can serve as a bridge between these two very different worldviews. Life is now lived one step removed from what is 'going on' and nothing in existence is serious or sacred any more. Kierkegaard saw in this sophisticated irony, aestheticism at its final or most evolved level.

This transitional zone of irony makes it far easier to move over to an ethical life, because it allows a person to understand the relative nature of all their endeavours. Sometimes, however, a person will get permanently stuck in this transitional zone and then irony may become a kind of existential life-view in its own right. To make the transition to the ethical, the intellectual state of irony needs to transform into a subjective direct experience of the truth of the ironical insights. The transition into an ethical way of existence requires the subordination of one's worldly ambitions and desires to *inner standards* guided by a strong sense of *commitment to one's moral duty*.

The ethical sphere of life

This requires a person to take a more active role in the shaping of his self and manner of living. Kierkegaard describes this as *choosing oneself*. In the ethical existence, the individual's *inner world* becomes of greater importance than his *outer* existence. He or she seeks self-knowledge and struggles to become a better human being – an *ideal* self. The fundamental distinction Kierkegaard makes between the aesthetic and ethical ways of life is that the former is 'outer', contingent, inconsistent and self-dissipating; the latter is 'inner', necessary, consistent and self-creating. The core idea of Kierkegaard's conception of 'ethical self-choice' is that a person must assume full responsibility for all aspects of his life. To do this requires detachment that allows him to break identification with his 'given' self whilst accepting that he possesses an *autonomous will* and *freedom of choice*.

At this stage he will be in a position consciously to *choose* his self. He now realises and accepts responsibility for all his past actions and behaviour. Kierkegaard's fictional character Judge William terms this retrospective movement 'repentance'. Above all, this person assumes responsibility as well as moral accountability for all the 'given' aspects of his self, and his present circumstances, whilst realising that these features do not determine his existence or limit his capacity for expressing freedom of choice; for his sense of self is now no longer identified with the 'given' self.

Finally, he takes full responsibility for his *future prospects* by treating his current life situation – character, inclinations, position in life – as the *raw material* that must be used to shape his existence according to his ideal conception of self that he has freely chosen. So the ethical self derives its sense of meaning not from the *outcome* or *result* of life, but through the full exercise of freedom of choice in terms of how a person *wills* his life. This allows one to develop a deep and enduring sense of personal identity.

According to Judge William, to live an *ideal* life requires adhering to the laws of social morality. A person living in the ethical sphere of consciousness has realised that all attempts to live a meaningful existence by satisfying sensual or intellectual desires are doomed to failure. Instead, he strives to embody in his existence enduring universal values such as freedom, justice, love and peace. This helps to detach and free him from the impulse to satisfy his own immediate interests. To achieve this aim, his personality becomes the 'absolute' and is 'its own end and purpose'. In other words, the ethical person *is* his own *goal*, his own *task*.

Unlike the aestheticist who is preoccupied with 'externals', his attention is directed towards his *inner being*, which he can learn to control and cultivate. Unlike the aestheticist who treats his personality attributes as unalterable facts of his nature to which he must submit, the ethical individual sees his character as a *challenge*. Through critical self-exploration he reaches an understanding of what he empirically *is* and what he is *capable of becoming*. Thus he constructs a conception of his 'ideal self' derived from a *realistic grasp* of inner potentials that are *not* dependent upon *external contingencies*, subject to unpredictable forces of change.

His sense of success or failure is therefore not dependent upon the success or failure of his worldly endeavours; instead he judges his achievements by the way in which he *carries out* these tasks, in terms of his *integrity*, strength of *spirit* and *personal commitment*. There is a sense of this attitude in the popular slogan 'it's not *what* you do, it's the *way* that you do it'.

Fundamentally this means that he makes commitments by being an active *participant* in society rather than an *outsider* or detached observer. The truly ethical person has a highly rational approach to reality and believes in the necessity of self-denial for the purpose of upholding one's obligations, for he has a strong sense of responsibility, duty and honour towards his friendships, family life and career. The ethical viewpoint offered by one of Kierkegaard's characters, Judge William, suggests that the power of human freedom lies in an individual's *spirit*, and is expressed through the freedom to choose one's self.

This does not mean to *re-create* oneself, which is an expression of the despair of defiance; rather it means *becoming* the person which 'the rational ordering of things' within the society has *determined* that one should be, and one must adopt this role in the spirit of complete self-acceptance. According to Judge William, this means choosing a job that coincides with one's talents and education, getting married, having children and assuming conscientiously all the responsibilities that these things entail.

Before one can choose *oneself* one must first choose *despair*. This means actively choosing to give up hope in the aesthetic way of life, which is simply a flight from one's true self and real calling in life. To will despair is to resign oneself to one's ethical duty to existence; only then can life be transformed into a work of art, a thing of beauty. For the ethical judge, the aesthete has no spirit and thus is *not* a full human being.

The weak points of the ethical approach

However, Kierkegaard's Judge overlooks the fact that the purely ethical approach to life does not always work, because life is filled with ambiguity and paradox. For instance, one might find oneself in a situation where one is confronted with two irreconcilable demands, or has to make a choice between two highly undesirable courses of action, or circumstances that demand one choice from amongst numerous possible alternatives. In all these situations there are no ethical principles or rules that can *determine conclusively* how one should respond. Clarity, order and harmony can be achieved in *pure thought*, but the moment one is faced with problems that arise from the constantly new, changing circumstances of existence, ambiguity is unavoidable.

Also, the ethical position is concerned with living in the 'right way', *doing one's duty*, which means to have done *enough*. But how can one be sure that one *has* done 'enough'? For instance, a person may be considered the epitome of social virtue in his society – honest in business, loyal to friends, family and the community and generous towards those in need. But how can this person be certain that from an objective *moral* standpoint he has done enough? For instance, Mother Teresa actually *lived* among the poor, and there are numerous other humans on this planet who give up all worldly, material benefits in order to take care of those in dire need.

So how can any ethical-minded individual really say they have done enough to satisfy the ethical requirement? All justifications that one *has* fulfilled one's moral obligations are merely self-deception – moral complacency that is achieved by judging oneself against those who have done less whilst ignoring the example of those who have done far more. Anyone who measures their existence against ethical standards must judge himself or herself a failure unless they live in self-deception. In addition, Kierkegaard discerns that when people completely submit to universal moral values, they lose their sense of individual responsibility.

The religious sphere of life

According to Kierkegaard, when someone truly acknowledges the truth of their ethical stance towards existence, they realise the 'contradiction' between the way they exist in their innermost soul and their failure to express this outwardly, and this leads to a state of 'ethical despair', which if intense enough can precipitate a leap to faith, resulting in the *religious outlook* on existence. Kierkegaard discloses a fundamentally important limitation of the ethical viewpoint which is evidenced in situations where the demands of religious faith and ethical duty *collide*. In *Fear and Trembling* Kierkegaard examines this collision as it is exemplified in the story of Abraham and Isaac. In stark contrast to the Romantics, who suggested that *individual conscience* should guide the moral life, and Hegel, who asserted that *rational ethical principles* are the only acceptable measure of morality, in the story of Abraham, *faith* is the deciding factor. Kierkegaard's use of this biblical story is like an explosion, utterly demolishing the view that ethics are the *ultimate standard* by which one should live. For in faith, the *single individual* and the human *will* (in obedience to God's will) take precedence over social morality and human reason.

The religious way of life is characterised by an awareness in which the individual realises the impossibility of truly fulfilling the ideals of the ethical existence. In *Concluding Unscientific Postscript*, Kierkegaard distinguishes between two types of religious life: a 'natural' religiosity (which he calls religiousness 'A'), in which the individual strives to relate to God and resolve the problem of guilt by relying exclusively upon one's natural 'immanent' idea of God; and Christianity (religiousness 'B'), which accepts that God is incarnated as a human being for the purpose of establishing a relation with humans. Religiousness 'B' – Christianity – can only be truly accepted via a 'leap to faith', for it is a transcendent religion based upon *revelation* rather than an *immanent* religion. The leap to faith is essential because the truth of the revelation that forms the basis of Christianity cannot be rationally demonstrated, because the incarnation of an infinite God in the finite form of man is a paradox that transcends all human reason.

So the genuinely religious person is someone who has utterly understood that the relative values from our finite worldly existence should never become our life's purpose, for worldly ambition *guarantees* an inner sense of emptiness. They have understood their utter *dependence* upon and *nothingness* in the face of the eternal force that created them. The religious person has mastered the 'balancing act' of maintaining, simultaneously, an *absolute* relation to the Eternal or Absolute and a *relative* relation to worldly life. For the aim in the religious sphere of consciousness is not to *deny* worldly life but to put in its rightful place.

The sign that someone has truly established a relation to the *eternal* aspect of existence is that their life becomes transformed by it. That person is not a religious *believer*, but a religious *exister* – their way of life is testimony to this fact, for they live *in the truth*. Theirs is also a life of 'objective uncertainty' because the validity of the genuine religious life cannot be rationally *proven* or justified.

Ultimately, what this leads to is a life based upon and rooted in *faith*. According to Kierkegaard, the decisive mark of the religious state of consciousness is the awareness of *total indebtedness* to the eternal – that we *owe ourselves to* and are rightly *owned* by the eternal.

Any other primary value is mere self-deception, which is double-mindedness, *two* wills, one that desires the *world* and the other – which one tries to ignore – that desires the *infinite*. But purity of heart is to will *one* thing – to have one goal, which in this case is the Eternal.

One cannot however make the Eternal the focus of one's life *in order* to improve one's position in the world, for again, this is double-mindedness, self-deception. According to Kierkegaard, Eternity is an 'either/or' choice. This means that all human relations, even those of family, are subordinate to the Eternal. One interacts with the world as an individual, inwardly divorced from the crowd, always conscious of one's *primary* responsibility to the *Eternal* as an individual who stands alone before the Eternal. This will obviously have an effect upon one's choice of career, for one could not live in this consciousness and work at something which was not a 'calling'.

The 'means' rather than the 'end' are now of central importance in all activities. As Kierkegaard states, man is not 'eternally responsible' for his successes or failures, 'But without exception, he is eternally responsible for the kind of means he uses' (*Purity of Heart*, p. 202, Torchbooks, 1956). According to Kierkegaard, the *moral behaviour* of a religious person is *not* due to self-disciplined adherence to social morality, rather it is the *natural consequence* of their *moral character*, which derives from their *inwardness* as an individual conscious of the Eternal. To sin, according to Kierkegaard, is to avoid intentionally one's calling to the Eternal. Kierkegaard asserts that consciousness of sin makes clear the 'infinite qualitative difference' between man and the Eternal.

The religious life, the 'call of the infinite', acts as a constant reminder that the laws and customs of any people are *finite*. Worldly values are *one-dimensional*, but humans are *not*. We are a synthesis of the finite *and* the infinite or eternal. Even if it were possible for a person to fulfil to perfection the requirements of social morality, they would still *not* have fulfilled the *infinite* requirement that ethics purports to express. Kierkegaard is convinced that this eternal aspect of one's being should become the central and *only* focus for one's existence, and then worldly values will have only a *relative* status in life and the fact of their *presence* or *absence* will no longer deeply concern one.

Death

The fear of death is the beginning of philosophy, and the final cause of religion. At the end of our life we meet death. When our experiences finally seem to have co-ordinated themselves into wisdom, our brain and body begins to decay. Just as our walking is in one sense a continuously prevented falling, so the life of our body is merely a continuous postponement of death.

The average person cannot reconcile themselves to death. The optimism of youth is partly due to the fact that whilst we are climbing the 'hill' of life our awareness of death is not prominent in our minds, for death lies on the other side of hill, at the very bottom. The prevalence of a belief in immortality is a token of mankind's awful fear of death.

Published the day before *Stages on Life's Way*, Kierkegaard's *Three Discourses* were written under his own name. In the third of these discourses, which provides the primary source for the discussion and the material used in this chapter, Kierkegaard discusses the educational value of the contemplation of death, particularly one's *own* death. This theme on the value of death-awareness also features in many of his later works, for he was acutely aware of 'the nothingness that pervades existence' and 'the possibility of death at any moment'.

Kierkegaard claimed that if an individual sincerely and intensely reflects upon the truth of the *inevitability* and *temporal unpredictability* of their own death, this can evoke the sincerity and passion that is necessary for the task of establishing true selfhood. 'Death in earnest gives life force as nothing else does; it makes one alert as nothing else does' (*TDO (E)*, V, p. 236).

With the exception of pathological cases, all humans understand that *eventually* they will die, because on a daily basis we are surrounded with abundant *objective proof* of this fact. In spite of this, the majority of human beings do not truly understand what their mortality *means*. According to Kierkegaard, the *meaning of death* is a *subjective truth* and therefore it can only be grasped *subjectively*, whereas most people possess only an *objective* understanding of their mortality – they view their death in a detached manner as something *outside* of them, that will happen to them one day, in their *future*.

To illustrate this point, Kierkegaard relates the story of a man who is invited to dinner by a friend he meets on a street corner in Copenhagen. A moment after this man enthusiastically promises to attend, he is struck down dead by a tile that happens to fall off a nearby roof. Kierkegaard mocks the dead man, and laughs at the irony of this event in which someone who has just made a firm commitment into the future has had their life taken away from them, quite suddenly and without any warning whatsoever. Kierkegaard then wonders if perhaps he is being too hard on the chap and suggests that we surely cannot have expected this man to have replied to the invitation with 'You can count on me, I shall certainly come; but I must make an exception for the contingency that a tile happens to blow down from a roof, and kills me; for in that case I cannot come' (*CUP (S.L.)*, p. 88).

It is clear, however, that Kierkegaard believes that the intensity of death-awareness, reflected by this rather exaggerated statement, is *essential* for grasping 'with inwardness' the subjective truth of our death. He asserts, 'A human being is only an instrument and never knows when the moment will come when he will be put aside. If he himself does not at times evoke this thought, he is a hireling, an unfaithful servant, who is trying to free himself and to cheat the Lord of the uncertainty in which he comprehends his own nothingness' (*EUD*, p. 282). In spite of this belief, the shock Kierkegaard experienced over his father's sudden demise indicates that at the time he was certainly *not* subjectively experiencing this truth, in spite of the fact that his father was in his eighties.

Even though Kierkegaard considered death-awareness to be of such central importance to the attainment of true selfhood, mysteriously, many introductory and advanced texts on Kierkegaardian philosophy, as well as collections of advanced essays on his work, ignore or pay little attention to his views on this crucial fact of life – even in the index of these texts there is frequently no reference to death. Astonishingly, in one particular *Dictionary of Philosophy*, which has a thousand pages, there is no entry for either 'death' or 'mortality'. It seems that even in the 'world of philosophy' there is confirmation of Kierkegaard's assertion that the majority of humans live in constant 'death denial'.

According to Kierkegaard, experiencing the subjective truth of one's own death is an essential prerequisite to experiencing one's true self. A genuine (subjective) understanding of our own mortality helps us to see what is truly important in our existence. Kierkegaard realised that *the positive* – existence – can only truly be subjectively understood via an acute awareness of *the negative* – 'the nothingness that pervades existence'. He asserted that the journey towards genuine selfhood requires a person to realise the urgency and fragility of life at the deepest level of his being, and each individual must discover this truth for himself and on his own, so that he truly treasures each day as a valuable step on his journey towards self-realisation. 'Even though the equality of all the dead is that now all is over, there is still one difference, my listener, a difference that cries aloud to heaven – the difference of what that life was that now in death is over' (*TDO (E)*, V, p. 238).

For Kierkegaard, a key beneficial consequence of death-awareness lies in its potential to inspire and motivate a religious state of consciousness. To illustrate this point, he cites the case of a man who had just been buried in his grave, pointing out that whilst this man was alive, he was deeply aware of the finality of his own death and it was *this* which inspired the man to devote his life to God. 'In the grave there is no recollection, not even of God. See, the man *did* know this ... because he knew this, he acted accordingly, and therefore *he recollected God* while he was living' (*TDO (E)*, V, p. 226).

Rather than being a source of depression, because this man's understanding of the finality of death inspired his devotion to the Eternal, God, it infused genuine joy into his life and true appreciation for his modest existence. Kierkegaard describes this man's final years: 'he was a man, old, he became aged, and then he died, but the recollection of God remained the same, a guide in all his activity, a quiet joy in his devout contemplation ... the deceased walked before him (God) and was better known by him than by anyone else' (*TDO (E)*, V, p. 227).

Kierkegaard clearly implies that this man's awareness of death had enriched every part of his life because it inspired him to view his finite existence in perspective, *relative* to Eternity – God. ('In the grave there is no recollection ... and therefore *he recollected God* while he was living.')

> He recollected God and became proficient in his work; he recollected God and became joyful in his work and joyful in his life; he recollected God and became happy in his modest home with his dear ones; he disturbed no one by indifference to public worship, disturbed no one by untimely zeal, but God's house was to him a second home – and now he has gone home (*TDO (E)*, V, p. 227).

Kierkegaard's own awareness of death, however, did not seem to provide him with this type of religious state of consciousness, for even when Kierkegaard lay on his deathbed, he was unable to forgive his brother and even refused to see him. He was, however, able to surrender peacefully to his own death.

The subjective/true understanding of death

Kierkegaard does not see our mortality as a basis for morbidity and despair; on the contrary, he considers that when a person reaches a true awareness of death, this can infuse their life with genuine appreciation, direction and even joy.

He realised that death is related to the entire way of living of each human being and therefore saw it as every person's task to realise this truth *existentially*, through *subjectively assimilating* this truth in moment-by-moment existence. He explains that the attainment of a true understanding of death requires continuous subjective awareness of only two essential facts: 1) death is an unavoidable certainty; 2) this certainty is a constant, but temporally unpredictable, possibility.

So genuine awareness of death – an essential condition of human freedom – entails the realisation that: it is certain that I shall die. I can never be certain *when* this will happen – I may die at any time and it could potentially happen suddenly and completely unexpectedly, without any warning.

> Uncertainty lends a hand and, like the teacher, points steadily to the object of learning and says to the learner, 'Pay close attention to the certainty' – then earnestness comes into existence. No teacher is able to teach the pupil to pay attention to what is said the way the uncertainty of death does when it points to the certainty of death; and no teacher is able to keep the pupil's thoughts concentrated on the one object of instruction the way the thought of the uncertainty of death does when it practices the thought of the certainty of death (*TDO (E)*, V, pp. 246–7).

Therefore, in every single instant of my existence, death is a possibility that hangs over everything I do. 'If death says, "Perhaps this very day", then earnest says, "Let it perhaps be today or not", but I say, "This very day" ' (*TDO (E)*, V, p. 238).

Death will end all my worldly possibilities, sever all my relationships and complete the story of my earthly existence. To achieve genuine individuality, to live as my true self, all the decisions I make in life must be based upon a clear subjective awareness of this truth, which provides a vantage point from where I am able to grasp my life as a whole, and differentiate clearly between what *is* and *is not* important to me. Because the *time* of my death is utterly uncertain this means that all the plans in my life that assume my future continuity – in other words *all* my plans – are merely *possibilities*, for they are constructed upon entirely unstable foundations.

> This is the way it is with death. The certainty is the unchanging, and the uncertainty is the brief statement: It is possible.... Every arrangement that wants to condition the certainty of death as to time and hour for the one who is acting, every condition, every agreement, every arrangement runs aground on this statement; and all passionateness and all cleverness and all defiance are rendered powerless by this statement (*TDO (E)*, V, p. 246).

In other words, I now live in companionship with my existential anxiety, for it is this mood that enables me to remain fully conscious of the fact that I stand on the very edge of a precipice facing personal extinction and eternity. 'Anxiety is freedom's possibility … because it consumes all finite ends and discovers all their deceptiveness' (*CA (E)*, IV, p. 422).

Even if I am young and healthy I now realise the pointlessness of placing my trust in a worldly existence where 'terrible perdition, and annihilation live next door to every man', for now I can see my life against the larger perspective of infinity. In the light of my death I can clearly see the shallowness of living as a self that is merely a false identity defined by the values of a finite, worldly existence; this inspires me to strive for genuine selfhood by grounding my self in its relation to the infinite. Each day is now of the greatest importance to me in terms of my spiritual task of true selfhood, because I can only work towards this whilst the gift of life still remains within me; 'it is a matter of understanding oneself, and the earnest understanding is that if death is night then life is day, that if no work can be done at night then work can be done during the day; and the terse but impelling cry of earnestness, like death's terse cry, is: This very day' (*TDO (E)*, V, p. 236).

Consequently I am only prepared to invest my time and energy in work and personal occupations that still have meaning when considered in the light of my temporally unpredictable death.

> The earnest person looks at himself. If he is young, the thought of death teaches him that a young person will become its booty here if it comes today…. The earnest person looks at himself; so he knows the nature of the one who would become death's booty here if it were to come today; he looks at his own work and so he knows what work it is that would be interrupted here if death were to come today (*TDO (E)*, V, p. 245).

Because I truly feel in the depths of my Being that each moment may be my last, this frees me from pettiness and the pressure to live as others expect me to live. I now value each day of my life and appreciate each moment of my existence as an individual, standing alone before the Eternal, exercising my freedom of choice. 'No bowstring can be tightened in such a way and is able to give the arrow such momentum the way the thought of death is able to accelerate the living when earnestness stretches the thought. Then earnestness grasps the present this very day' (*TDO (E)*, V, p. 237).

Inauthentic death awareness

Kierkegaard points out that to ignore the complete uncertainty of life, and view death *only* in terms of it being an 'actual event', is the root source of our inaccurate understanding of death. However, the door to this 'teacher' of life can always be opened when a person feels ready to learn.

> The thought of death, that teacher of earnestness who at birth is appointed to everyone for a whole lifetime and who in the uncertainty is always ready to begin the instruction when it is requested. Death does not come because someone calls it (for the weaker one to order the stronger one in that way would be only a jest), but as soon as someone opens the door to uncertainty, the teacher is there, the teacher who will at some time come to give a test and examine the pupil: whether he has wanted to use his instruction or not. And this testing by death – or with a more commonly used foreign word to designate the same thing – this final examination of life, is equally difficult for all ... because it is the test of earnestness (*TDO (E)*, V, pp. 252–3).

Instead of taking advantage of death as 'the teacher of earnestness', through acknowledging the utter insecurity of human existence, the normal member of society ignores his mortality due to his *fear* of the *specific* or *actual event* of death which causes him to escape into everyday worldly concerns. Death is now viewed merely as a remote possibility in the future that for the moment only happens to others. This does not mean that he won't be prepared to acknowledge openly the fact that 'life is short, we don't live forever', but such words will be merely empty, meaningless gestures that are excluded from his *subjective feeling-awareness*. This self-deception results in an illusory or confused perception of reality. 'The ordinary view of death only confuses thought' (*TDO (E)*, V, p. 245).

According to Kierkegaard, even if a person regularly acknowledges to himself the brevity and uncertainty of his existence, he has still not *subjectively* understood the meaning of death if his reaction is to cram as much pleasure as possible into his 'short' life. Kierkegaard sees this merely as the frightened response of sensual individuals. 'Death induces the sensual person to say: Let us eat and drink, because tomorrow we shall die – but this is sensuality's cowardly lust for life, that contemptible order of things where one lives in order to eat and drink instead of eating and drinking in order to live' (*TDO (E)*, V, p. 236).

Kierkegaard points to another shallow response to death, which is seen in 'profound thinkers', whose deep introspective but *passive* response to the realities of death are in fact a symptom of weakness that has been induced by the shock of their perceptions. 'The idea of death may induce weakness in the more profound person so that he sinks relaxed in mood' (*TDO (E)*, V, p. 236).

Both the above examples stand in sharp contrast to the genuine awareness of death which is defined by genuine 'earnestness' – sincere, intense focus on the truth of death that is bravely accepted and assimilated in manner that guides and energises the entire approach to existence, 'the thought of death gives the earnest person the right momentum in life and the right goal toward which he directs his momentum' (*TDO (E)*, V, p. 236).

However, this condition of genuine death-awareness is not something which *once gained* is never lost; rather it needs to be maintained constantly, for there is always the temptation to relapse again into a superficial awareness of death, which arises from the dramatic contrast between the thought of death and a person's vibrant sense of being alive. This potentially can create in him a false sense of security about his personal survival into the future, and thus he may once again turn his back on the fact that he is constantly overshadowed by the possibility of sudden death, which may occur *at any moment*. As a result, the sense of urgency to life may evaporate, causing him to feel that he has time enough to suspend temporarily his task of genuine selfhood:

> supported by the earnest thought of death, the earnest person says, 'All is not over.' But if this bright prospect is tempting, if he once again merely glimpses it in the half-light of contemplation, if it puts distance between him and the task, if time does not become a scarcity, if the possession of it is secure for him – then again he is not earnest (*TDO (E)*, V, p. 238).

Kierkegaard observed that some individuals are inclined to think obsessively and morbidly about death, and are convinced that their perception of death is the absolute truth. He was, however, convinced of the fact that this type of intense and continual death-awareness was a manifestation of intense despair, and thus a clear indication of a misconception or *superficial understanding* of the true significance of death. He regarded this condition as being a 'death worse than death', in the sense that a human in this state fears the depths of despair even more than they fear death. This is evidenced by the fact that a person in this state is prone to moods of depression or anger that express themselves either in fierce aggression towards others or self-destructive thoughts and behaviour that can lead to suicidal despair: 'When death is the greatest danger, we hope for life; but when we learn to know the even greater danger, we hope for death. When the danger is so great that death becomes the hope, then despair is the hopelessness of not even being able to die' (*SUD (E)*, XI, p. 132).

The Christian's metaphorical death

Due to his Christian beliefs, Kierkegaard held the view that death is the end of our *finite* existence but not a *final* end. 'Christianly understood, death itself is a passing into life ... death is not the end' (*SUD (E)*, XI, p. 131). He considered the normal earthly existence as being nothing more than an illusory façade concealing our true spiritual essence:

> Just look at the world that lies before you in all its variegated multi-fariousness; it is like looking at a play, except that the multifari-ousness is much, much greater. Because of his dissimilarity, every single one of these innumerable individuals is something particular, represents something particular, but essentially he is something else. Yet this you do not get to see here in life; here you see only what the individual represents and how he does it. It is just as in the play. But when the curtain falls on the stage, then the one who played the king and the one who played the beggar etc. are all alike; all are one and the same – actors. When at death the curtain falls on the stage of actuality (it is confusing use of language to say that at death the curtain is raised on the stage of eternity, since eternity is not a stage at all; it is truth) then they, too, are all one, they are human beings. All of them

213

are what they essentially were, what you did not see because of the dissimilarity that you saw – they are human beings (*Works of Love*, IX, p. 86, trans. Howard V. Hong and Edna H. Hong in *The Essential Kierkegaard*).

Kierkegaard believed that total commitment to Christianity meant surrendering entirely the personality with its egotistical desires and ambition, and this means giving up all attachment to worldly existence.

Christianity teaches that you must die. Your power must be dismantled. And the life-giving Spirit is the very one who slays you. The first thing this Spirit says is that you must enter into death, you must die to yourself. The life-giving Spirit – that is the invitation. Who would not willingly take hold of it? But die first – there's the rub! You must first die to every earthly hope, to every merely *human* confidence. You must die to your selfishness, and to the world, because it is only through your selfishness that the world has power over you. Naturally there is nothing a human being hangs on to so firmly – indeed, with his whole self – as to this selfishness! Ah, the separation of soul and body at the hour of death is not as painful as being forced to be separated from our flesh when we are alive! Yes, we human beings do not hang on to this physical life as firmly as we do to our selfishness! (*For Self-Examination and Judge for Yourself* (abridged), pp. 76–87, trans. Howard V. Hong and Edna H. Hong, Princeton University Press, 1990).

Because of the intensity with which human beings hold on to their worldly values, Kierkegaard believed that only intense suffering could pry loose this grip on the world: 'Not until a person has become so wretched that his only wish, his only consolation, is to die – not until then does Christianity truly begin' (*JP*, I, p. 216).

It seems fairly obvious that Kierkegaard's preoccupation with the immense significance and utter unpredictability of death was greatly influenced by his own tragic experiences. When he was six years old, his brother (Søren Michael), who was only twelve, died very suddenly and unexpectedly from a brain haemorrhage following a playground accident, and by the age of twenty-one, Søren had experienced the sad loss of his mother and five of his six siblings, four of these deaths occurring during the tragically short span of about two years, between 1832 and 1834.

His journals, which he began in 1834, contain brief entries recording his reactions to these deaths. In the case of his brother Niels, he writes that he felt no real grief, but expected the impact to arrive later. However, in 1835 whilst on a summer vacation, one can sense the closeness he felt to the dead family members and the great depth to which he was affected. It also appears that he may have harboured a death wish so that he could join them. During a walk at a favourite coastal spot north of Gilleleje, he records that

> the few dear departed (Nicoline, Ane, Petrea, Niels) rose from the grave before me, or rather it seemed as though they were not dead. I felt so much at ease in their midst, I rested in their embrace, and felt as though I were outside my body and floated about with them in a higher ether – until the seagull's screech reminded me that I stood alone (*Pap.*, I A 68, dated 29 July 1835; *Papers and Journals: A Selection*, p. 26).

Søren Kierkegaard died peacefully on 11 November 1855. On his deathbed he felt that his earthly task had been completed and had prayed that despair would not overcome him at the end, for he wished his death to become a meaningful act. The hospital records describing his condition recorded:

> He considers the sickness fatal. His death is necessary for the cause which he has devoted all his intellectual strength to resolving.... If he is to go on living, he must continue his religious battle; but in that case it will peter out, while, on the contrary, by his death it will maintain its strength and, he believes, its victory (*Breveog Aktstykker*, I, pp. 21 (28), 21–4 (28–32).

A fitting epitaph that seems to summarise wonderfully the significance of his life and his death appears in a passage he wrote himself in *Either/Or.*

> Something marvellous has happened to me. I was transported to the seventh heaven. There sat all the gods assembled. As a special dispensation, I was granted the favour of making a wish. 'What do you want,' asked Mercury. 'Do you want youth, or beauty, or power, or a long life, or the most beautiful girl, or any one of the other glorious things we have in the treasure chest? Choose – but only one thing.' For a moment I was bewildered; then I addressed the gods, saying:

My esteemed contemporaries, I choose one thing – that I may always have the laughter on my side. Not one of the gods said a word; instead, all of them began to laugh. From that I concluded that my wish was granted and decided that the gods knew how to express themselves with good taste, for it would indeed have been inappropriate to reply solemnly: It is granted to you (*EO 1*, p. 27).

Further reading

Kierkegaard's writings

A scholarly English edition of Kierkegaard's complete collected works has been published by Princeton University Press and edited by H. V. and E. H. Hong. It consists of 26 volumes, 1978–2000.

An excellent, comprehensive single-volume anthology of Kierkegaard's writings available in English is *The Essential Kierkegaard* (edited by H. V. and E. H. Hong, 2000), which traces the development of his work with chronologically presented generous selections from all his key texts.

Finally, *The Laughter is on My Side*, edited by Roger Poole and Henrik Stangerup (Princeton University Press, 1989), provides an unconventional but highly innovative assortment of Kierkegaard's writings that ignores chronology in its selection in order to provide the reader with highly entertaining pieces from Kierkegaard's works that show him at his aesthetic best.

Biographies of Kierkegaard

An excellent and recently published 'intellectual biography' of Kierkegaard is A. Hannay's *Kierkegaard: A Biography* (Cambridge University Press, 2001).

Josiah Thompson's *Kierkegaard* (Gollancz, 1974) is another reliable and insightful biographical study.

In addition there is Joakim Garff's Danish biography, which is due to be published in English.

Other recommended secondary sources

Collins, James. *The Mind of Kierkegaard* (Princeton University Press, 1983).

Hannay, Alastair. *Kierkegaard* (Routledge and Kegan Paul, 1982).

Hannay, A. and Marino, G. (eds). *The Cambridge Companion to Kierkegaard* (Cambridge University Press, 1998).

Index

Note: page numbers in *italics* refer to illustrations